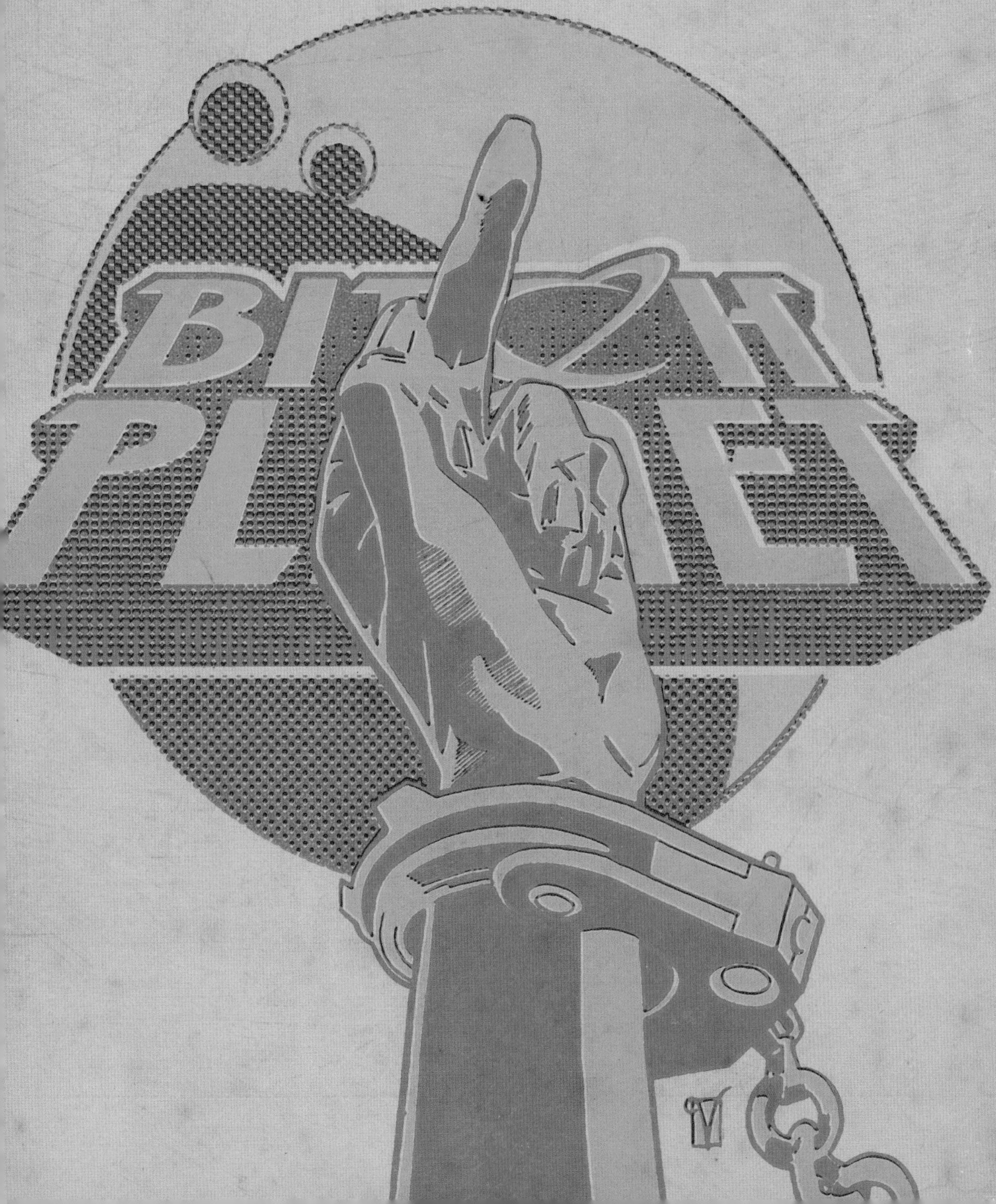

PRESENTS

KELLY SUE DeCONNICK
SCRIPT / CO-CREATOR

VALENTINE DE LANDRO
ART & COVERS / CO-CREATOR

EARTH IS THE FATHER ... SPACE IS THE MOTHER

...WHERE WICKEDNESS YOUR FATHER HAS CAST YOU OUT

TAKI SOMA
ART (ISSUE #6)

WITH

KELLY FITZPATRICK
COLORS

CLAYTON COWLES
LETTERS

RIAN HUGHES
LOGO, ORIGINAL COVERS DESIGN. BOOK DESIGN

LAURENN McCUBBIN
BACKMATTER DESIGN

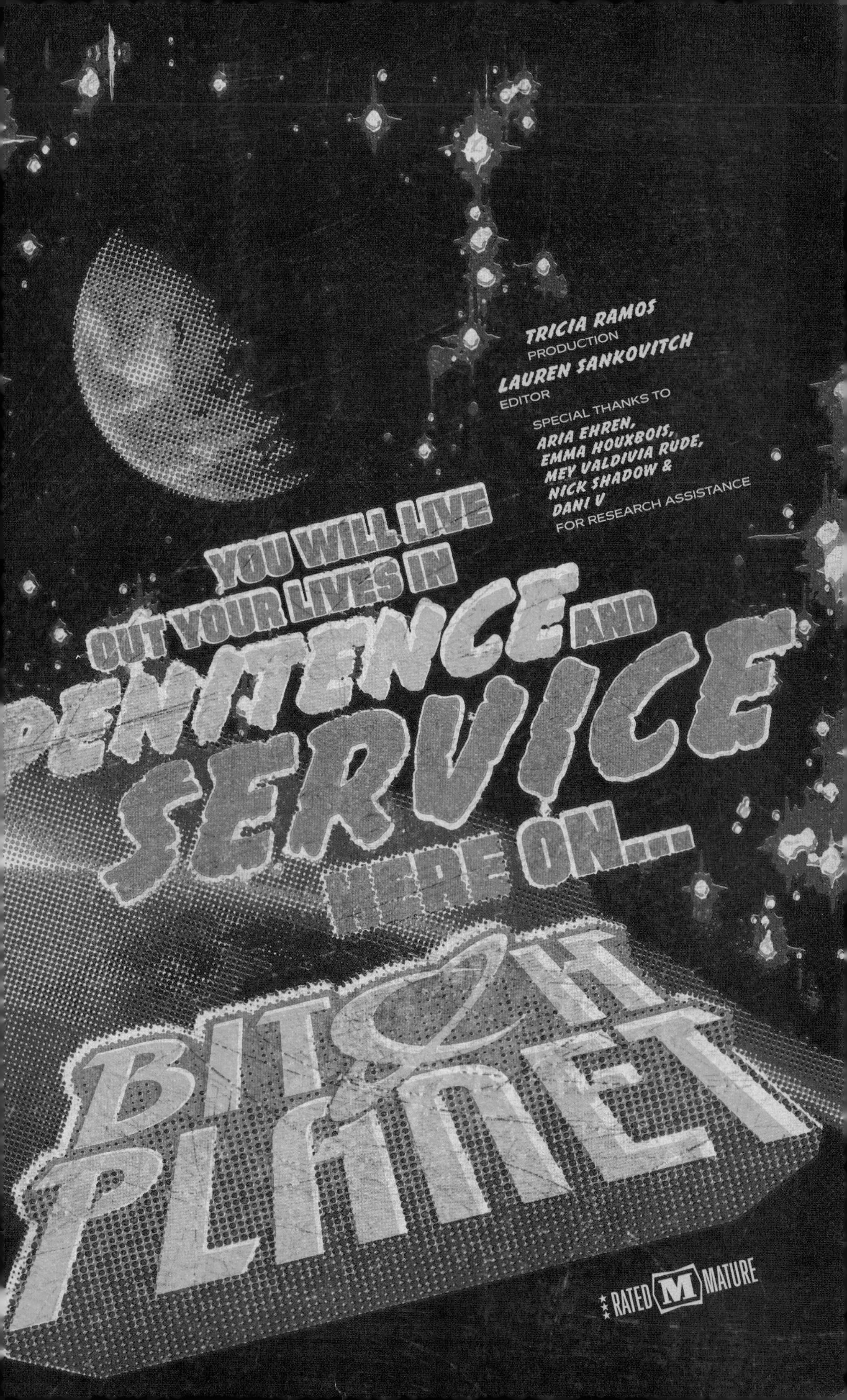

TRICIA RAMOS
PRODUCTION
LAUREN SANKOVITCH
EDITOR
SPECIAL THANKS TO
ARIA EHREN,
EMMA HOUXBOIS,
MEY VALDIVIA RUDE,
NICK SHADOW &
DANI V
FOR RESEARCH ASSISTANCE
YOU WILL LIVE
OUT YOUR LIVES IN
PENITENCE AND
SERVICE
HERE ON...
BITCH
PLANET
RATED M MATURE

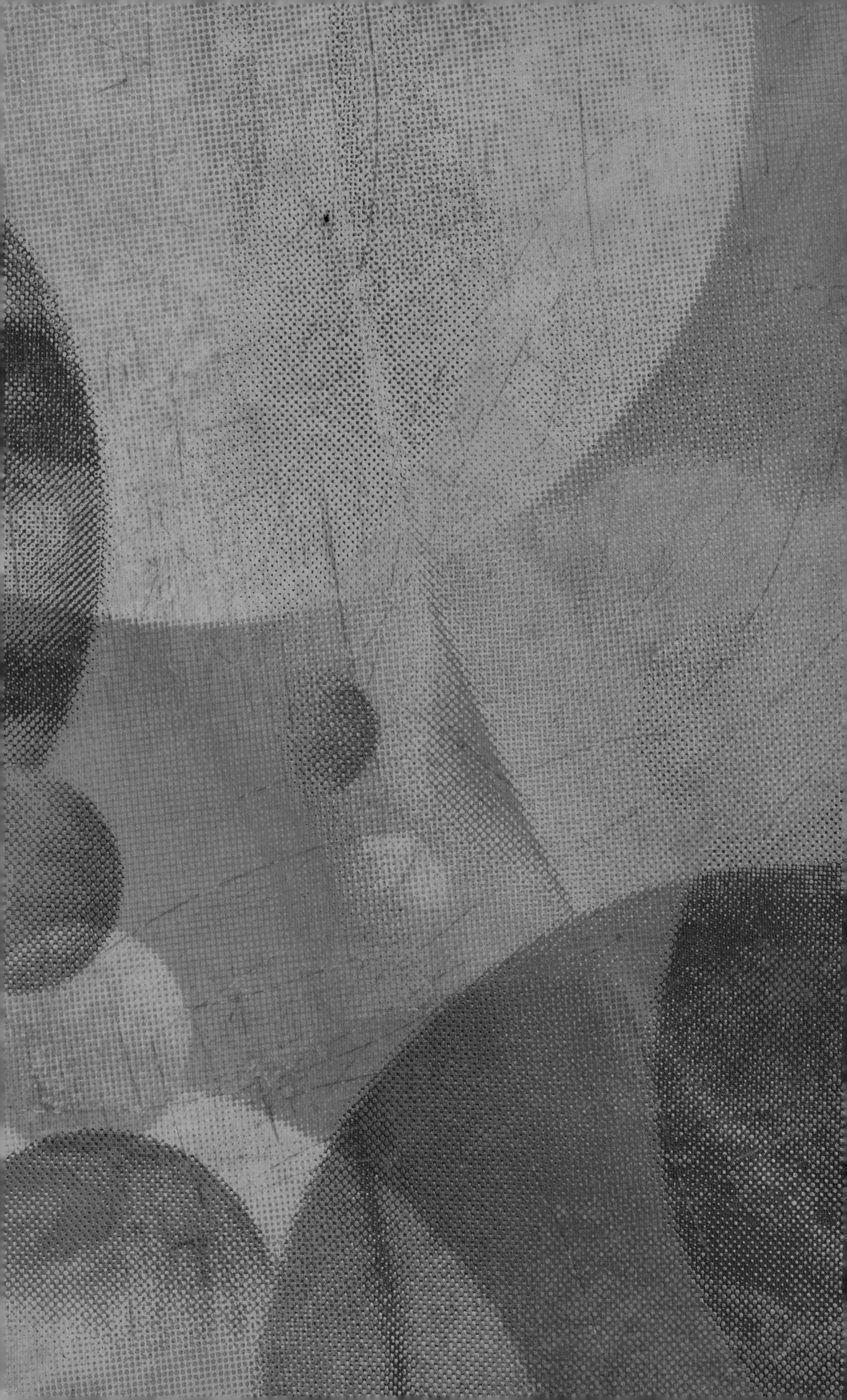

CONTENT ADVISORY:

THE FOLLOWING IS A FLASHBACK ISSUE, COVERING THE EVENTS THAT LED TO MEIKO MAKI'S INCARCERATION. IT CONTAINS PLOT ELEMENTS AND IMAGES RELATING TO SEXUAL ASSAULT.

WE ENCOURAGE YOU TO EVALUATE YOUR COMFORT LEVEL BEFORE DECIDING TO CONTINUE.

BITCH PLANET'S MAIN NARRATIVE RESUMES WITH ISSUE 7 AND DOES NOT RECOUNT THE ASSAULT.

IN A 2008 DEPARTMENT OF JUSTICE SURVEY OF FORMER PRISONERS, 1 IN 16 FEMALE PRISONERS REPORTED BEING SEXUALLY ASSAULTED WHILE INCARCERATED.

http://tinyurl.com/hxjrwx6

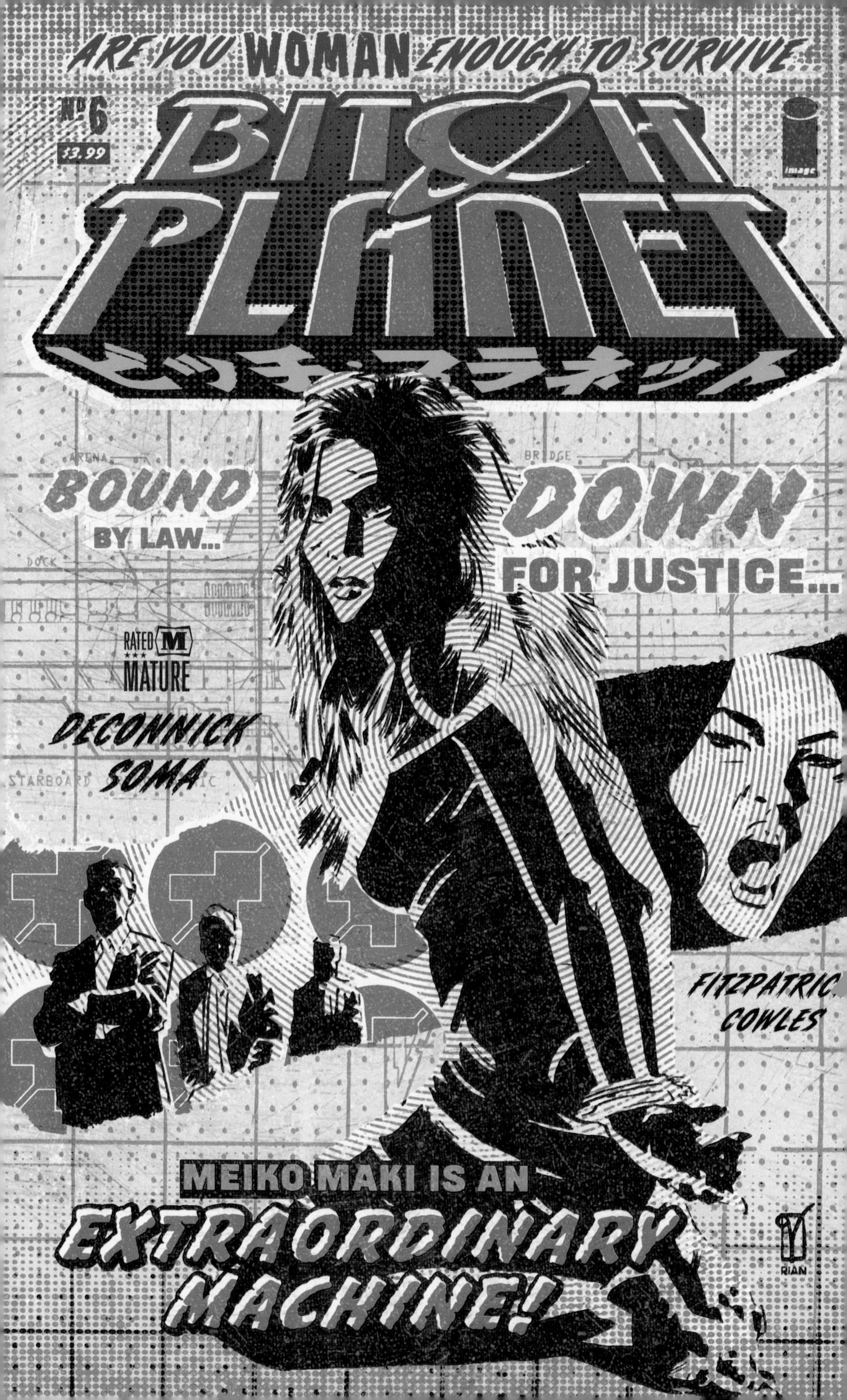
ARE YOU WOMAN ENOUGH TO SURVIVE
Nº 6
$3.99
BITCH PLANET
ビッチプラネット
image
ARENA
BRIDGE
BOUND
BY LAW...
DOWN
FOR JUSTICE...
DOCK
RATED M MATURE
DECONNICK
SOMA
STARBOARD
FITZPATRIC
COWLES
MEIKO MAKI IS AN
EXTRAORDINARY
MACHINE!
RIAN

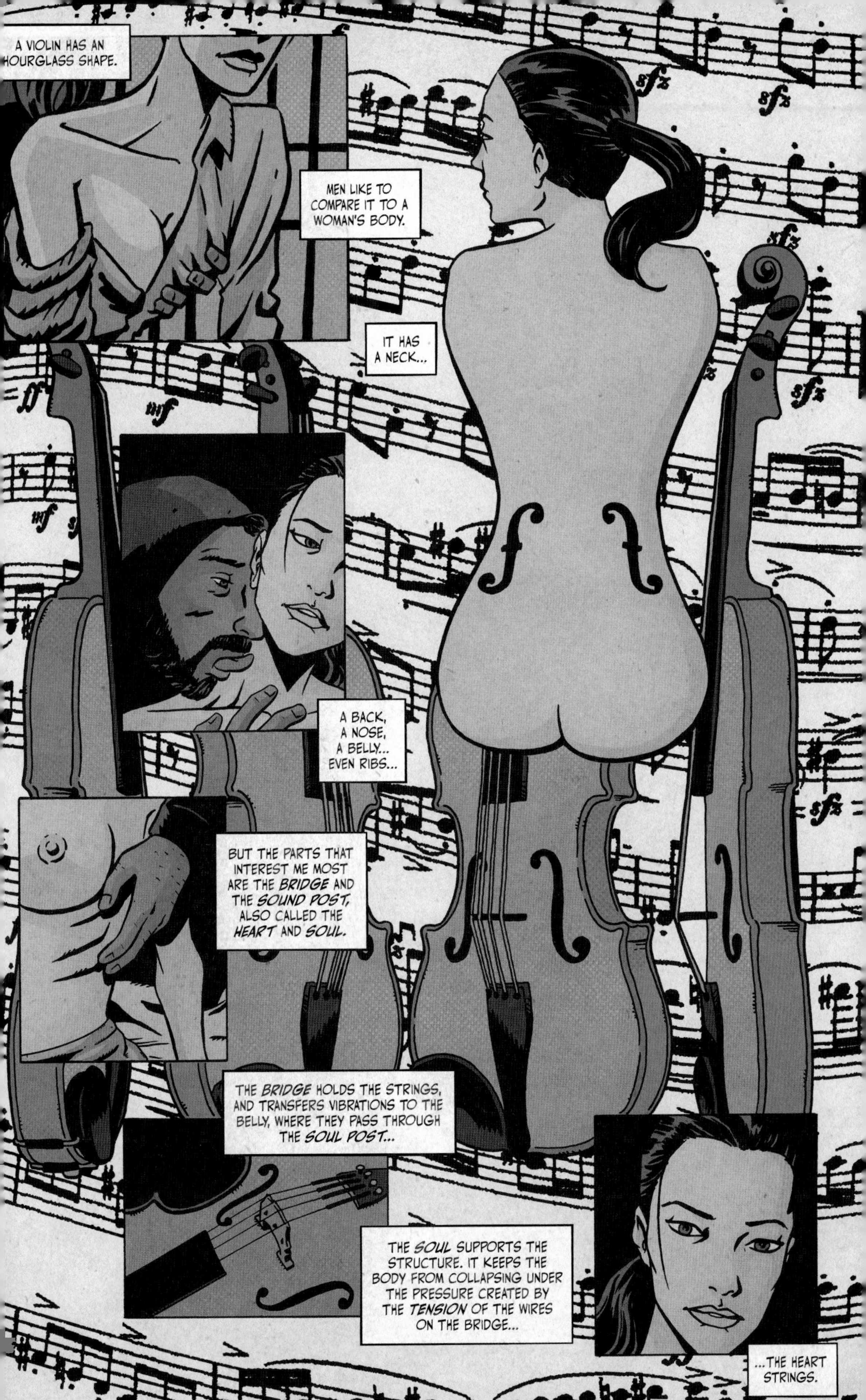
A VIOLIN HAS AN HOURGLASS SHAPE.
MEN LIKE TO COMPARE IT TO A WOMAN'S BODY.
IT HAS A NECK...
A BACK, A NOSE, A BELLY... EVEN RIBS...
BUT THE PARTS THAT INTEREST ME MOST ARE THE *BRIDGE* AND THE *SOUND POST*, ALSO CALLED THE *HEART* AND *SOUL*.
THE *BRIDGE* HOLDS THE STRINGS, AND TRANSFERS VIBRATIONS TO THE BELLY, WHERE THEY PASS THROUGH THE *SOUL POST*...
THE *SOUL* SUPPORTS THE STRUCTURE. IT KEEPS THE BODY FROM COLLAPSING UNDER THE PRESSURE CREATED BY THE *TENSION* OF THE WIRES ON THE BRIDGE...
...THE HEART STRINGS.

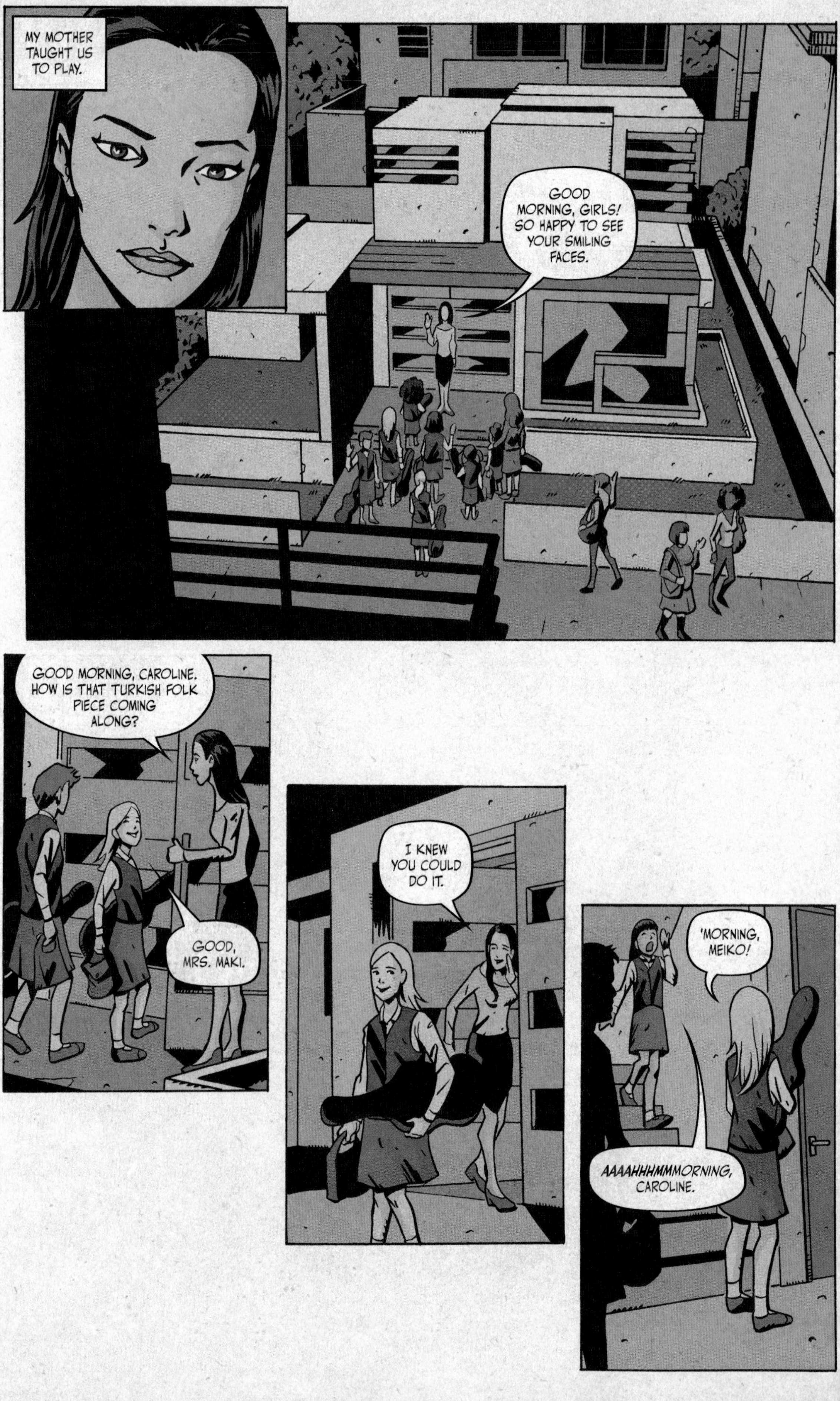
MY MOTHER TAUGHT US TO PLAY.
GOOD MORNING, GIRLS! SO HAPPY TO SEE YOUR SMILING FACES.
GOOD MORNING, CAROLINE. HOW IS THAT TURKISH FOLK PIECE COMING ALONG?
GOOD, MRS. MAKI.
I KNEW YOU COULD DO IT.
'MORNING, MEIKO!
AAAAHHHMMMORNING, CAROLINE.

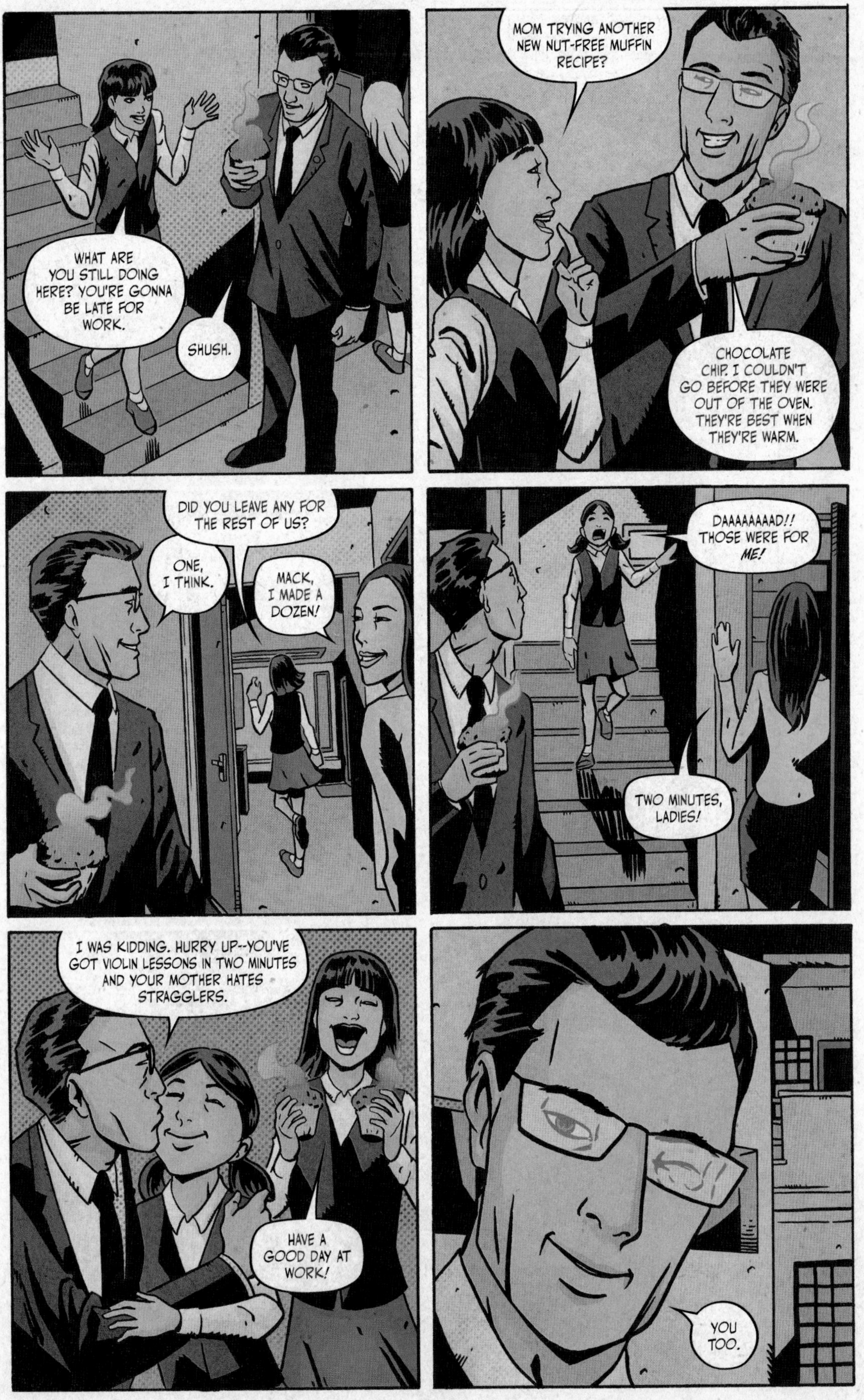
WHAT ARE YOU STILL DOING HERE? YOU'RE GONNA BE LATE FOR WORK.
SHUSH.
MOM TRYING ANOTHER NEW NUT-FREE MUFFIN RECIPE?
CHOCOLATE CHIP. I COULDN'T GO BEFORE THEY WERE OUT OF THE OVEN. THEY'RE BEST WHEN THEY'RE WARM.
DID YOU LEAVE ANY FOR THE REST OF US?
ONE, I THINK.
MACK, I MADE A DOZEN!
DAAAAAAAAD!! THOSE WERE FOR *ME!*
TWO MINUTES, LADIES!
I WAS KIDDING. HURRY UP--YOU'VE GOT VIOLIN LESSONS IN TWO MINUTES AND YOUR MOTHER HATES STRAGGLERS.
HAVE A GOOD DAY AT WORK!
YOU TOO.

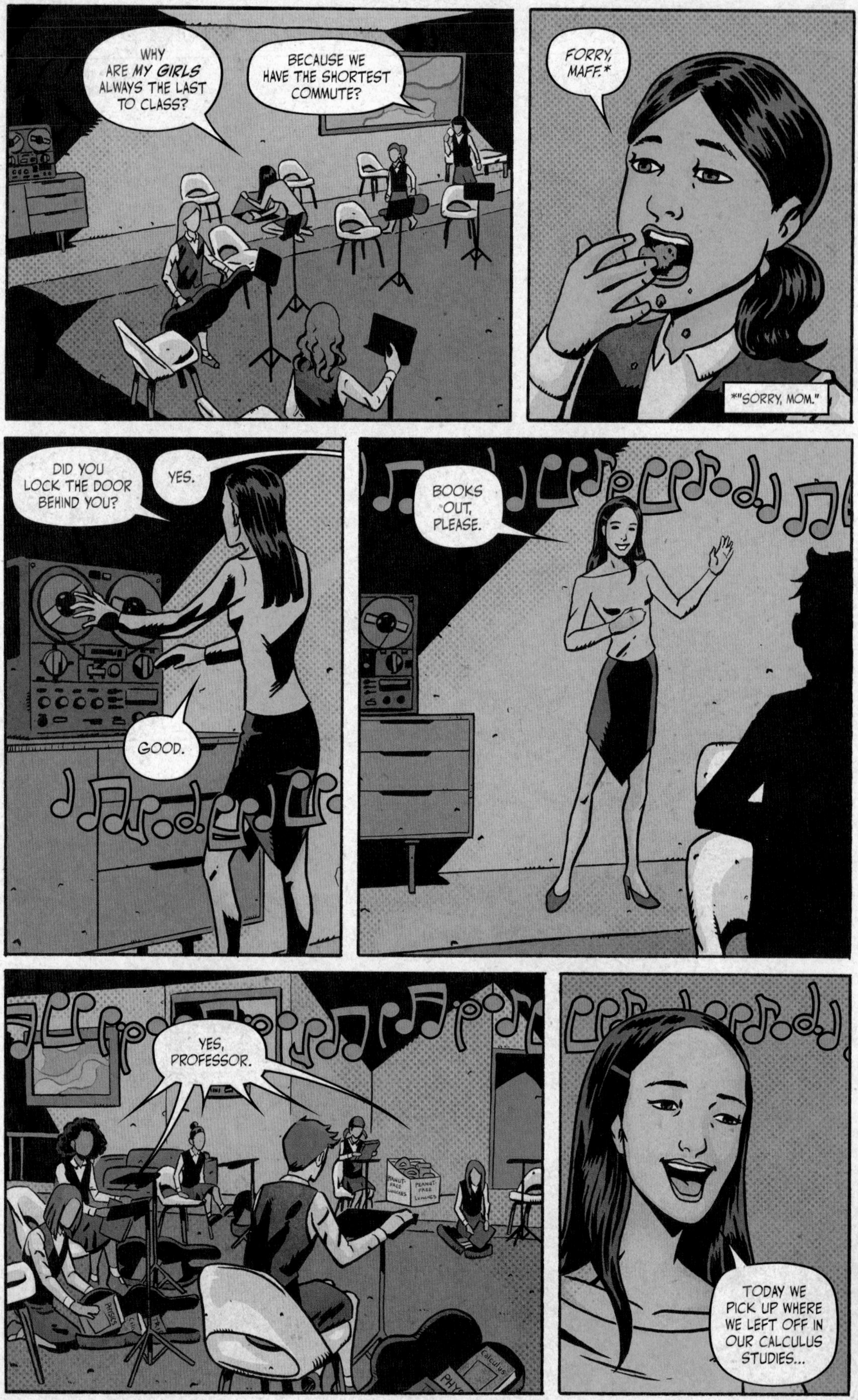
WHY ARE MY GIRLS ALWAYS THE LAST TO CLASS?
BECAUSE WE HAVE THE SHORTEST COMMUTE?
FORRY, MAFF.*
*"SORRY, MOM."
DID YOU LOCK THE DOOR BEHIND YOU?
YES.
GOOD.
BOOKS OUT, PLEASE.
YES, PROFESSOR.
TODAY WE PICK UP WHERE WE LEFT OFF IN OUR CALCULUS STUDIES...

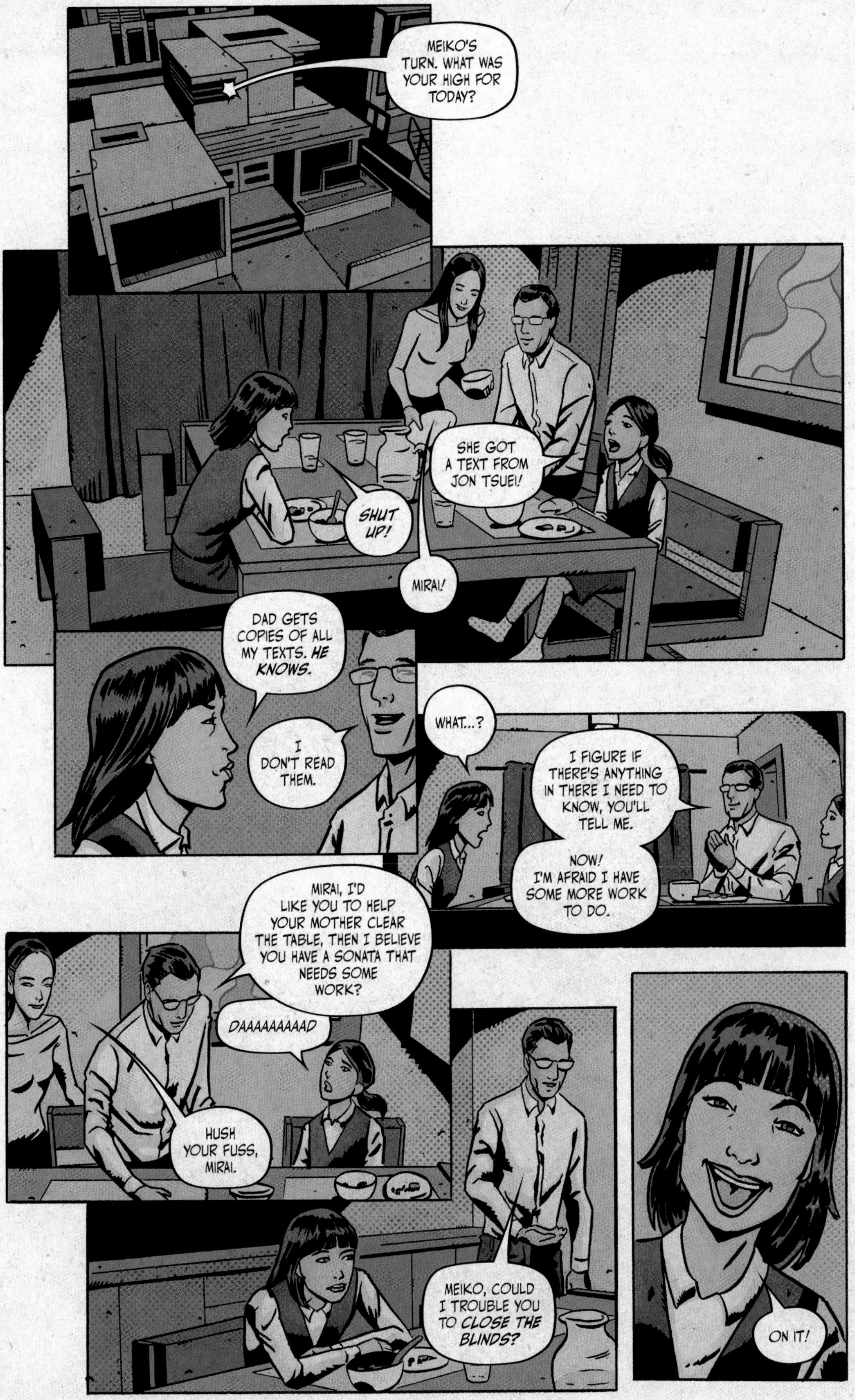
MEIKO'S TURN. WHAT WAS YOUR HIGH FOR TODAY?
SHE GOT A TEXT FROM JON TSUEI!
SHUT UP!
MIRAI!
DAD GETS COPIES OF ALL MY TEXTS. HE KNOWS.
I DON'T READ THEM.
WHAT...?
I FIGURE IF THERE'S ANYTHING IN THERE I NEED TO KNOW, YOU'LL TELL ME.
NOW! I'M AFRAID I HAVE SOME MORE WORK TO DO.
MIRAI, I'D LIKE YOU TO HELP YOUR MOTHER CLEAR THE TABLE, THEN I BELIEVE YOU HAVE A SONATA THAT NEEDS SOME WORK?
DAAAAAAAAAD
HUSH YOUR FUSS, MIRAI.
MEIKO, COULD I TROUBLE YOU TO CLOSE THE BLINDS?
ON IT!

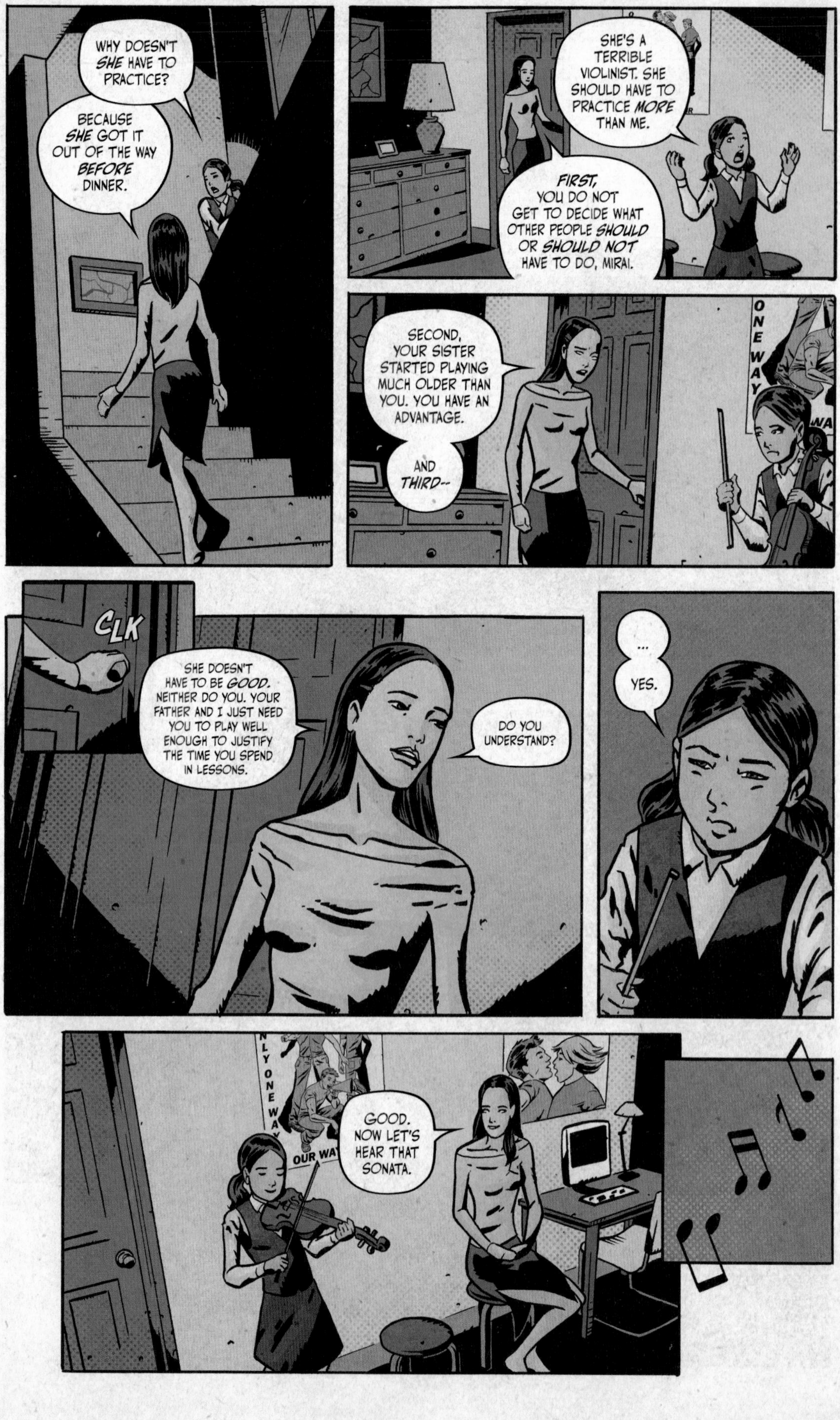
WHY DOESN'T SHE HAVE TO PRACTICE?
BECAUSE SHE GOT IT OUT OF THE WAY BEFORE DINNER.
SHE'S A TERRIBLE VIOLINIST. SHE SHOULD HAVE TO PRACTICE MORE THAN ME.
FIRST, YOU DO NOT GET TO DECIDE WHAT OTHER PEOPLE SHOULD OR SHOULD NOT HAVE TO DO, MIRAI.
SECOND, YOUR SISTER STARTED PLAYING MUCH OLDER THAN YOU. YOU HAVE AN ADVANTAGE.
AND THIRD--
ONE WAY
CLK
SHE DOESN'T HAVE TO BE GOOD. NEITHER DO YOU. YOUR FATHER AND I JUST NEED YOU TO PLAY WELL ENOUGH TO JUSTIFY THE TIME YOU SPEND IN LESSONS.
DO YOU UNDERSTAND?
...
YES.
ONE WAY
OUR WAY
GOOD. NOW LET'S HEAR THAT SONATA.

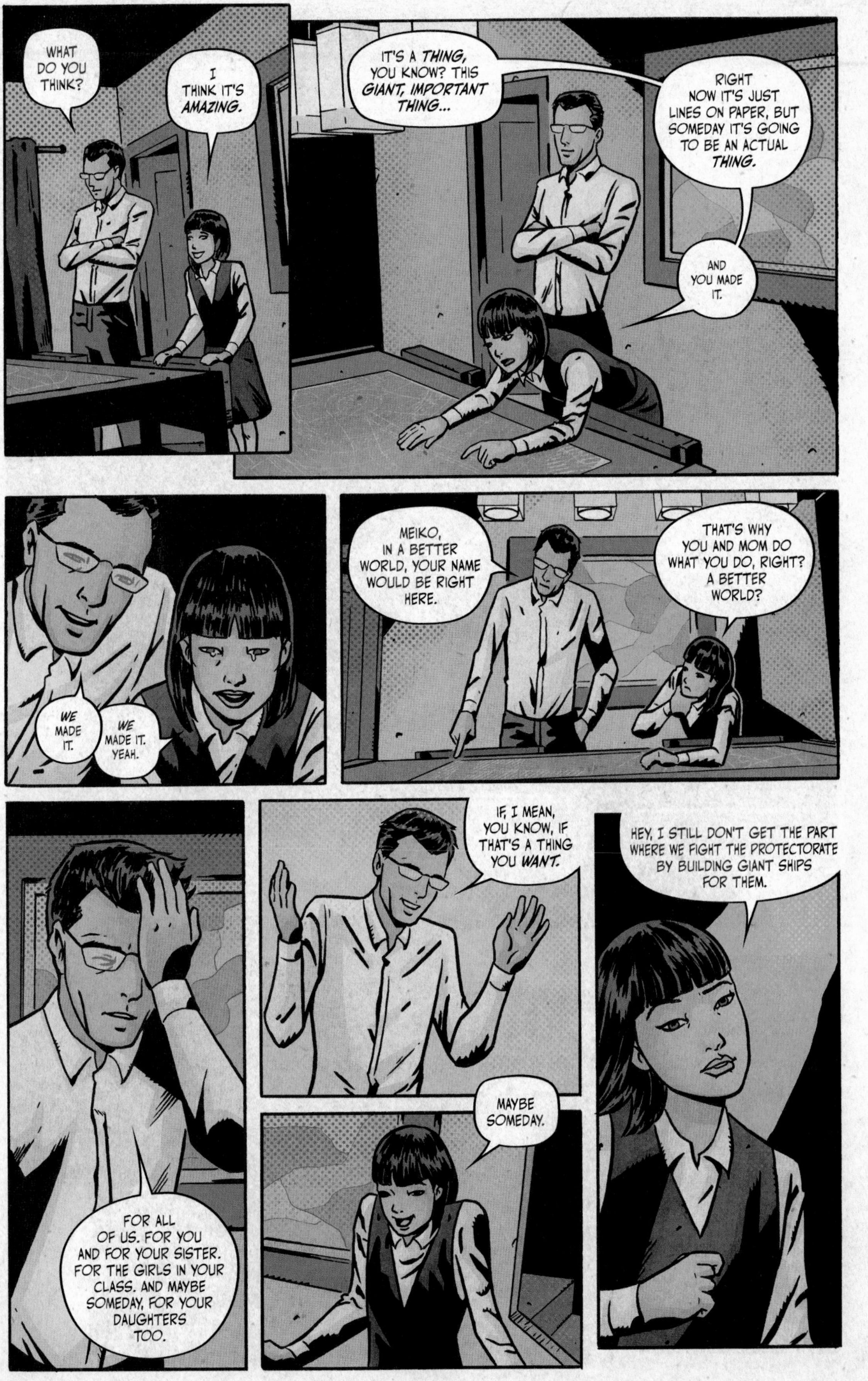

WHAT DO YOU THINK?
I THINK IT'S *AMAZING.*
IT'S A *THING,* YOU KNOW? THIS *GIANT, IMPORTANT THING...*
RIGHT NOW IT'S JUST LINES ON PAPER, BUT SOMEDAY IT'S GOING TO BE AN ACTUAL *THING.*
AND YOU MADE IT.
WE MADE IT.
WE MADE IT. YEAH.
MEIKO, IN A BETTER WORLD, YOUR NAME WOULD BE RIGHT HERE.
THAT'S WHY YOU AND MOM DO WHAT YOU DO, RIGHT? A BETTER WORLD?
FOR ALL OF US. FOR YOU AND FOR YOUR SISTER. FOR THE GIRLS IN YOUR CLASS. AND MAYBE SOMEDAY, FOR YOUR DAUGHTERS TOO.
IF, I MEAN, YOU KNOW, IF THAT'S A THING YOU *WANT.*
MAYBE SOMEDAY.
HEY, I STILL DON'T GET THE PART WHERE WE FIGHT THE PROTECTORATE BY BUILDING GIANT SHIPS FOR THEM.

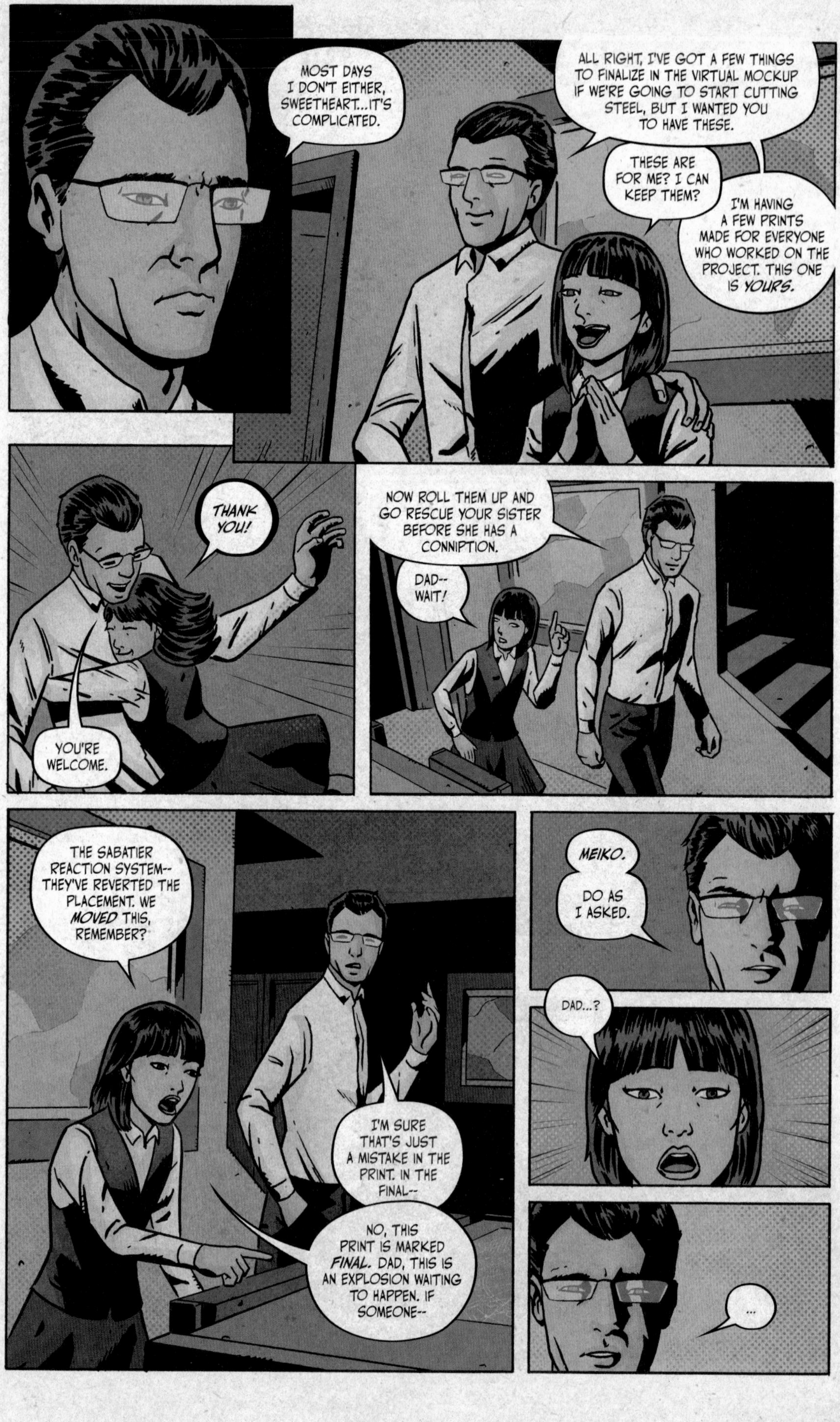
MOST DAYS I DON'T EITHER, SWEETHEART...IT'S COMPLICATED.
ALL RIGHT, I'VE GOT A FEW THINGS TO FINALIZE IN THE VIRTUAL MOCKUP IF WE'RE GOING TO START CUTTING STEEL, BUT I WANTED YOU TO HAVE THESE.
THESE ARE FOR ME? I CAN KEEP THEM?
I'M HAVING A FEW PRINTS MADE FOR EVERYONE WHO WORKED ON THE PROJECT. THIS ONE IS *YOURS.*
THANK YOU!
YOU'RE WELCOME.
NOW ROLL THEM UP AND GO RESCUE YOUR SISTER BEFORE SHE HAS A CONNIPTION.
DAD-- WAIT!
THE SABATIER REACTION SYSTEM-- THEY'VE REVERTED THE PLACEMENT. WE *MOVED* THIS, REMEMBER?
I'M SURE THAT'S JUST A MISTAKE IN THE PRINT. IN THE FINAL--
NO, THIS PRINT IS MARKED *FINAL.* DAD, THIS IS AN EXPLOSION WAITING TO HAPPEN. IF SOMEONE--
MEIKO.
DO AS I ASKED.
DAD...?
...

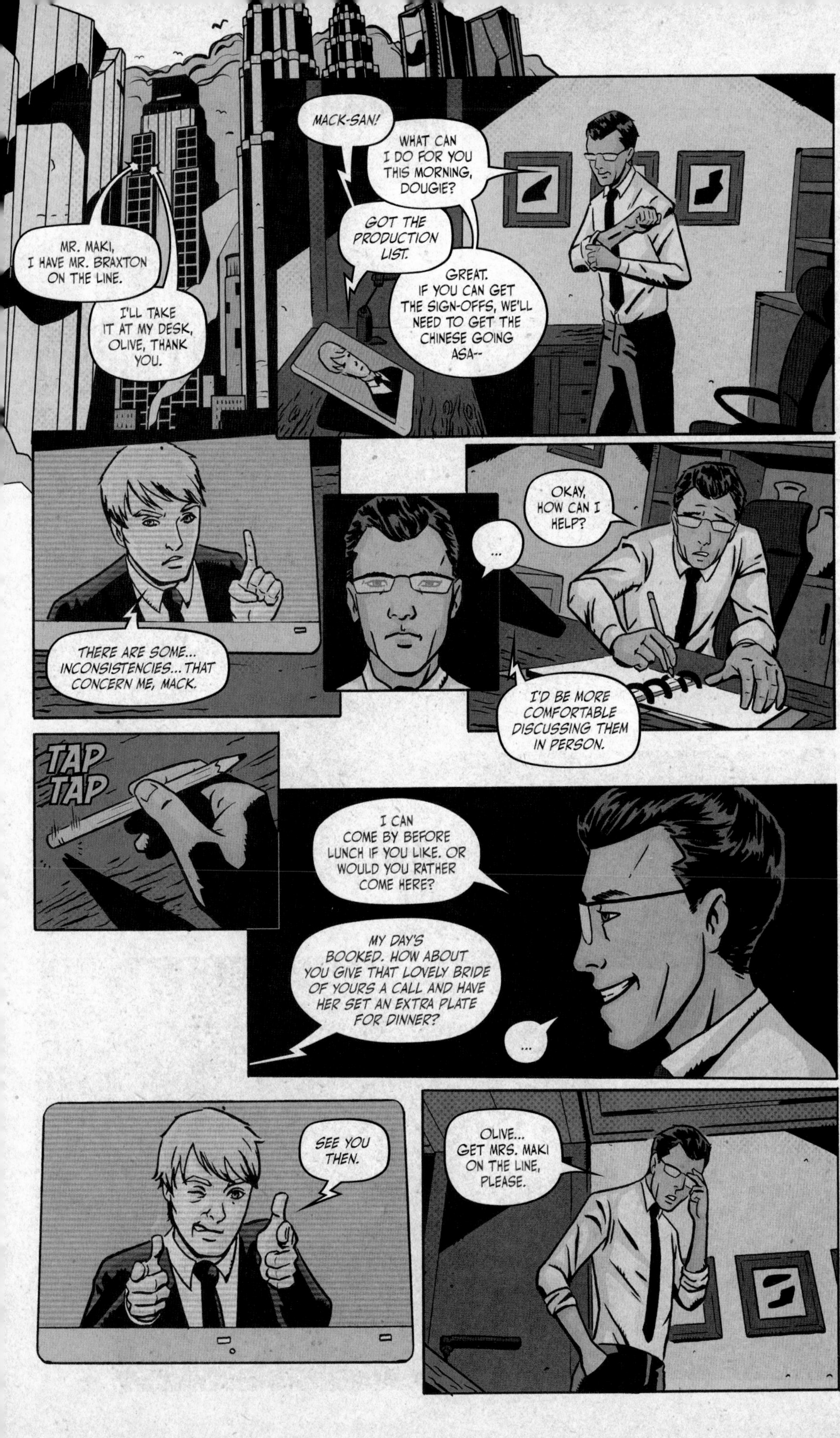
MR. MAKI, I HAVE MR. BRAXTON ON THE LINE.
I'LL TAKE IT AT MY DESK, OLIVE, THANK YOU.
MACK-SAN!
WHAT CAN I DO FOR YOU THIS MORNING, DOUGIE?
GOT THE PRODUCTION LIST.
GREAT. IF YOU CAN GET THE SIGN-OFFS, WE'LL NEED TO GET THE CHINESE GOING ASA--
THERE ARE SOME... INCONSISTENCIES... THAT CONCERN ME, MACK.
...
OKAY, HOW CAN I HELP?
I'D BE MORE COMFORTABLE DISCUSSING THEM IN PERSON.
TAP TAP
I CAN COME BY BEFORE LUNCH IF YOU LIKE. OR WOULD YOU RATHER COME HERE?
MY DAY'S BOOKED. HOW ABOUT YOU GIVE THAT LOVELY BRIDE OF YOURS A CALL AND HAVE HER SET AN EXTRA PLATE FOR DINNER?
...
SEE YOU THEN.
OLIVE... GET MRS. MAKI ON THE LINE, PLEASE.

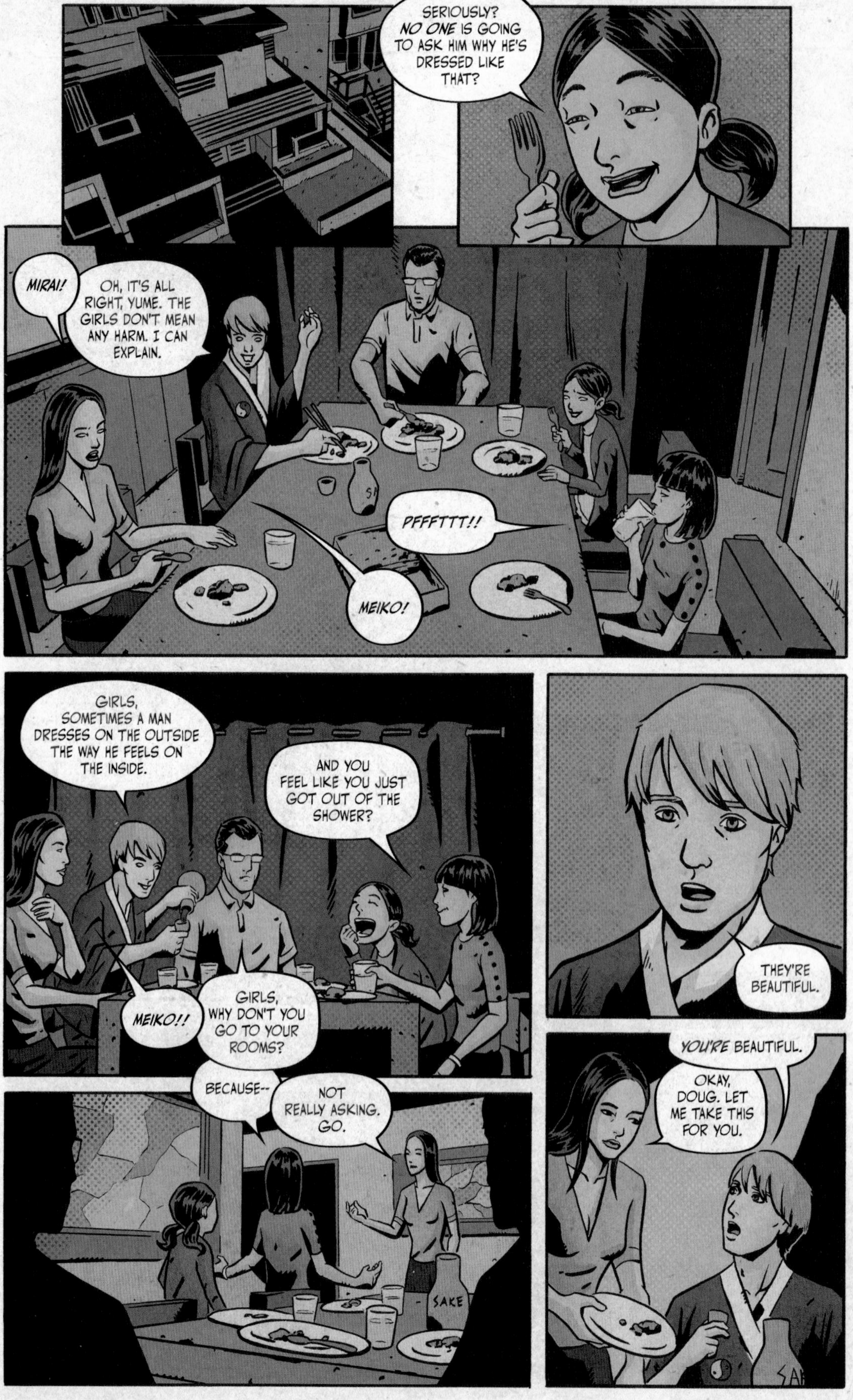
SERIOUSLY? NO ONE IS GOING TO ASK HIM WHY HE'S DRESSED LIKE THAT?
MIRAI!
OH, IT'S ALL RIGHT, YUME. THE GIRLS DON'T MEAN ANY HARM. I CAN EXPLAIN.
PFFFTTT!!
MEIKO!
GIRLS, SOMETIMES A MAN DRESSES ON THE OUTSIDE THE WAY HE FEELS ON THE INSIDE.
AND YOU FEEL LIKE YOU JUST GOT OUT OF THE SHOWER?
MEIKO!!
GIRLS, WHY DON'T YOU GO TO YOUR ROOMS?
THEY'RE BEAUTIFUL.
YOU'RE BEAUTIFUL.
OKAY, DOUG. LET ME TAKE THIS FOR YOU.
BECAUSE--
NOT REALLY ASKING. GO.
SAKE

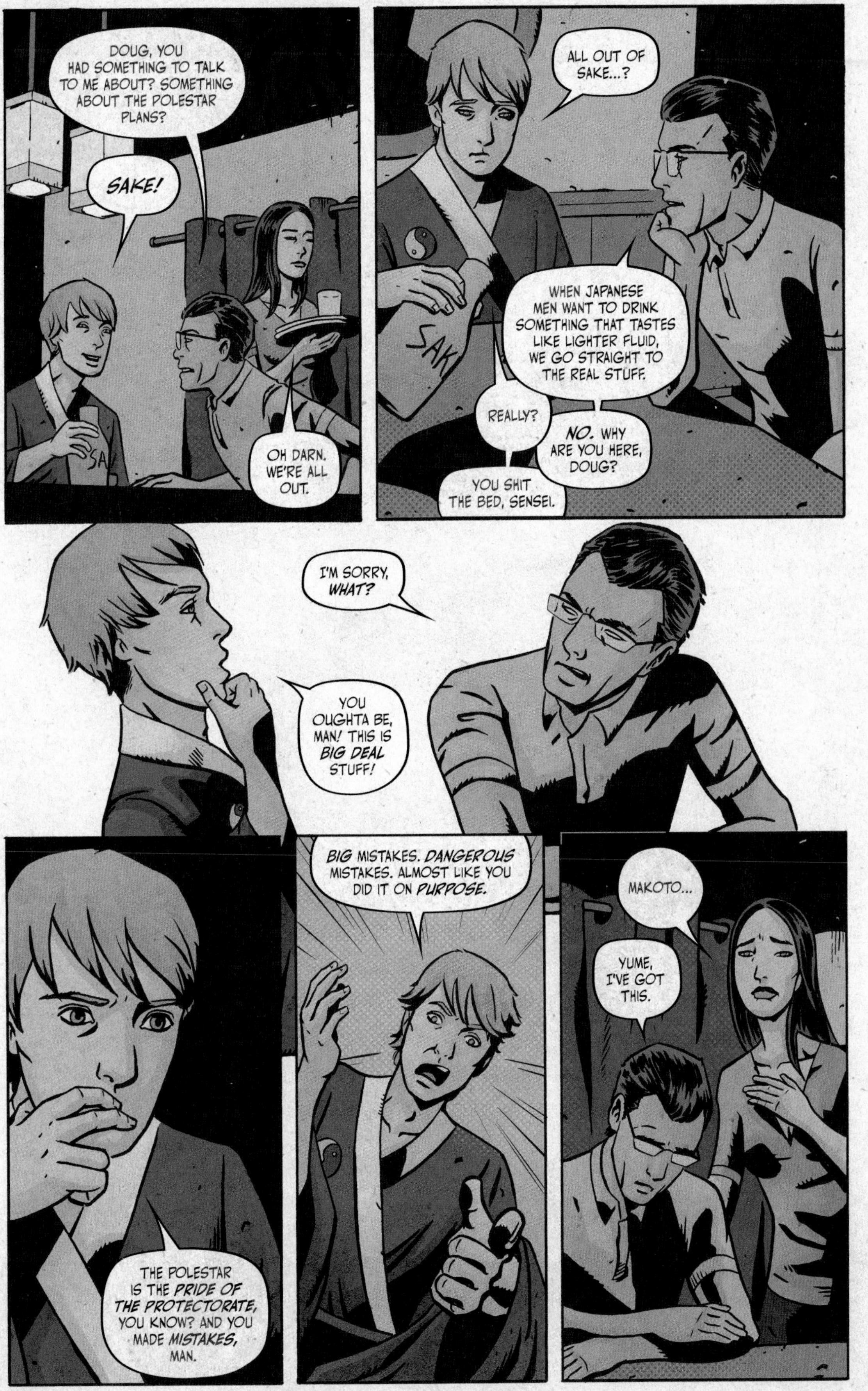
DOUG, YOU HAD SOMETHING TO TALK TO ME ABOUT? SOMETHING ABOUT THE POLESTAR PLANS?
SAKE!
OH DARN. WE'RE ALL OUT.
ALL OUT OF SAKE...?
WHEN JAPANESE MEN WANT TO DRINK SOMETHING THAT TASTES LIKE LIGHTER FLUID, WE GO STRAIGHT TO THE REAL STUFF.
REALLY?
NO. WHY ARE YOU HERE, DOUG?
YOU SHIT THE BED, SENSEI.
I'M SORRY, WHAT?
YOU OUGHTA BE, MAN! THIS IS BIG DEAL STUFF!
THE POLESTAR IS THE PRIDE OF THE PROTECTORATE, YOU KNOW? AND YOU MADE MISTAKES, MAN.
BIG MISTAKES. DANGEROUS MISTAKES. ALMOST LIKE YOU DID IT ON PURPOSE.
MAKOTO...
YUME, I'VE GOT THIS.

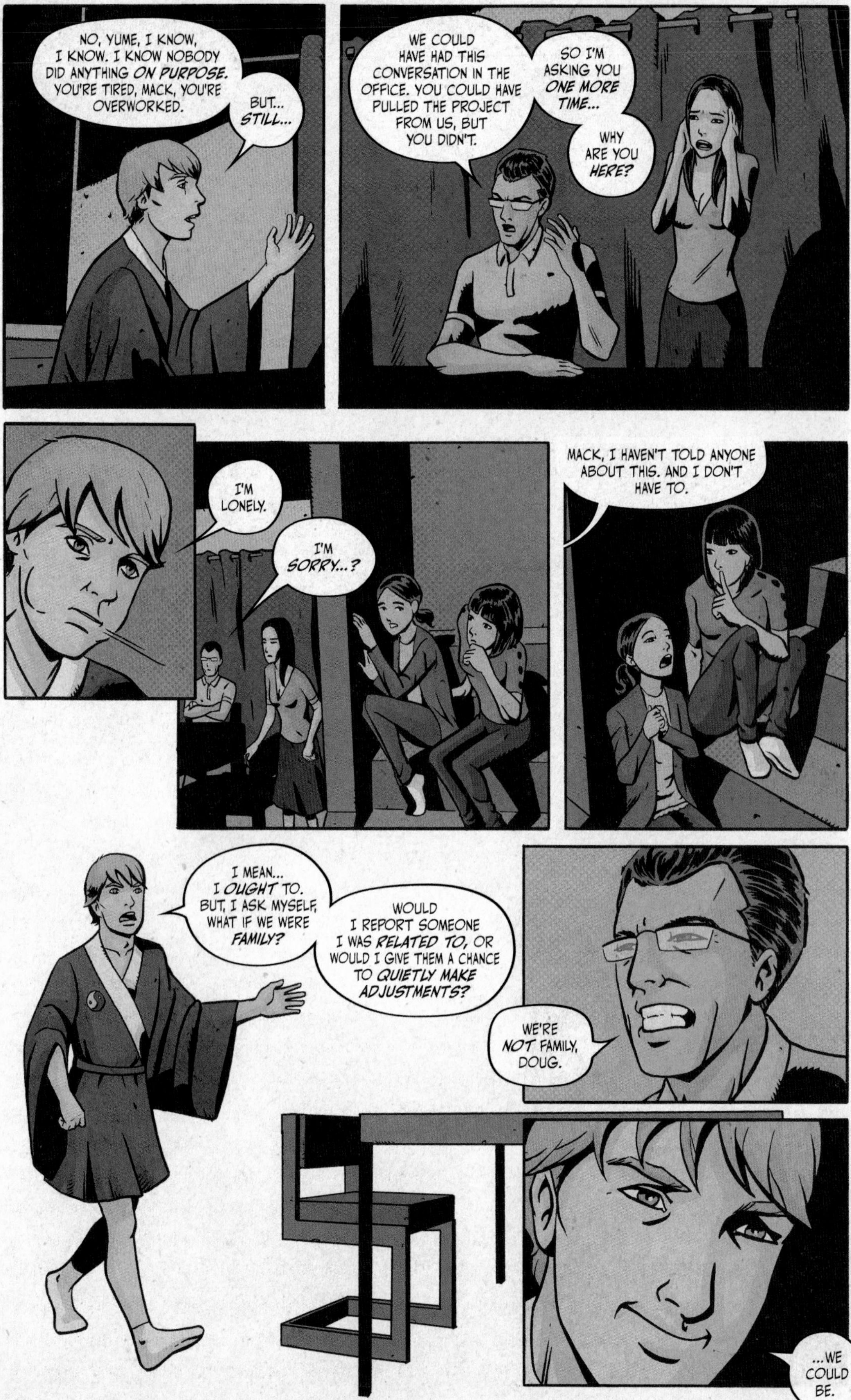
NO, YUME, I KNOW, I KNOW. I KNOW NOBODY DID ANYTHING ON PURPOSE. YOU'RE TIRED, MACK, YOU'RE OVERWORKED.
BUT... STILL...
WE COULD HAVE HAD THIS CONVERSATION IN THE OFFICE. YOU COULD HAVE PULLED THE PROJECT FROM US, BUT YOU DIDN'T.
SO I'M ASKING YOU ONE MORE TIME...
WHY ARE YOU HERE?
I'M LONELY.
I'M SORRY...?
MACK, I HAVEN'T TOLD ANYONE ABOUT THIS. AND I DON'T HAVE TO.
I MEAN... I OUGHT TO. BUT, I ASK MYSELF, WHAT IF WE WERE FAMILY?
WOULD I REPORT SOMEONE I WAS RELATED TO, OR WOULD I GIVE THEM A CHANCE TO QUIETLY MAKE ADJUSTMENTS?
WE'RE NOT FAMILY, DOUG.
...WE COULD BE.

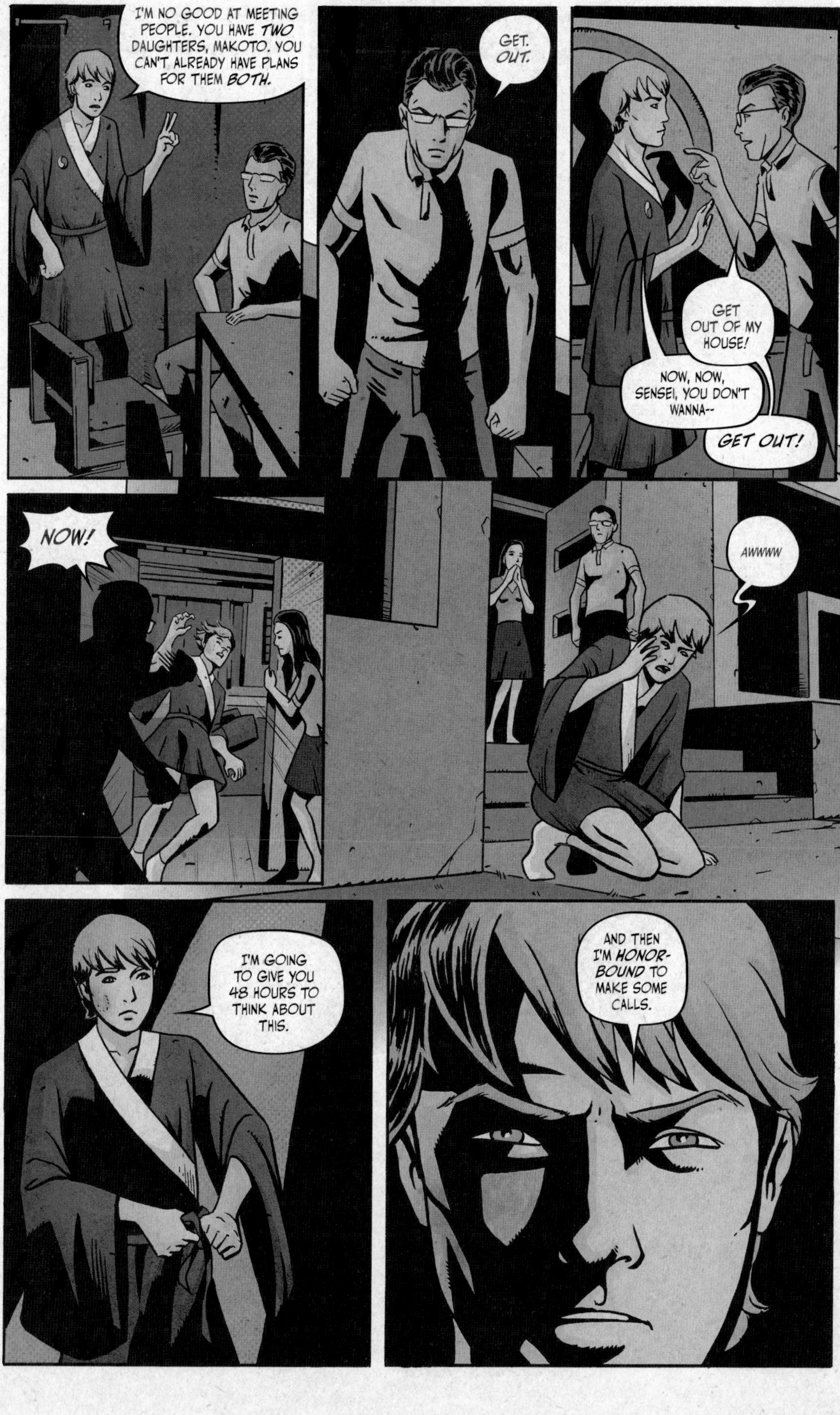
I'M NO GOOD AT MEETING PEOPLE. YOU HAVE TWO DAUGHTERS, MAKOTO. YOU CAN'T ALREADY HAVE PLANS FOR THEM BOTH.
GET. OUT.
GET OUT OF MY HOUSE!
NOW, NOW, SENSEI, YOU DON'T WANNA--
GET OUT!
NOW!
AWWWW
I'M GOING TO GIVE YOU 48 HOURS TO THINK ABOUT THIS.
AND THEN I'M HONOR-BOUND TO MAKE SOME CALLS.

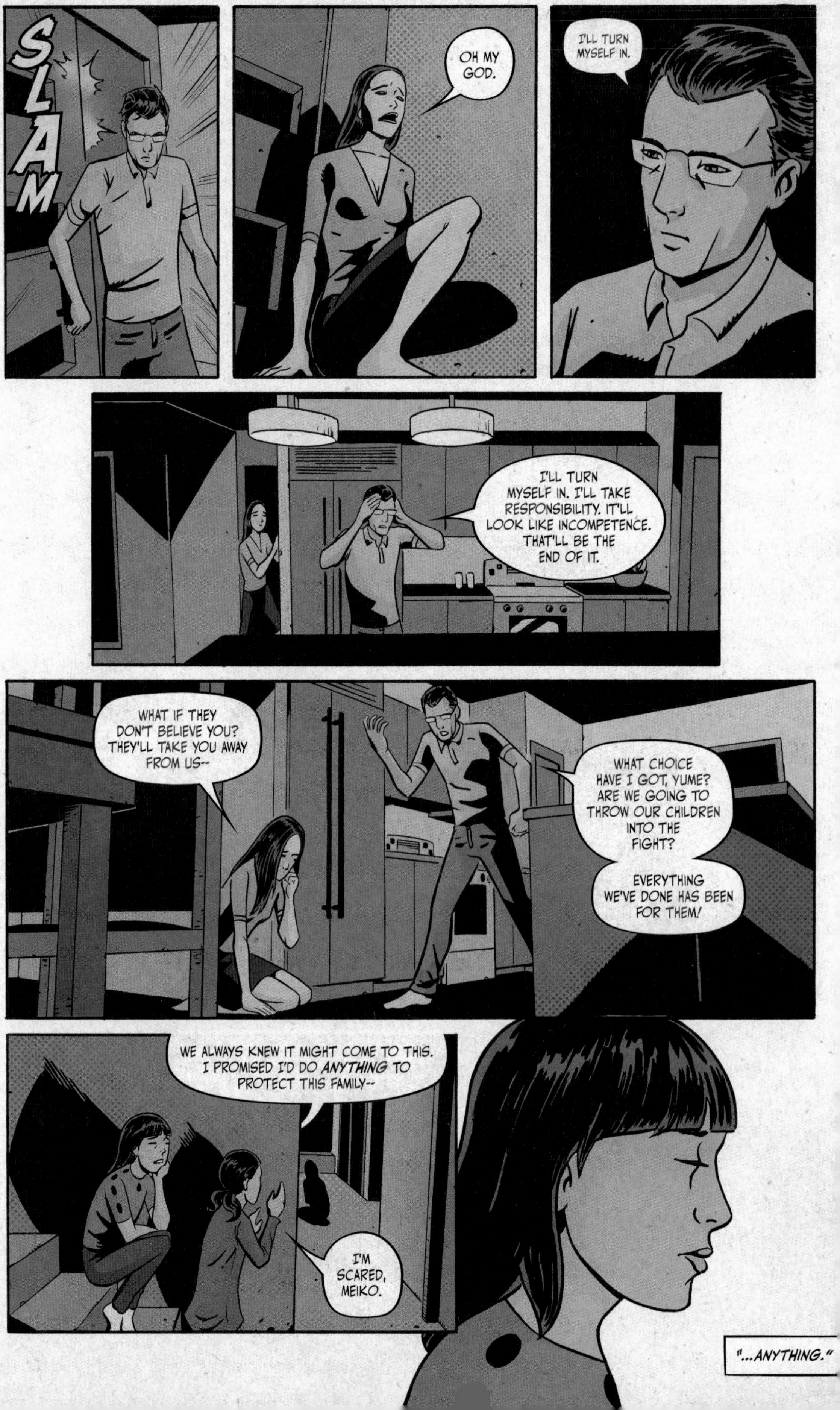
SLAM
OH MY GOD.
I'LL TURN MYSELF IN.
I'LL TURN MYSELF IN. I'LL TAKE RESPONSIBILITY. IT'LL LOOK LIKE INCOMPETENCE. THAT'LL BE THE END OF IT.
WHAT IF THEY DON'T BELIEVE YOU? THEY'LL TAKE YOU AWAY FROM US--
WHAT CHOICE HAVE I GOT, YUME? ARE WE GOING TO THROW OUR CHILDREN INTO THE FIGHT?
EVERYTHING WE'VE DONE HAS BEEN FOR THEM!
WE ALWAYS KNEW IT MIGHT COME TO THIS. I PROMISED I'D DO ANYTHING TO PROTECT THIS FAMILY--
I'M SCARED, MEIKO.
"...ANYTHING."

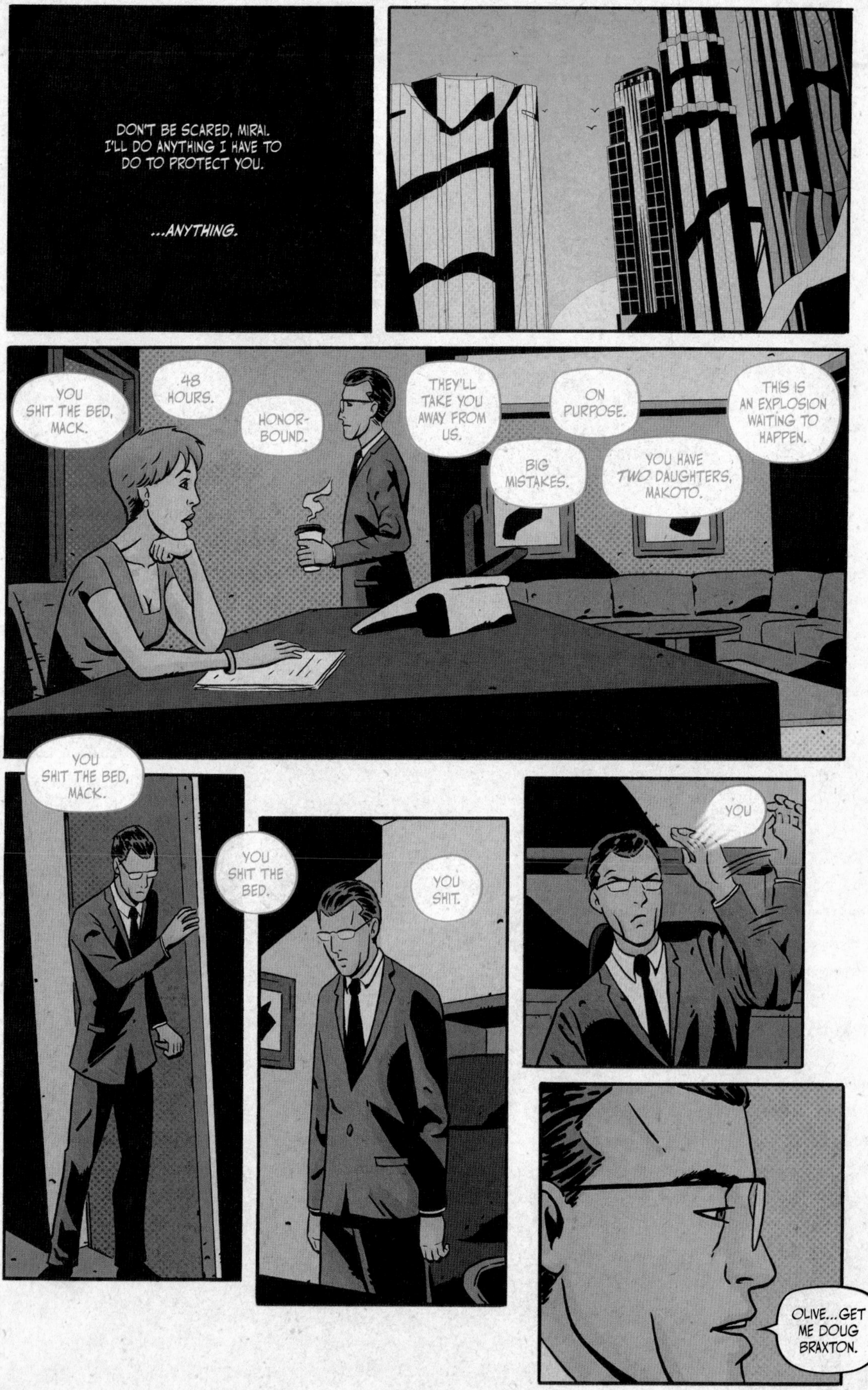
DON'T BE SCARED, MIRAI. I'LL DO ANYTHING I HAVE TO DO TO PROTECT YOU.
...ANYTHING.
YOU SHIT THE BED, MACK.
48 HOURS.
HONOR-BOUND.
THEY'LL TAKE YOU AWAY FROM US.
BIG MISTAKES.
ON PURPOSE.
YOU HAVE TWO DAUGHTERS, MAKOTO.
THIS IS AN EXPLOSION WAITING TO HAPPEN.
YOU SHIT THE BED, MACK.
YOU SHIT THE BED.
YOU SHIT.
YOU
OLIVE...GET ME DOUG BRAXTON.

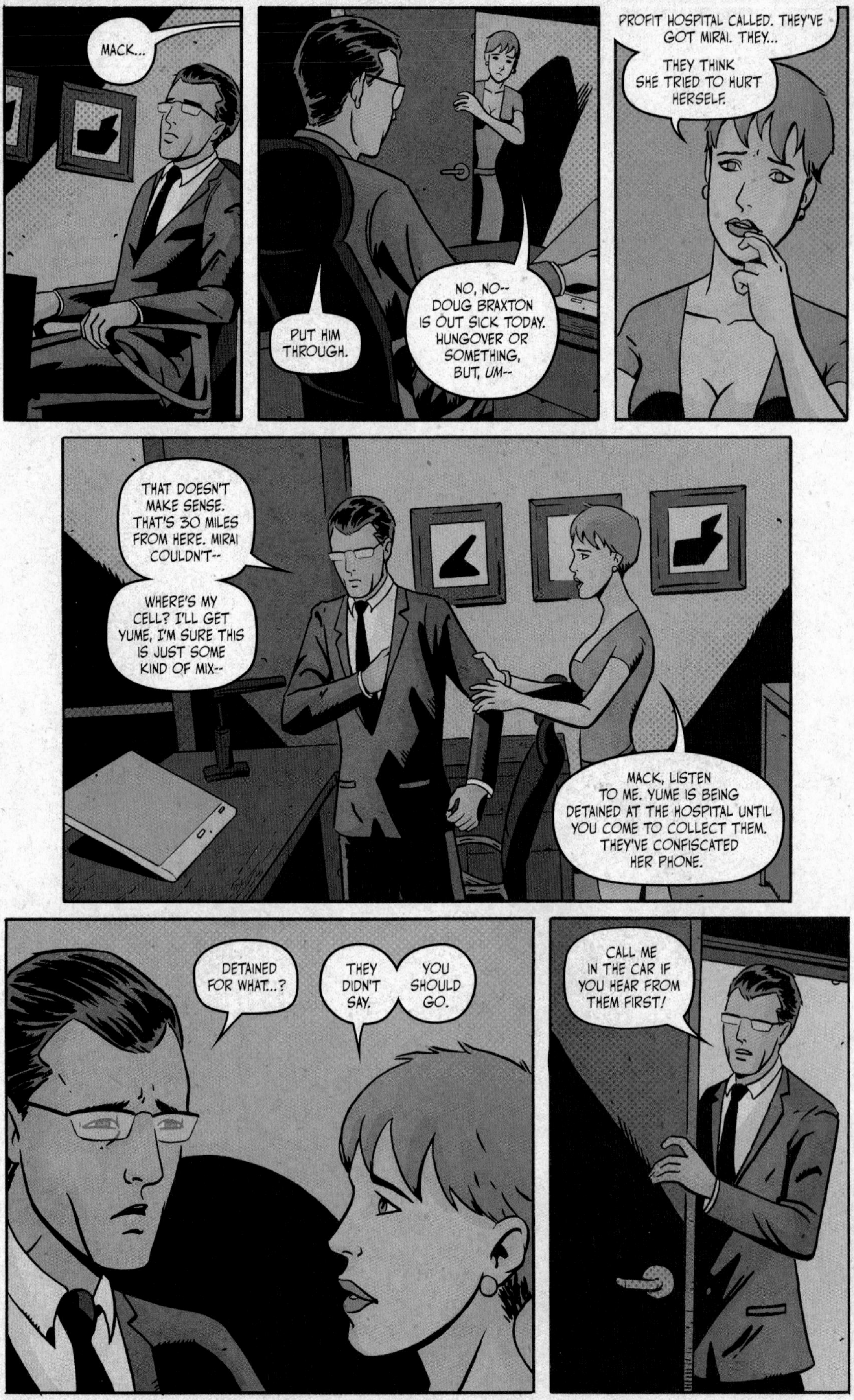
MACK...
PUT HIM THROUGH.
NO, NO-- DOUG BRAXTON IS OUT SICK TODAY. HUNGOVER OR SOMETHING, BUT, UM--
PROFIT HOSPITAL CALLED. THEY'VE GOT MIRAI. THEY...
THEY THINK SHE TRIED TO HURT HERSELF.
THAT DOESN'T MAKE SENSE. THAT'S 30 MILES FROM HERE. MIRAI COULDN'T--
WHERE'S MY CELL? I'LL GET YUME, I'M SURE THIS IS JUST SOME KIND OF MIX--
MACK, LISTEN TO ME. YUME IS BEING DETAINED AT THE HOSPITAL UNTIL YOU COME TO COLLECT THEM. THEY'VE CONFISCATED HER PHONE.
DETAINED FOR WHAT...?
THEY DIDN'T SAY.
YOU SHOULD GO.
CALL ME IN THE CAR IF YOU HEAR FROM THEM FIRST!

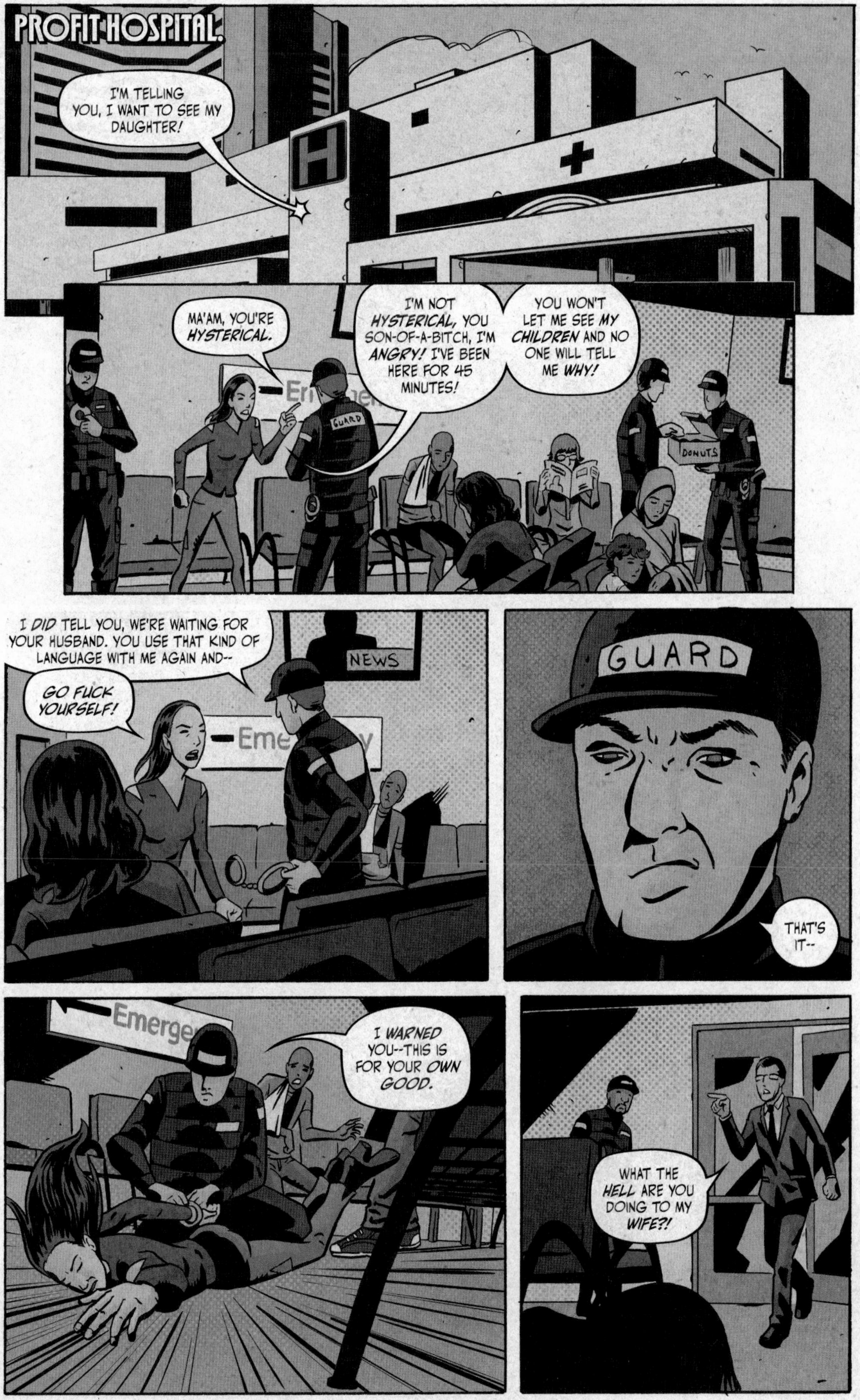
PROFIT HOSPITAL.
I'M TELLING YOU, I WANT TO SEE MY DAUGHTER!
MA'AM, YOU'RE HYSTERICAL.
I'M NOT HYSTERICAL, YOU SON-OF-A-BITCH, I'M ANGRY! I'VE BEEN HERE FOR 45 MINUTES!
YOU WON'T LET ME SEE MY CHILDREN AND NO ONE WILL TELL ME WHY!
GUARD
DONUTS
I DID TELL YOU, WE'RE WAITING FOR YOUR HUSBAND. YOU USE THAT KIND OF LANGUAGE WITH ME AGAIN AND--
GO FUCK YOURSELF!
NEWS
GUARD
THAT'S IT--
Emergen
I WARNED YOU--THIS IS FOR YOUR OWN GOOD.
WHAT THE HELL ARE YOU DOING TO MY WIFE?!

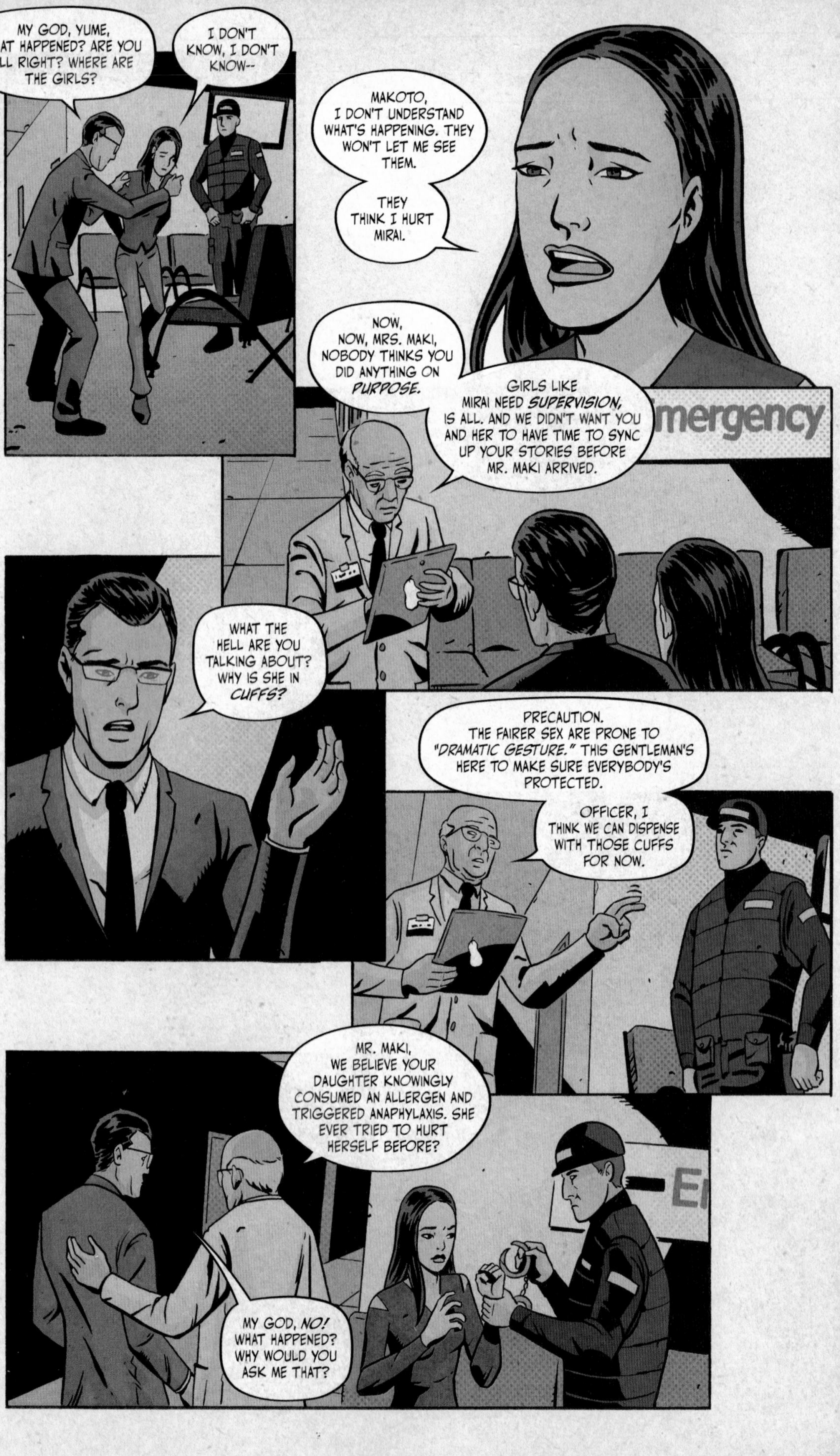

MY GOD, YUME, WHAT HAPPENED? ARE YOU ALL RIGHT? WHERE ARE THE GIRLS?
I DON'T KNOW, I DON'T KNOW--
MAKOTO, I DON'T UNDERSTAND WHAT'S HAPPENING. THEY WON'T LET ME SEE THEM.
THEY THINK I HURT MIRAI.
NOW, NOW, MRS. MAKI, NOBODY THINKS YOU DID ANYTHING ON *PURPOSE.*
GIRLS LIKE MIRAI NEED *SUPERVISION,* IS ALL. AND WE DIDN'T WANT YOU AND HER TO HAVE TIME TO SYNC UP YOUR STORIES BEFORE MR. MAKI ARRIVED.
Emergency
WHAT THE HELL ARE YOU TALKING ABOUT? WHY IS SHE IN *CUFFS?*
PRECAUTION. THE FAIRER SEX ARE PRONE TO *"DRAMATIC GESTURE."* THIS GENTLEMAN'S HERE TO MAKE SURE EVERYBODY'S PROTECTED.
OFFICER, I THINK WE CAN DISPENSE WITH THOSE CUFFS FOR NOW.
MR. MAKI, WE BELIEVE YOUR DAUGHTER KNOWINGLY CONSUMED AN ALLERGEN AND TRIGGERED ANAPHYLAXIS. SHE EVER TRIED TO HURT HERSELF BEFORE?
MY GOD, *NO!* WHAT HAPPENED? WHY WOULD YOU ASK ME THAT?

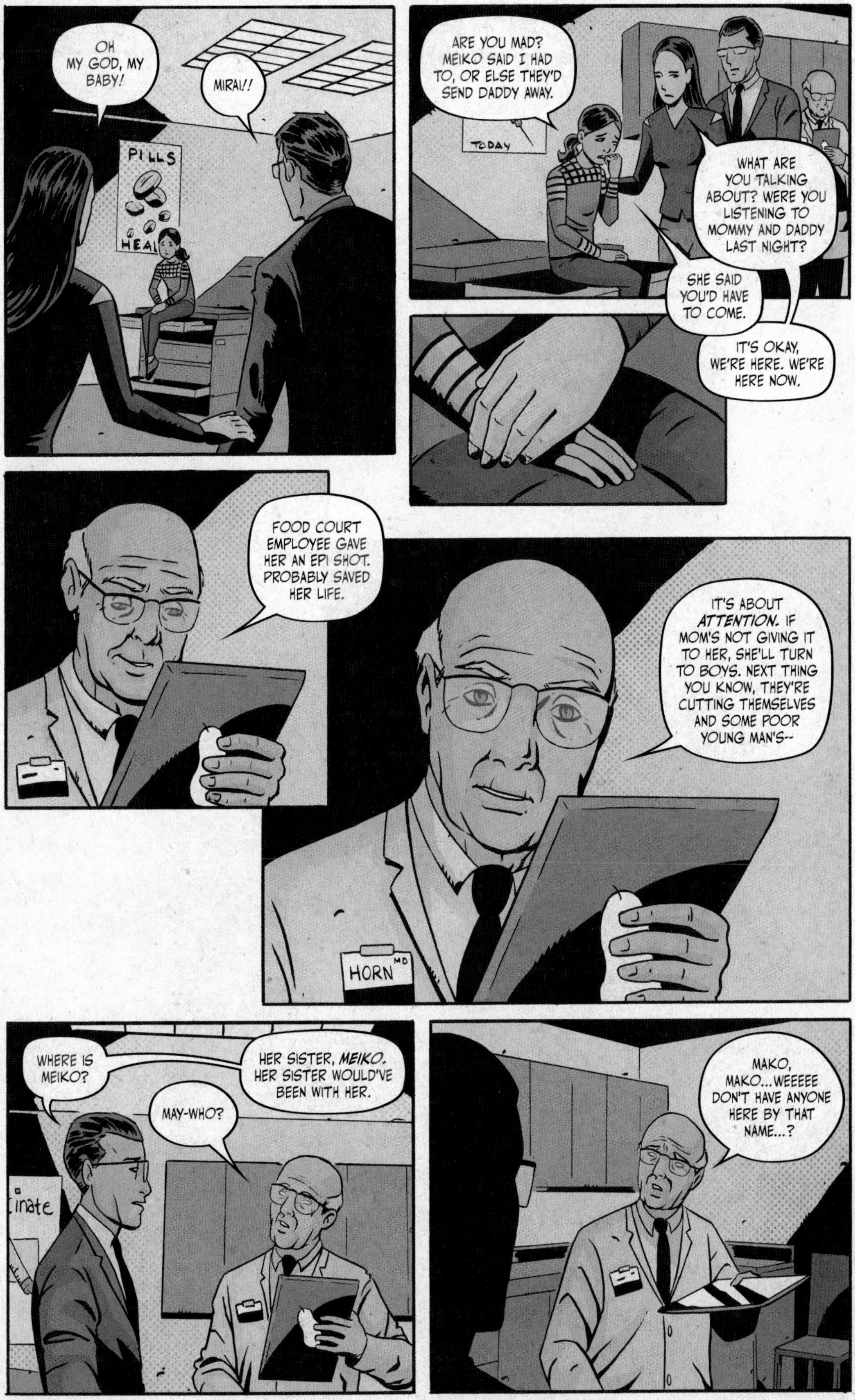
OH MY GOD, MY BABY!
MIRAI!!
PILLS
HEAL
ARE YOU MAD? MEIKO SAID I HAD TO, OR ELSE THEY'D SEND DADDY AWAY.
TODAY
WHAT ARE YOU TALKING ABOUT? WERE YOU LISTENING TO MOMMY AND DADDY LAST NIGHT?
SHE SAID YOU'D HAVE TO COME.
IT'S OKAY, WE'RE HERE. WE'RE HERE NOW.
FOOD COURT EMPLOYEE GAVE HER AN EPI SHOT. PROBABLY SAVED HER LIFE.
IT'S ABOUT *ATTENTION.* IF MOM'S NOT GIVING IT TO HER, SHE'LL TURN TO BOYS. NEXT THING YOU KNOW, THEY'RE CUTTING THEMSELVES AND SOME POOR YOUNG MAN'S--
HORN MD
WHERE IS MEIKO?
HER SISTER, *MEIKO.* HER SISTER WOULD'VE BEEN WITH HER.
MAY-WHO?
MAKO, MAKO...WEEEEE DON'T HAVE ANYONE HERE BY THAT NAME...?

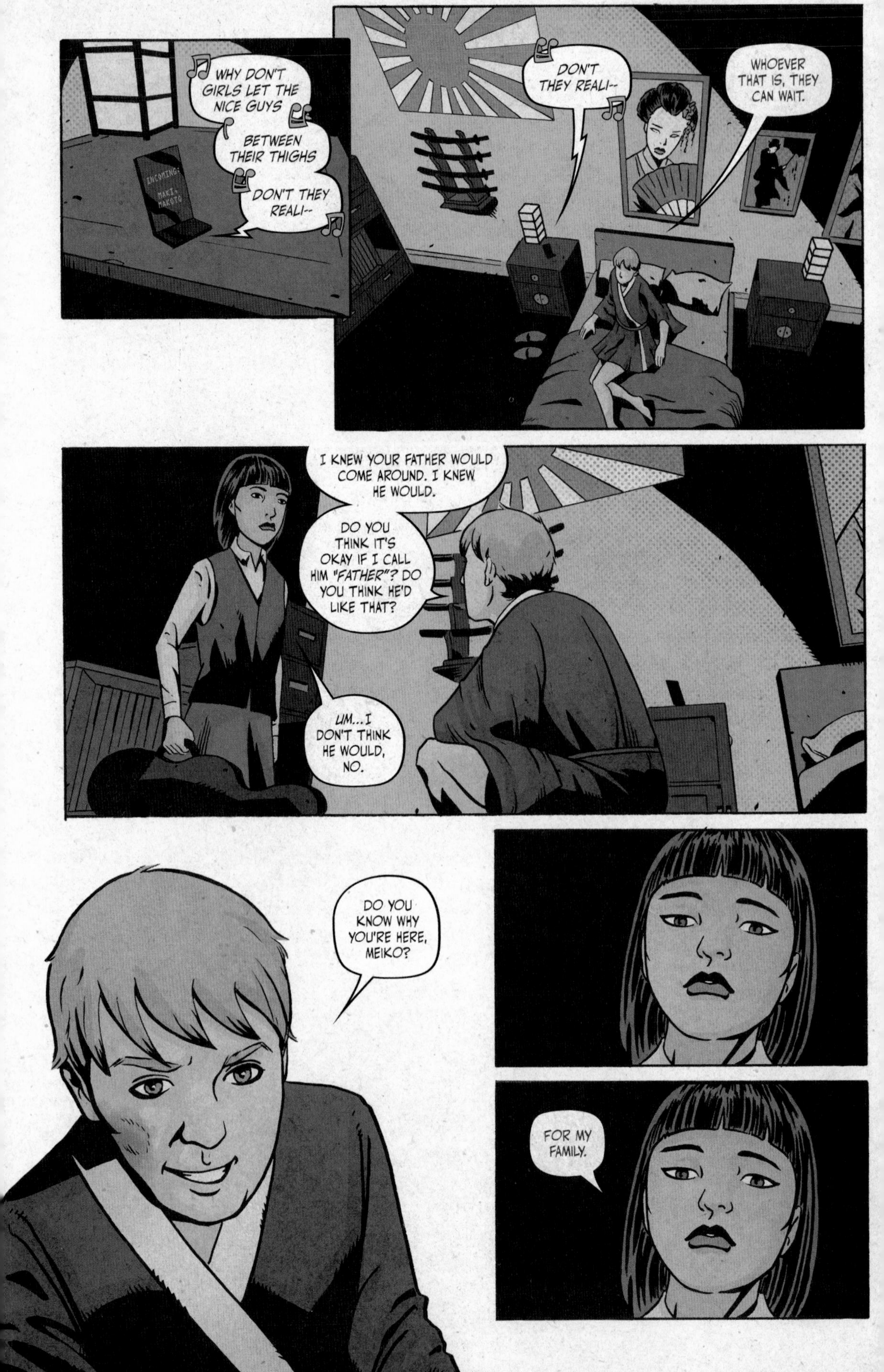
INCOMING:
MAKI, MAKOTO
WHY DON'T GIRLS LET THE NICE GUYS
BETWEEN THEIR THIGHS
DON'T THEY REALI--
DON'T THEY REALI--
WHOEVER THAT IS, THEY CAN WAIT.
I KNEW YOUR FATHER WOULD COME AROUND. I KNEW HE WOULD.
DO YOU THINK IT'S OKAY IF I CALL HIM "FATHER"? DO YOU THINK HE'D LIKE THAT?
UM...I DON'T THINK HE WOULD, NO.
DO YOU KNOW WHY YOU'RE HERE, MEIKO?
FOR MY FAMILY.

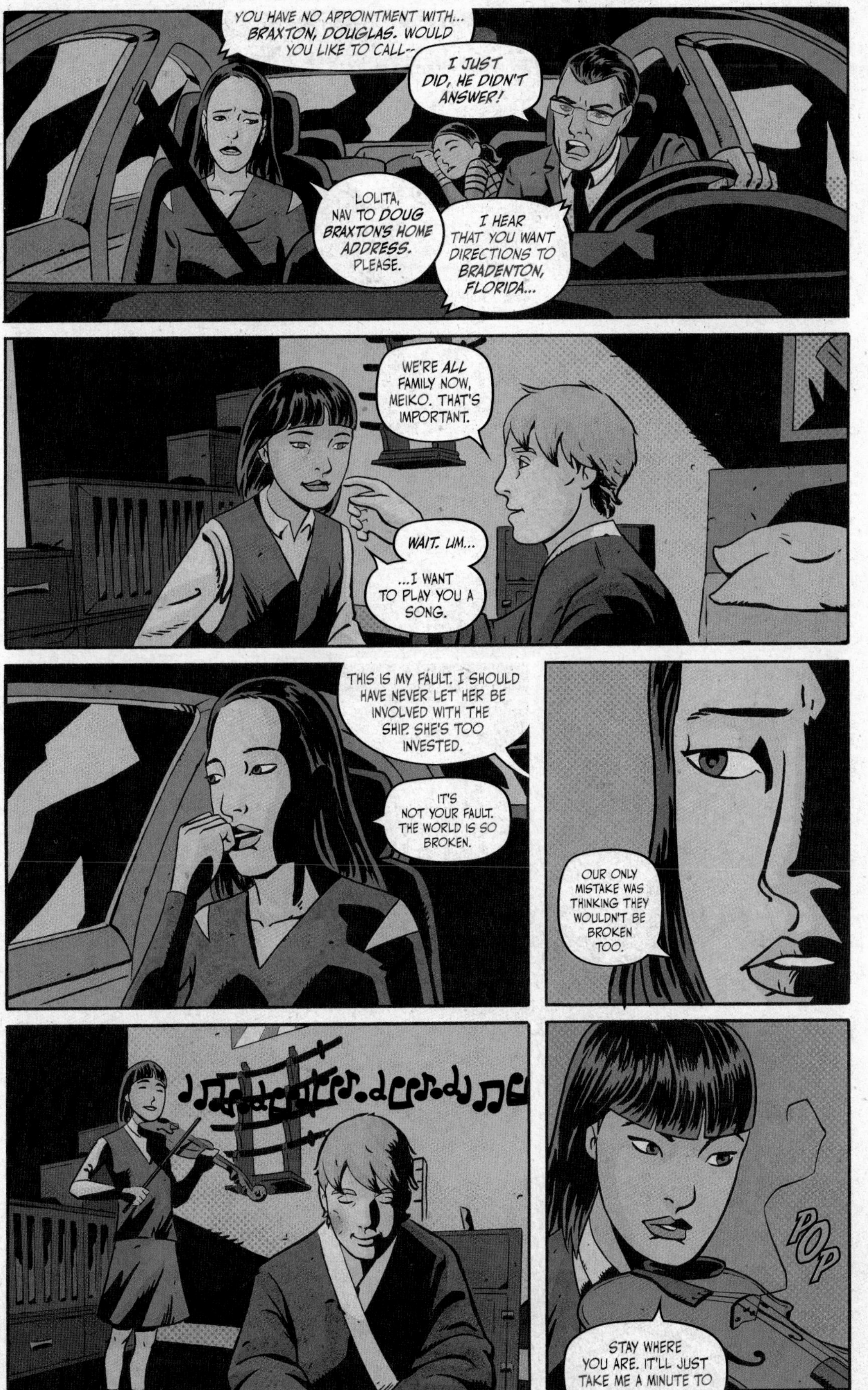
YOU HAVE NO APPOINTMENT WITH... BRAXTON, DOUGLAS. WOULD YOU LIKE TO CALL--
I JUST DID, HE DIDN'T ANSWER!
LOLITA, NAV TO DOUG BRAXTON'S HOME ADDRESS. PLEASE.
I HEAR THAT YOU WANT DIRECTIONS TO BRADENTON, FLORIDA...
WE'RE ALL FAMILY NOW, MEIKO. THAT'S IMPORTANT.
WAIT. UM...
...I WANT TO PLAY YOU A SONG.
THIS IS MY FAULT. I SHOULD HAVE NEVER LET HER BE INVOLVED WITH THE SHIP. SHE'S TOO INVESTED.
IT'S NOT YOUR FAULT. THE WORLD IS SO BROKEN.
OUR ONLY MISTAKE WAS THINKING THEY WOULDN'T BE BROKEN TOO.
POP
STAY WHERE YOU ARE. IT'LL JUST TAKE ME A MINUTE TO FIX THIS...

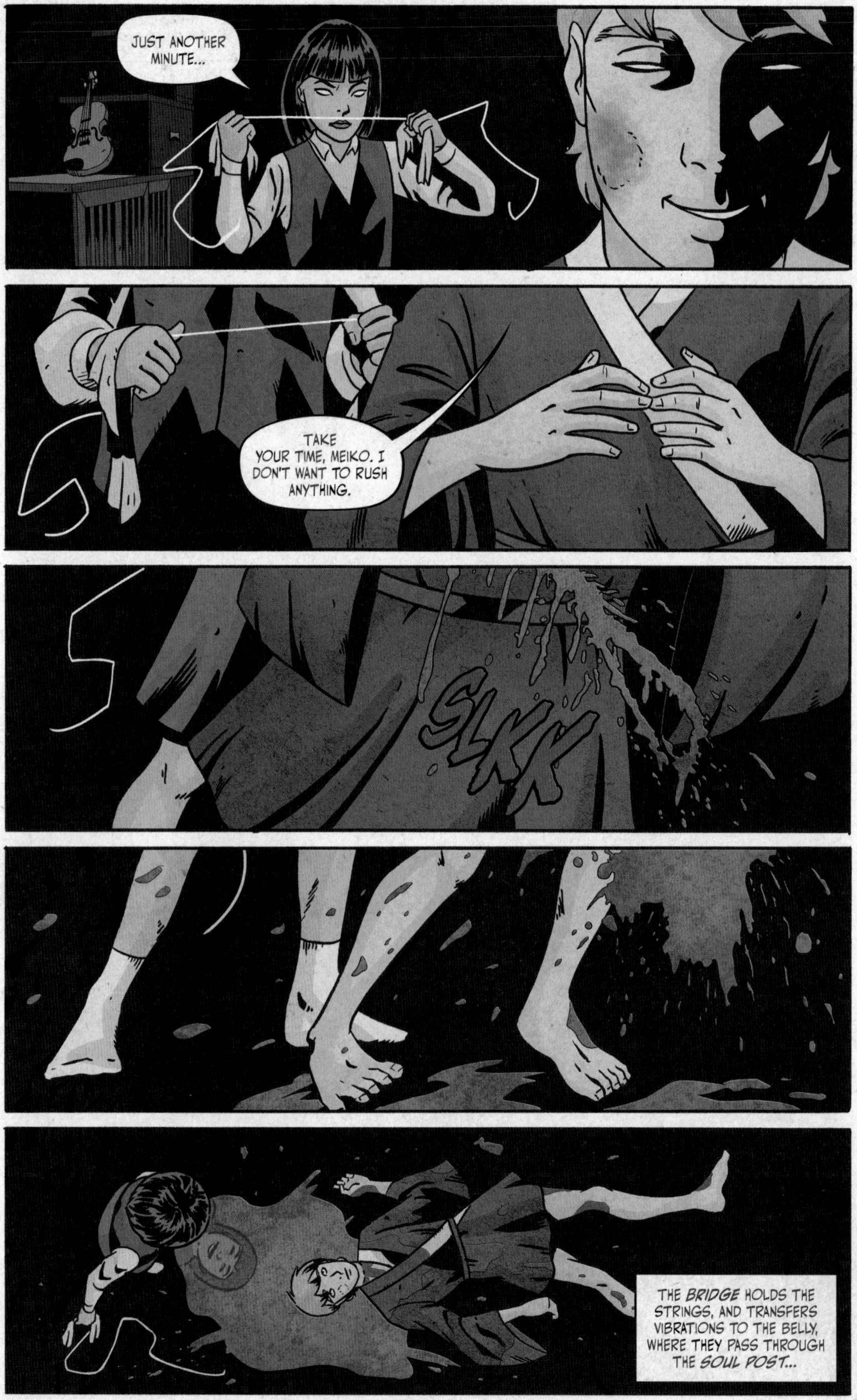
JUST ANOTHER MINUTE...
TAKE YOUR TIME, MEIKO. I DON'T WANT TO RUSH ANYTHING.
SLKK
THE *BRIDGE* HOLDS THE STRINGS, AND TRANSFERS VIBRATIONS TO THE BELLY, WHERE THEY PASS THROUGH THE *SOUL POST*...

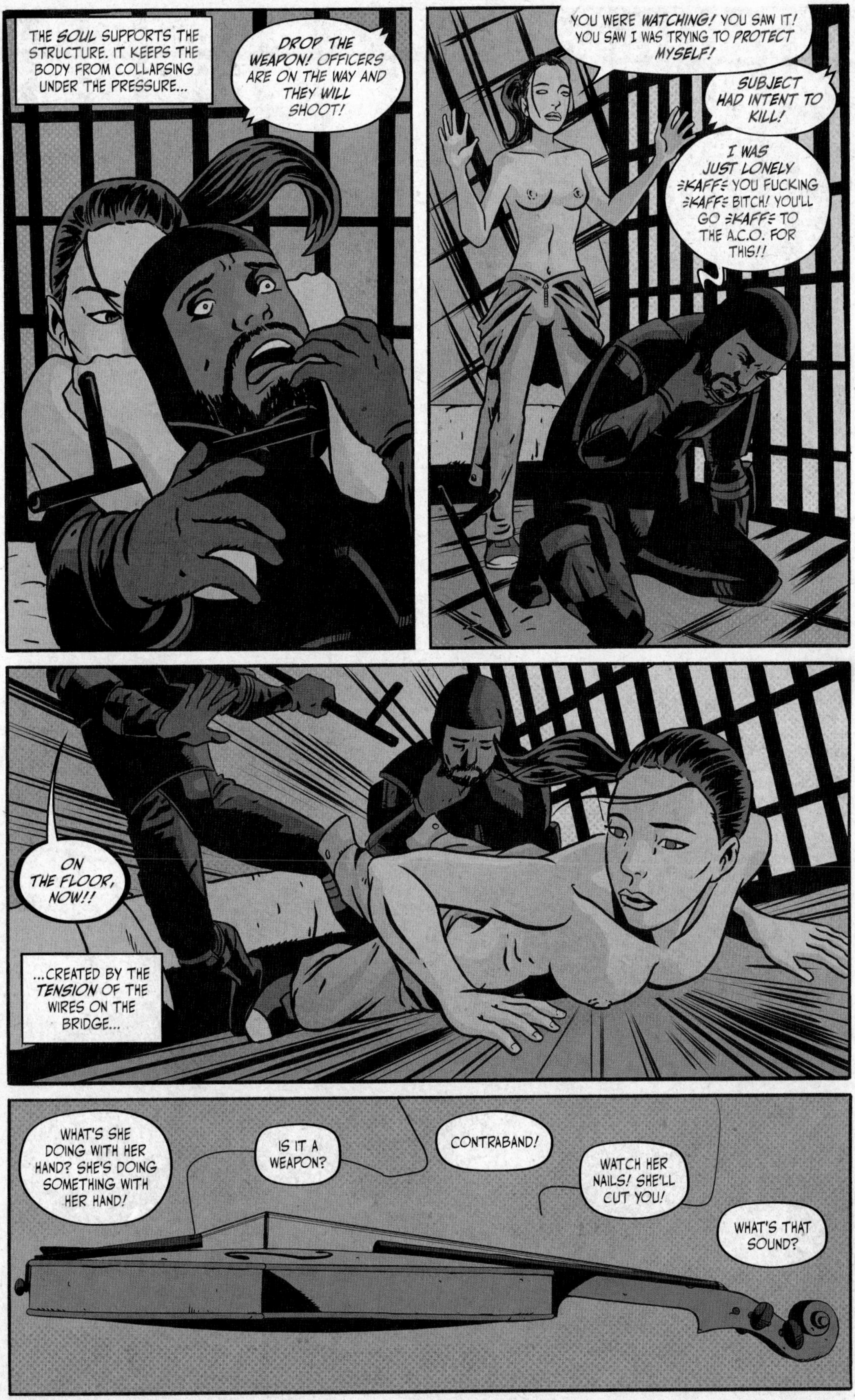
THE SOUL SUPPORTS THE STRUCTURE. IT KEEPS THE BODY FROM COLLAPSING UNDER THE PRESSURE...
DROP THE WEAPON! OFFICERS ARE ON THE WAY AND THEY WILL SHOOT!
YOU WERE WATCHING! YOU SAW IT! YOU SAW I WAS TRYING TO PROTECT MYSELF!
SUBJECT HAD INTENT TO KILL!
I WAS JUST LONELY *KAFF* YOU FUCKING *KAFF* BITCH! YOU'LL GO *KAFF* TO THE A.C.O. FOR THIS!!
ON THE FLOOR, NOW!!
...CREATED BY THE TENSION OF THE WIRES ON THE BRIDGE...
WHAT'S SHE DOING WITH HER HAND? SHE'S DOING SOMETHING WITH HER HAND!
IS IT A WEAPON?
CONTRABAND!
WATCH HER NAILS! SHE'LL CUT YOU!
WHAT'S THAT SOUND?

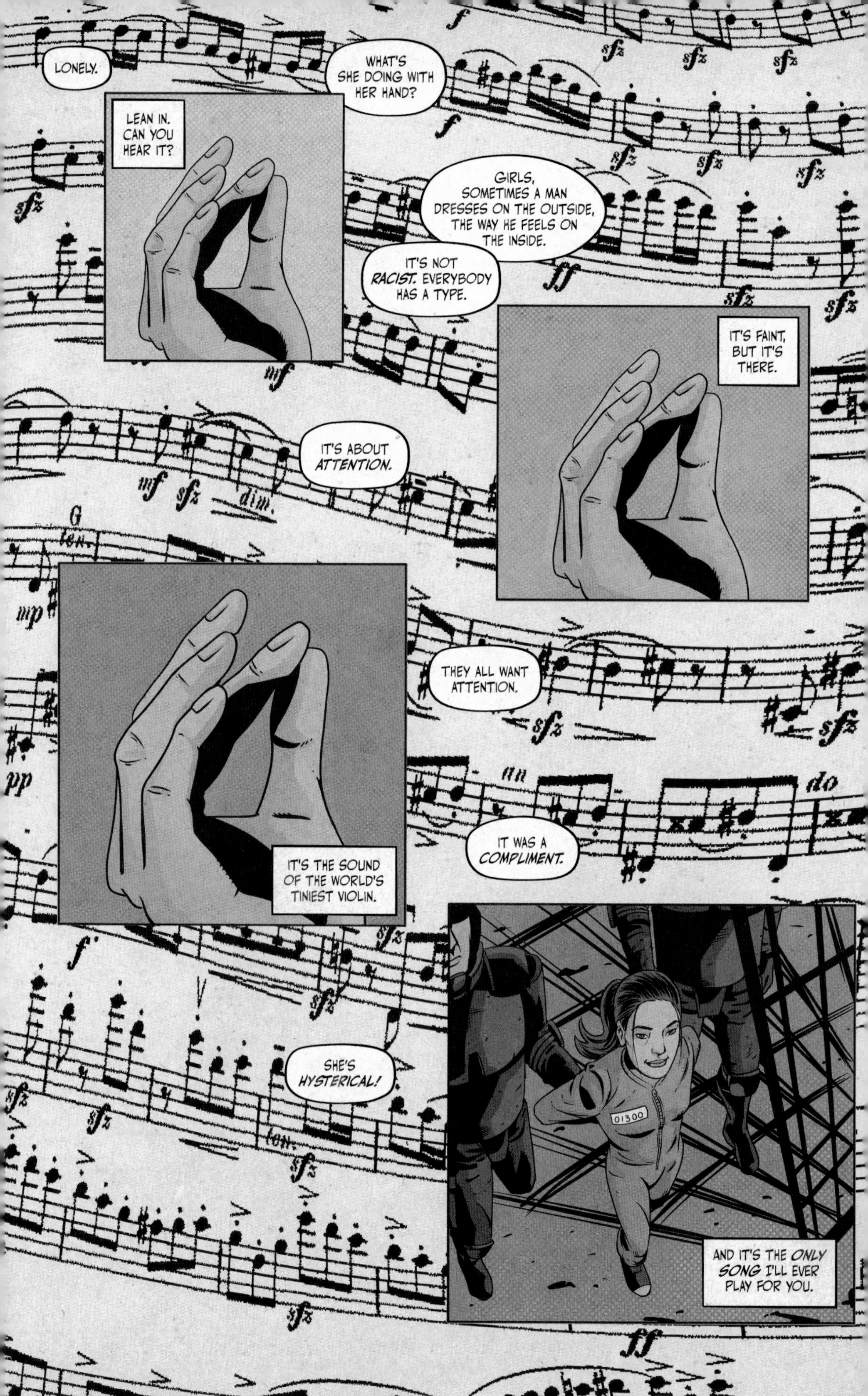
LONELY.
WHAT'S SHE DOING WITH HER HAND?
LEAN IN. CAN YOU HEAR IT?
GIRLS, SOMETIMES A MAN DRESSES ON THE OUTSIDE, THE WAY HE FEELS ON THE INSIDE.
IT'S NOT *RACIST.* EVERYBODY HAS A TYPE.
IT'S FAINT, BUT IT'S THERE.
IT'S ABOUT *ATTENTION.*
THEY ALL WANT ATTENTION.
IT'S THE SOUND OF THE WORLD'S TINIEST VIOLIN.
IT WAS A *COMPLIMENT.*
SHE'S *HYSTERICAL!*
01300
AND IT'S THE *ONLY SONG* I'LL EVER PLAY FOR YOU.

Welcome to Womanhood

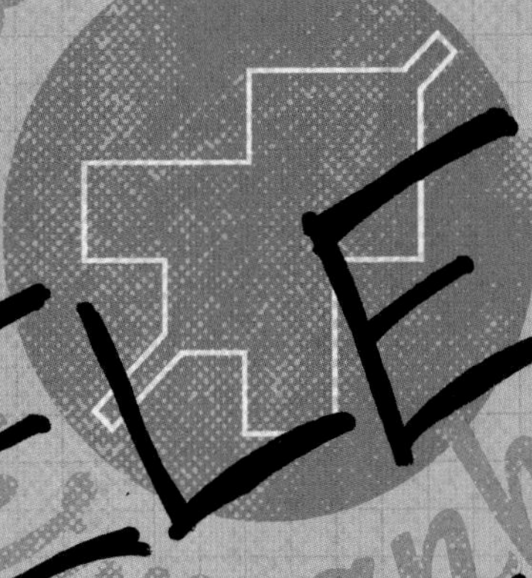

ELEANOR LIVES!

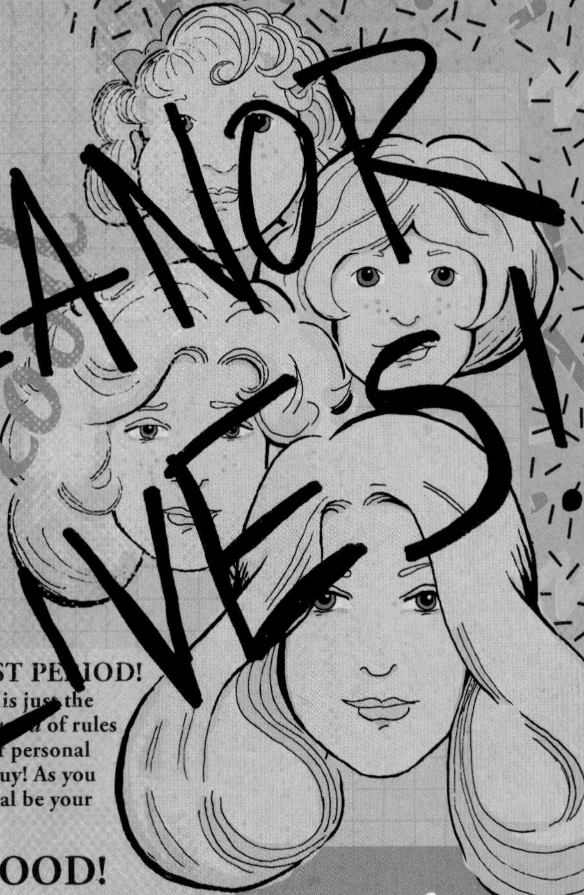

Congratulations on achieving your FIRST PERIOD!
This special time in the life of every young lady is just the beginning: your first step into a fabulous *new world* of rules to follow, people to please, an endless catalog of personal shortcomings and—*OF COURSE*—things to buy! As you try to navigate your way through, let this manual be your Companion and Guide, welcoming you to—

THE AGE OF WOMANHOOD!

The Chapters that follow lay out **Principles of Compliance**, the ultimate goals of which are, of course, your happiness and fulfillment. These Principles will help you decide everything from "Should I wear makeup?" (You can't feel your best unless look your best!) to "How many children should I have?" (As many as your husband, your body and your fiscal fitness will allow!)

Herein you'll find advice on topics ranging from Homemaking to Child Rearing (and everything in between!), plus introductions to Floral Arrangement, Basic Nursing, Advanced Interrogation Techniques and more.

But it's not ***all*** fun and games, First Blood means you have officially become a woman in the eyes of the law. Like all gifts, this one is two-fold. It comes with ***opportunities***, but also ***responsibilities***– to your family, your extended family, your future husband, your unborn children, your community, your teachers, your employers, your co-workers, your strangers on the street, your face in the mirror, that guy who sent you that email that one time, and, of course, your Protectorate.

Turn the page to begin your JOURNEY into the WONDERFUL WORLD OF WOMANHOOD.

Resources for Better Compliance

Do you need help with the **Principles of Compliance?**

A legacy of our days as hunters and gatherers, women's brains are organized for communal endeavors and shared successes (which is the ***scientific*** reason why women, more than men, excel in supporting roles). If you find these principles challenging at first, consider joining a study group led by one of your homeschool mothers. It's like a club, but one you have to bleed to join—what a bond!

While it's true that most men prefer that certain mysteries of womanhood remain just that, it's also true sometimes there's just no substitute for the guidance of a strong and loving man. If you or one of your friends needs counsel, consider consulting —

- Your Father or Older Brother
- Your Husband (or Fiancé!)
- Your Pastor, Priest, Rabbi or Imam
- Your Boss
- Your Doctor
- Your Mechanic
- Any City, State or Federal Official

Welcome to Compliance!

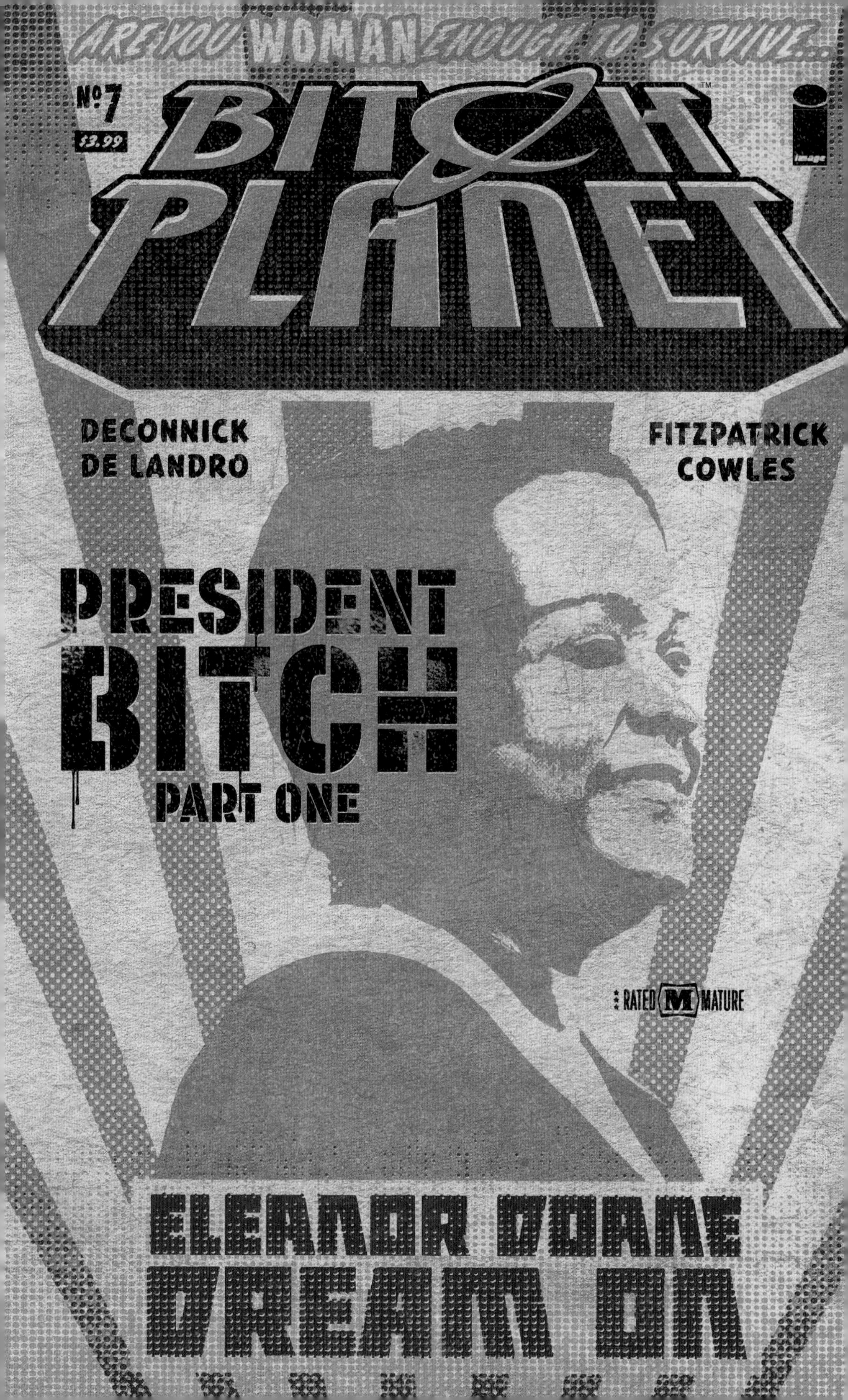
ARE YOU WOMAN ENOUGH TO SURVIVE...
Nº7
$3.99
BITCH PLANET™
image
DECONNICK
DE LANDRO
FITZPATRICK
COWLES
PRESIDENT
BITCH
PART ONE
RATED M MATURE
ELEANOR DOANE
DREAM ON

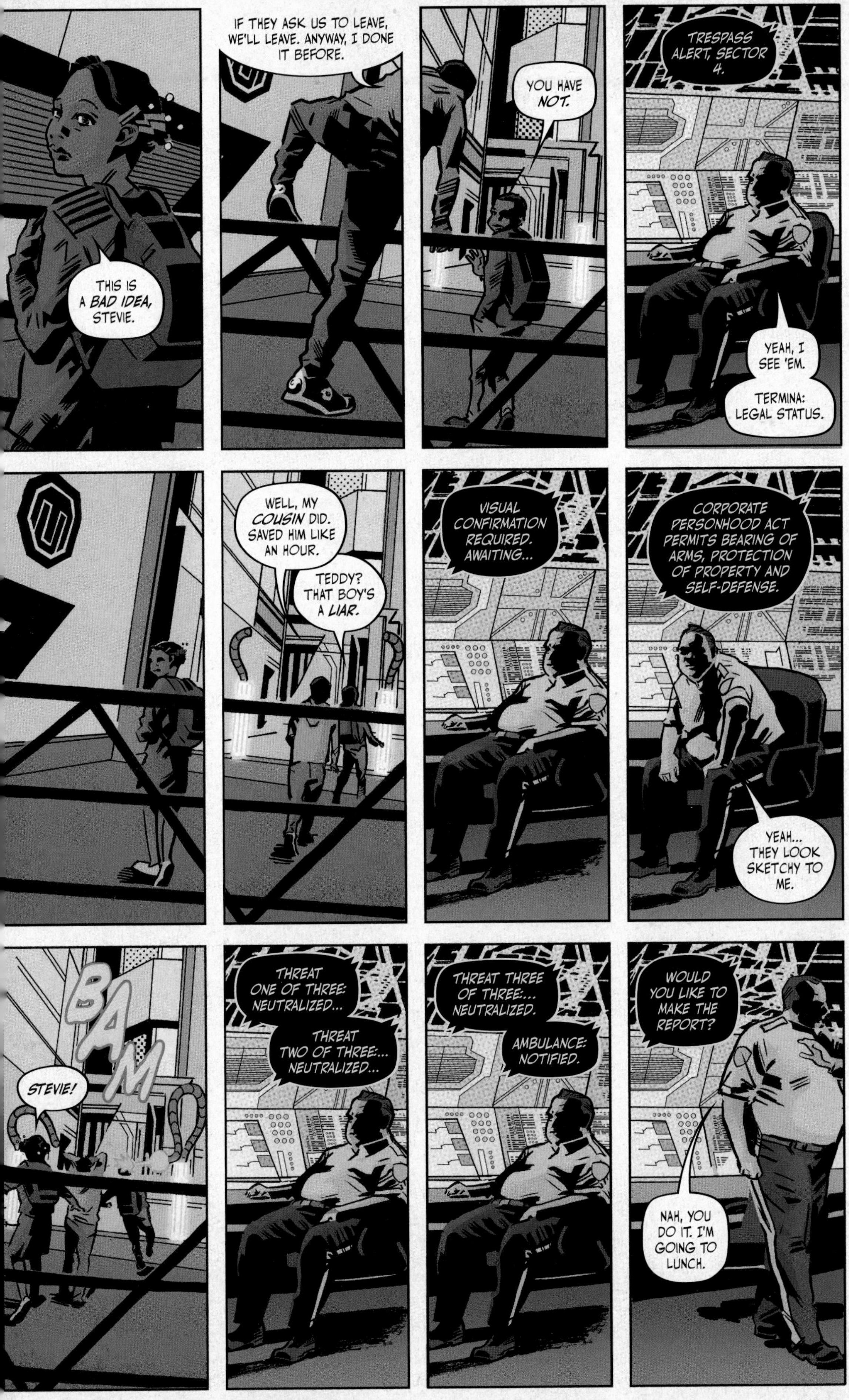
THIS IS A BAD IDEA, STEVIE.
IF THEY ASK US TO LEAVE, WE'LL LEAVE. ANYWAY, I DONE IT BEFORE.
YOU HAVE NOT.
TRESPASS ALERT, SECTOR 4.
YEAH, I SEE 'EM.
TERMINA: LEGAL STATUS.
WELL, MY COUSIN DID. SAVED HIM LIKE AN HOUR.
TEDDY? THAT BOY'S A LIAR.
VISUAL CONFIRMATION REQUIRED. AWAITING...
CORPORATE PERSONHOOD ACT PERMITS BEARING OF ARMS, PROTECTION OF PROPERTY AND SELF-DEFENSE.
YEAH... THEY LOOK SKETCHY TO ME.
BAM
STEVIE!
THREAT ONE OF THREE: NEUTRALIZED...
THREAT TWO OF THREE:... NEUTRALIZED...
THREAT THREE OF THREE:... NEUTRALIZED.
AMBULANCE: NOTIFIED.
WOULD YOU LIKE TO MAKE THE REPORT?
NAH, YOU DO IT. I'M GOING TO LUNCH.

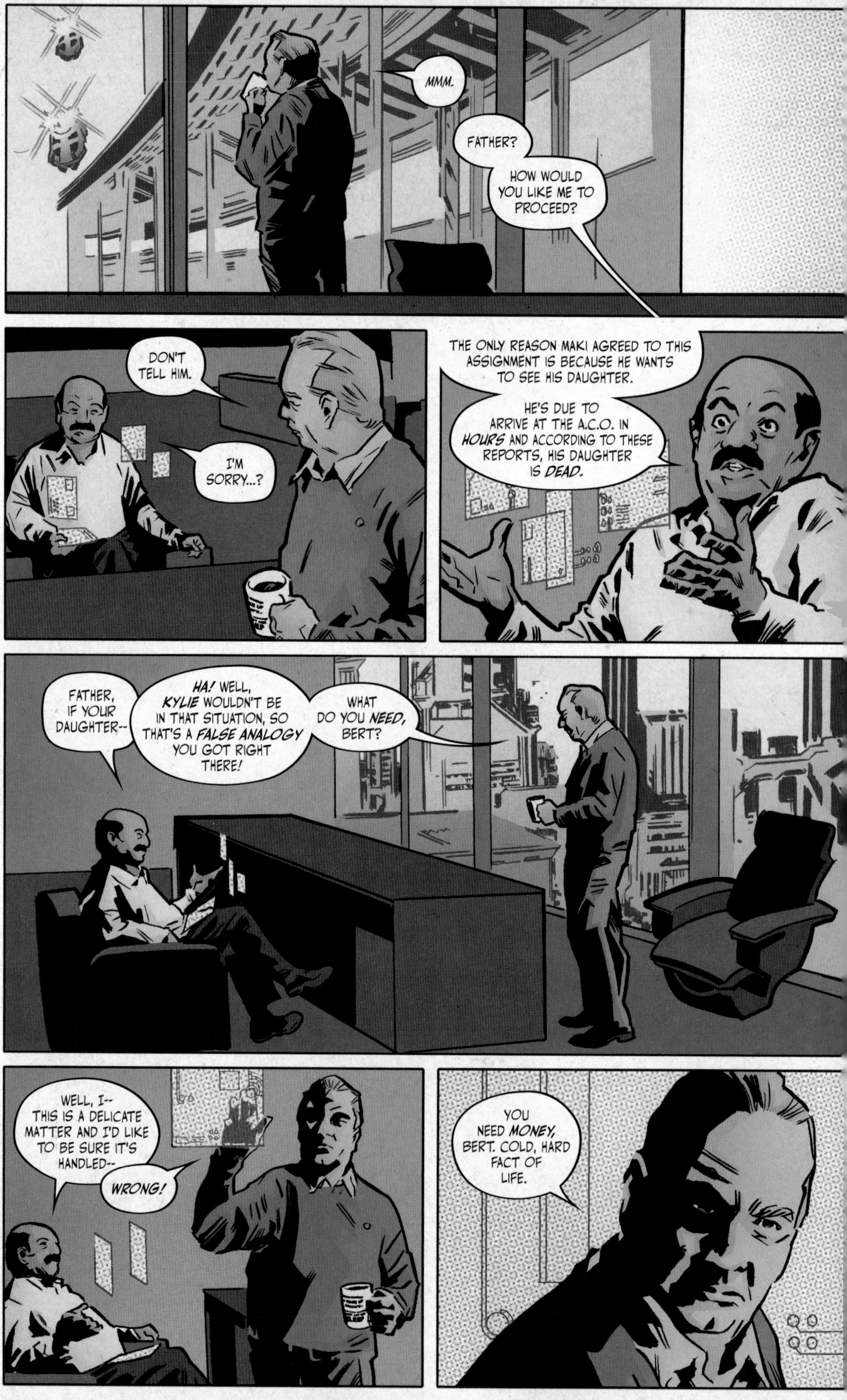
MMM.
FATHER?
HOW WOULD YOU LIKE ME TO PROCEED?
DON'T TELL HIM.
I'M SORRY...?
THE ONLY REASON MAKI AGREED TO THIS ASSIGNMENT IS BECAUSE HE WANTS TO SEE HIS DAUGHTER.
HE'S DUE TO ARRIVE AT THE A.C.O. IN HOURS AND ACCORDING TO THESE REPORTS, HIS DAUGHTER IS DEAD.
FATHER, IF YOUR DAUGHTER--
HA! WELL, KYLIE WOULDN'T BE IN THAT SITUATION, SO THAT'S A FALSE ANALOGY YOU GOT RIGHT THERE!
WHAT DO YOU NEED, BERT?
WELL, I-- THIS IS A DELICATE MATTER AND I'D LIKE TO BE SURE IT'S HANDLED--
WRONG!
YOU NEED MONEY, BERT. COLD, HARD FACT OF LIFE.

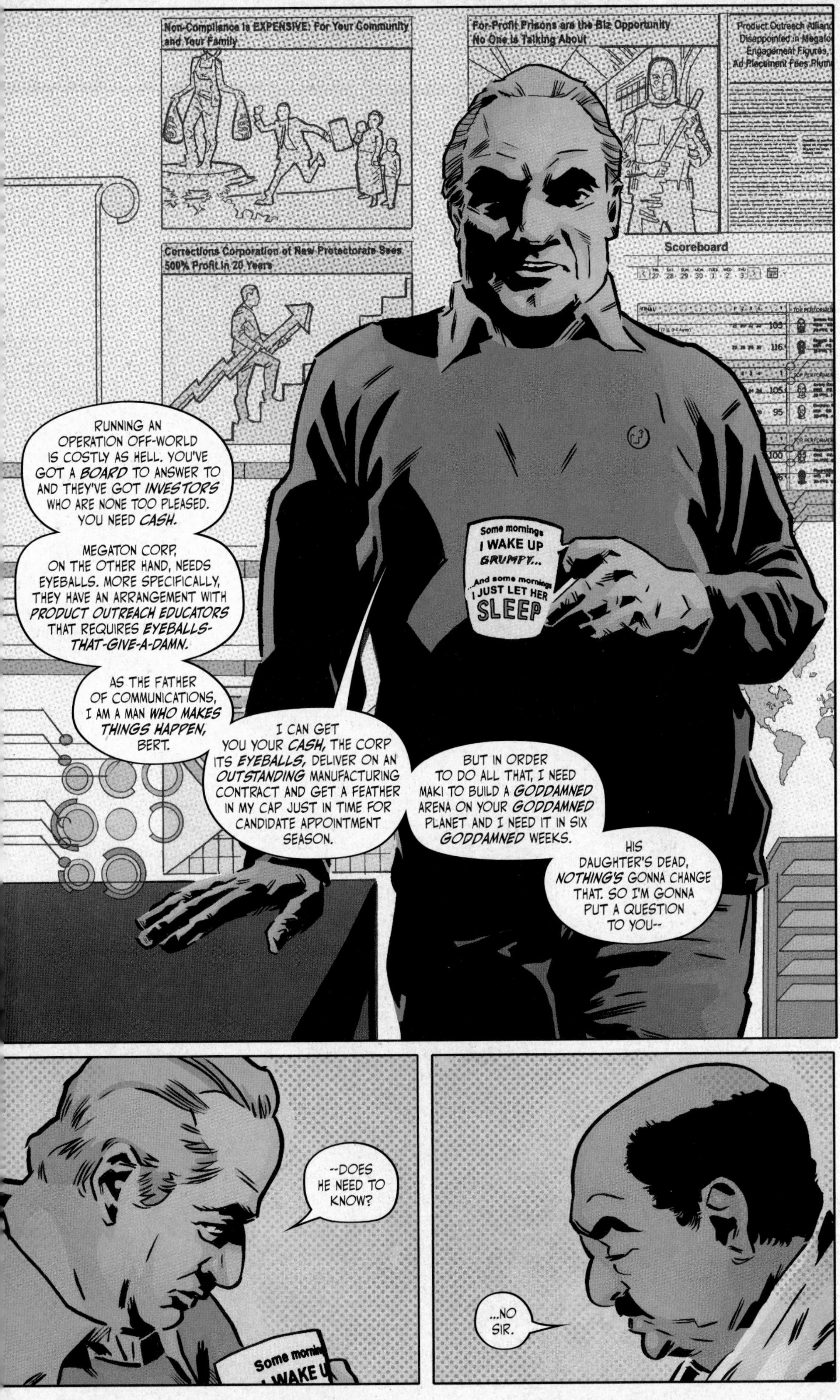
Non-Compliance is EXPENSIVE: For Your Community and Your Family
For-Profit Prisons are the Biz Opportunity No One is Talking About
Corrections Corporation of New Protectorate Sees 500% Profit in 20 Years
Scoreboard
RUNNING AN OPERATION OFF-WORLD IS COSTLY AS HELL. YOU'VE GOT A BOARD TO ANSWER TO AND THEY'VE GOT INVESTORS WHO ARE NONE TOO PLEASED. YOU NEED CASH.
MEGATON CORP, ON THE OTHER HAND, NEEDS EYEBALLS. MORE SPECIFICALLY, THEY HAVE AN ARRANGEMENT WITH PRODUCT OUTREACH EDUCATORS THAT REQUIRES EYEBALLS-THAT-GIVE-A-DAMN.
AS THE FATHER OF COMMUNICATIONS, I AM A MAN WHO MAKES THINGS HAPPEN, BERT.
Some mornings I WAKE UP GRUMPY... ...And some mornings I JUST LET HER SLEEP
I CAN GET YOU YOUR CASH, THE CORP ITS EYEBALLS, DELIVER ON AN OUTSTANDING MANUFACTURING CONTRACT AND GET A FEATHER IN MY CAP JUST IN TIME FOR CANDIDATE APPOINTMENT SEASON.
BUT IN ORDER TO DO ALL THAT, I NEED MAKI TO BUILD A GODDAMNED ARENA ON YOUR GODDAMNED PLANET AND I NEED IT IN SIX GODDAMNED WEEKS.
HIS DAUGHTER'S DEAD, NOTHING'S GONNA CHANGE THAT. SO I'M GONNA PUT A QUESTION TO YOU--
--DOES HE NEED TO KNOW?
...NO SIR.

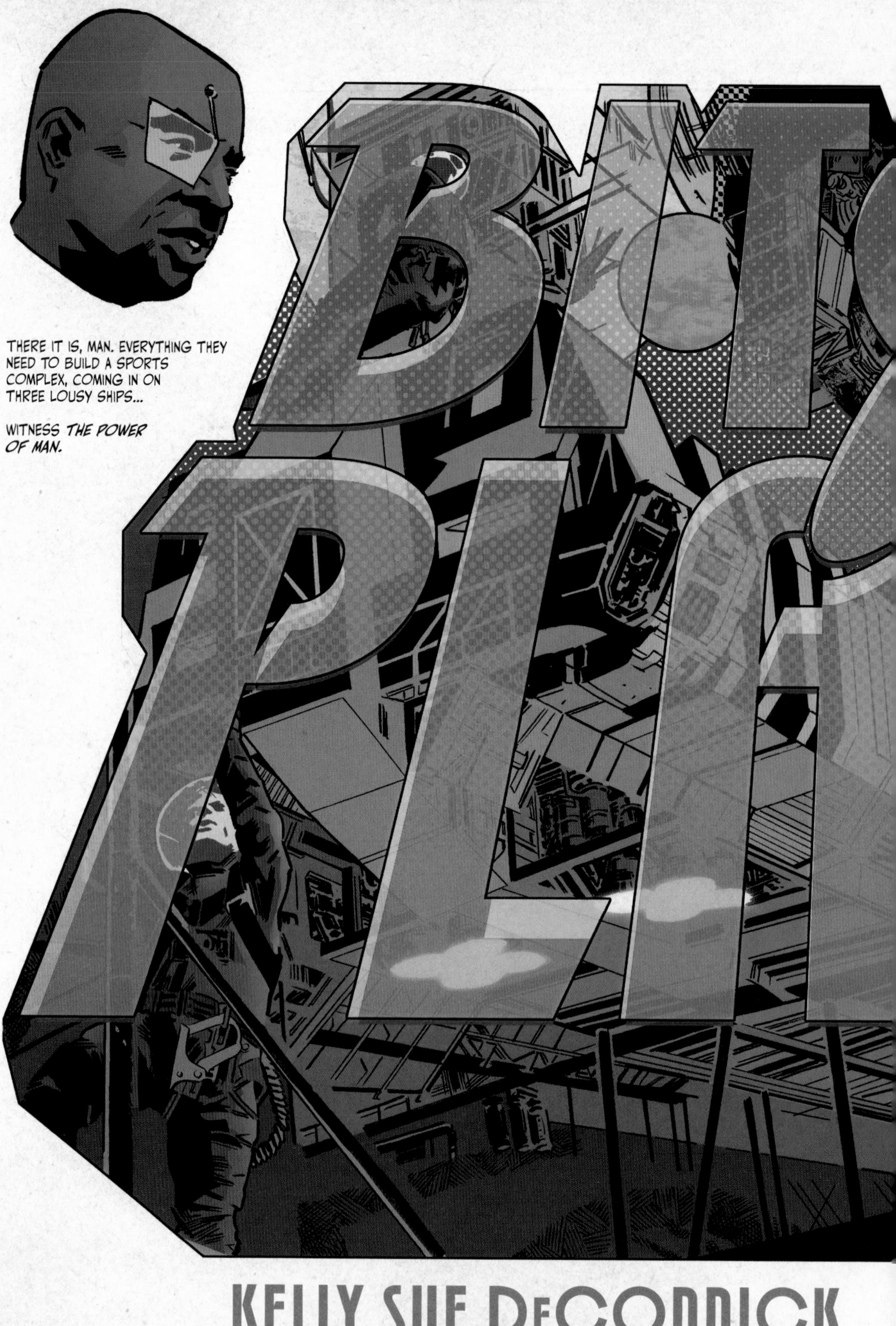
THERE IT IS, MAN. EVERYTHING THEY NEED TO BUILD A SPORTS COMPLEX, COMING IN ON THREE LOUSY SHIPS...
WITNESS *THE POWER OF MAN.*

KELLY SUE DeCONNICK
SCRIPT

KELLY FITZPATRICK
COLORS

CLAYTON COWLES
LETTERS

RIAN HUGHES
COVER DESIGN & LOGO DESIGN

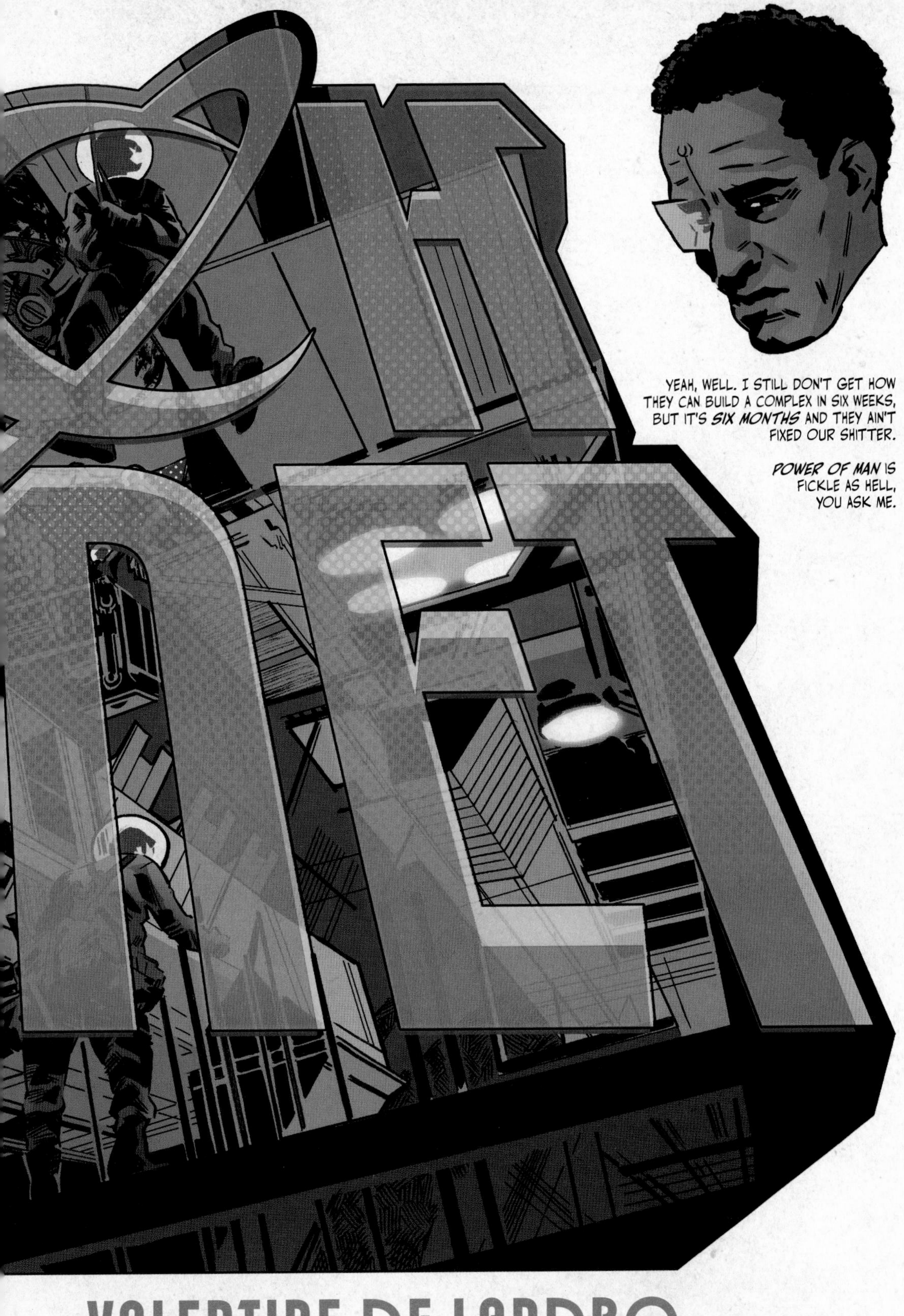
YEAH, WELL. I STILL DON'T GET HOW THEY CAN BUILD A COMPLEX IN SIX WEEKS, BUT IT'S *SIX MONTHS* AND THEY AIN'T FIXED OUR SHITTER.
POWER OF MAN IS FICKLE AS HELL, YOU ASK ME.

VALENTINE DE LANDRO
ART/COVERS

LAURENN McCUBBIN
BACKMATTER DESIGN

LAUREN SANKOVITCH
EDITOR

GRRRNNNRRRN

HEH. WELL, IT *IS* CHILLY IN THE STASIS TUBE.

WELCOME TO THE AUXILIARY COMPLIANCE OUTPOST, INTAKE FACILITY TWO, GENTLEMEN. PLEASE HELP YOURSELVES TO TEA AND ROBES AND FOLLOW THE CONCOURSE TO YOUR QUARTERS...

MM. SURE, THAT MUST BE IT.

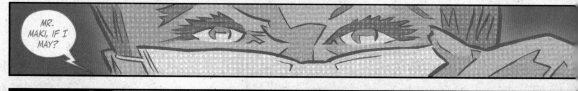

MR. MAKI, IF I MAY?

THIS WAY, SIR...

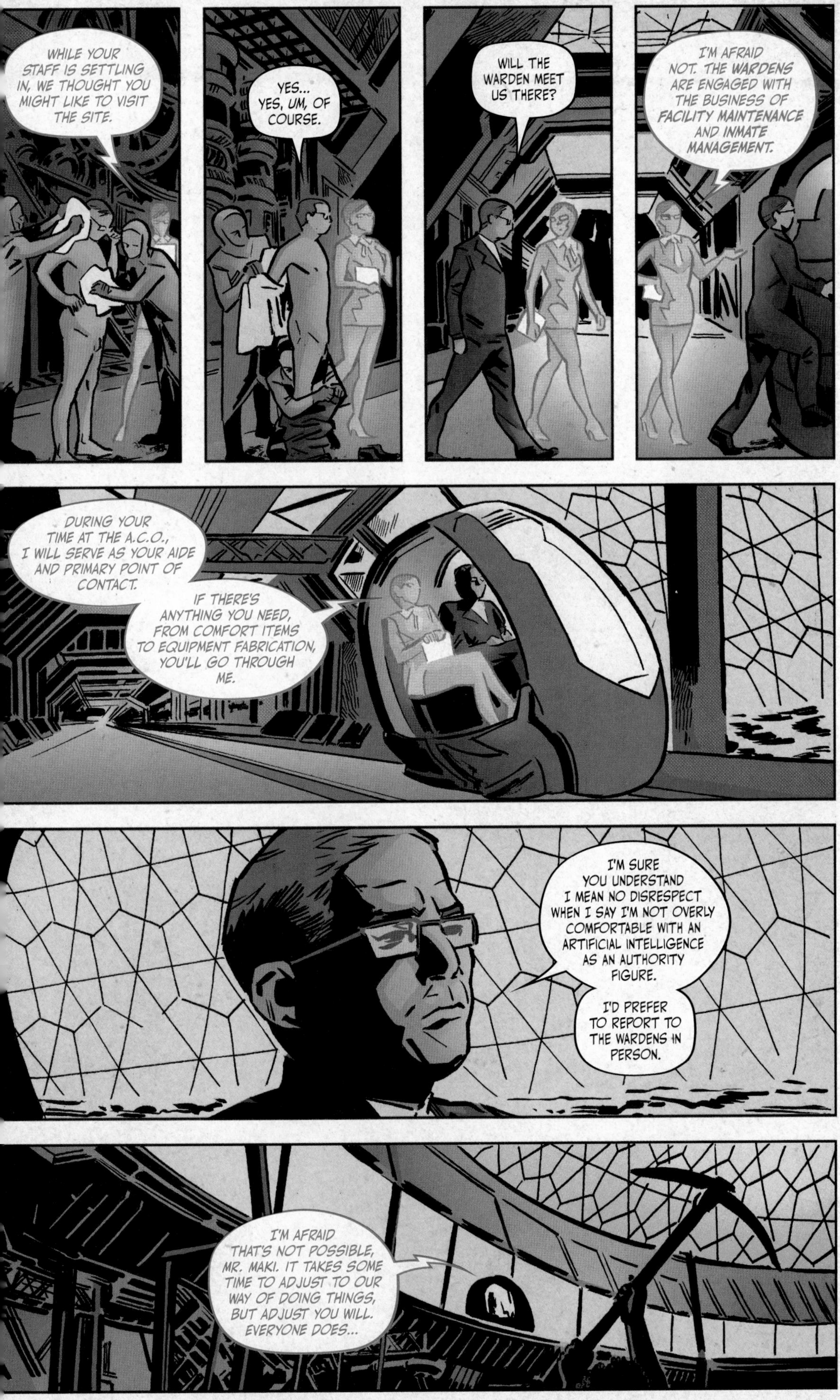
WHILE YOUR STAFF IS SETTLING IN, WE THOUGHT YOU MIGHT LIKE TO VISIT THE SITE.
YES... YES, UM, OF COURSE.
WILL THE WARDEN MEET US THERE?
I'M AFRAID NOT. THE WARDENS ARE ENGAGED WITH THE BUSINESS OF FACILITY MAINTENANCE AND INMATE MANAGEMENT.
DURING YOUR TIME AT THE A.C.O., I WILL SERVE AS YOUR AIDE AND PRIMARY POINT OF CONTACT.
IF THERE'S ANYTHING YOU NEED, FROM COMFORT ITEMS TO EQUIPMENT FABRICATION, YOU'LL GO THROUGH ME.
I'M SURE YOU UNDERSTAND I MEAN NO DISRESPECT WHEN I SAY I'M NOT OVERLY COMFORTABLE WITH AN ARTIFICIAL INTELLIGENCE AS AN AUTHORITY FIGURE.
I'D PREFER TO REPORT TO THE WARDENS IN PERSON.
I'M AFRAID THAT'S NOT POSSIBLE, MR. MAKI. IT TAKES SOME TIME TO ADJUST TO OUR WAY OF DOING THINGS, BUT ADJUST YOU WILL. EVERYONE DOES...

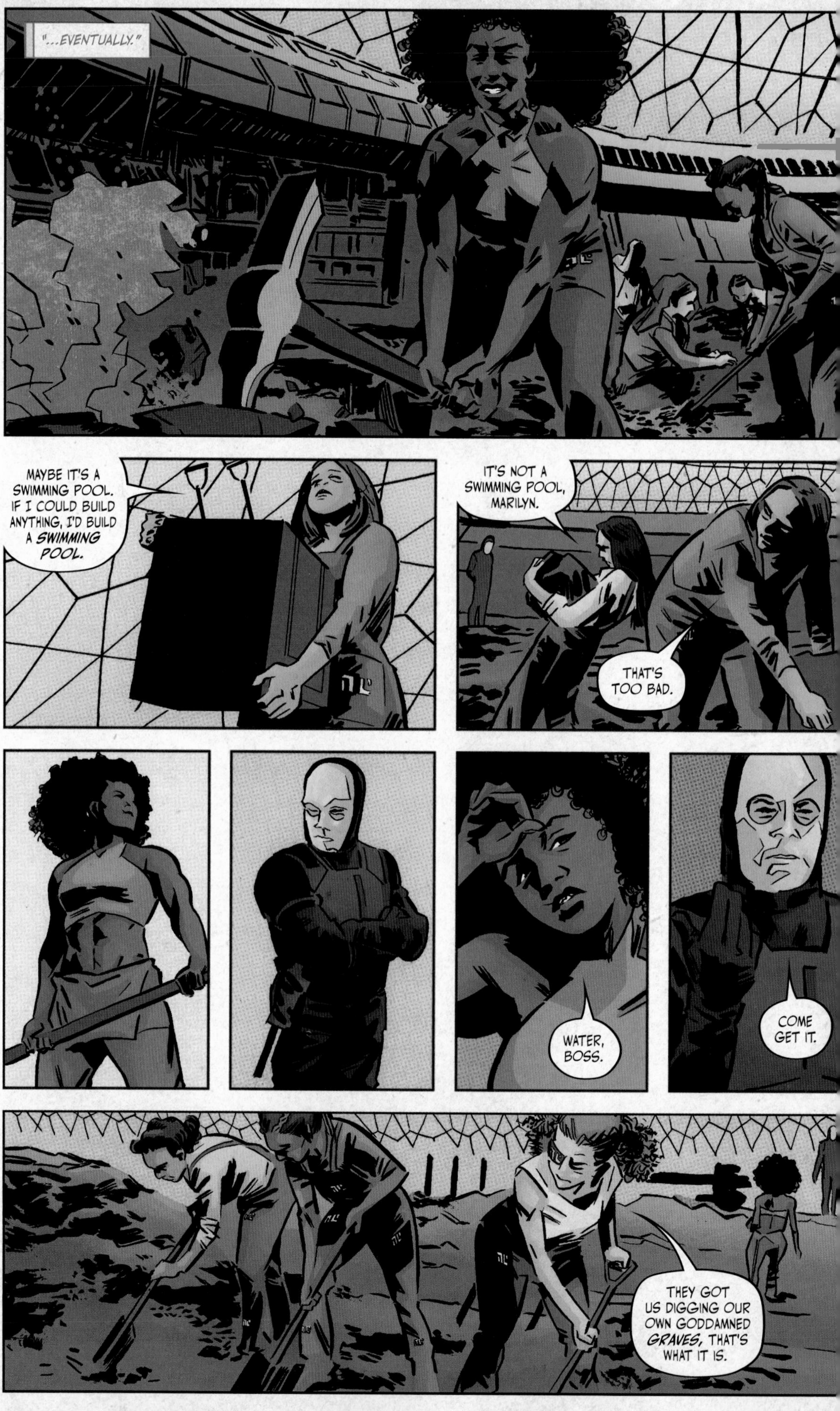
"...EVENTUALLY."
MAYBE IT'S A SWIMMING POOL. IF I COULD BUILD ANYTHING, I'D BUILD A *SWIMMING POOL.*
IT'S NOT A SWIMMING POOL, MARILYN.
THAT'S TOO BAD.
WATER, BOSS.
COME GET IT.
THEY GOT US DIGGING OUR OWN GODDAMNED *GRAVES*, THAT'S WHAT IT IS.

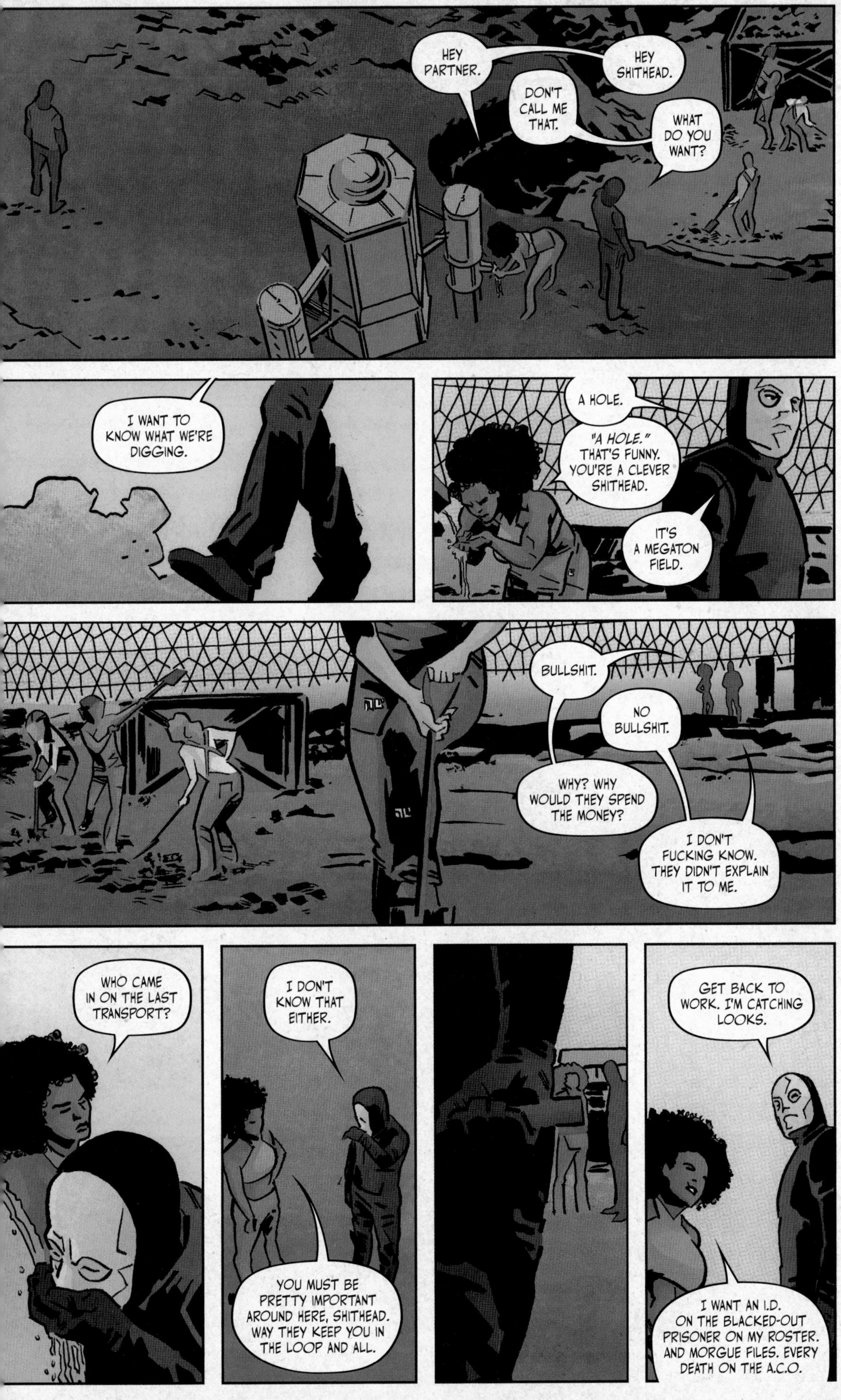
HEY PARTNER.
HEY SHITHEAD.
DON'T CALL ME THAT.
WHAT DO YOU WANT?
I WANT TO KNOW WHAT WE'RE DIGGING.
A HOLE.
"A HOLE." THAT'S FUNNY. YOU'RE A CLEVER SHITHEAD.
IT'S A MEGATON FIELD.
BULLSHIT.
NO BULLSHIT.
WHY? WHY WOULD THEY SPEND THE MONEY?
I DON'T FUCKING KNOW. THEY DIDN'T EXPLAIN IT TO ME.
WHO CAME IN ON THE LAST TRANSPORT?
I DON'T KNOW THAT EITHER.
YOU MUST BE PRETTY IMPORTANT AROUND HERE, SHITHEAD. WAY THEY KEEP YOU IN THE LOOP AND ALL.
GET BACK TO WORK. I'M CATCHING LOOKS.
I WANT AN I.D. ON THE BLACKED-OUT PRISONER ON MY ROSTER. AND MORGUE FILES. EVERY DEATH ON THE A.C.O.

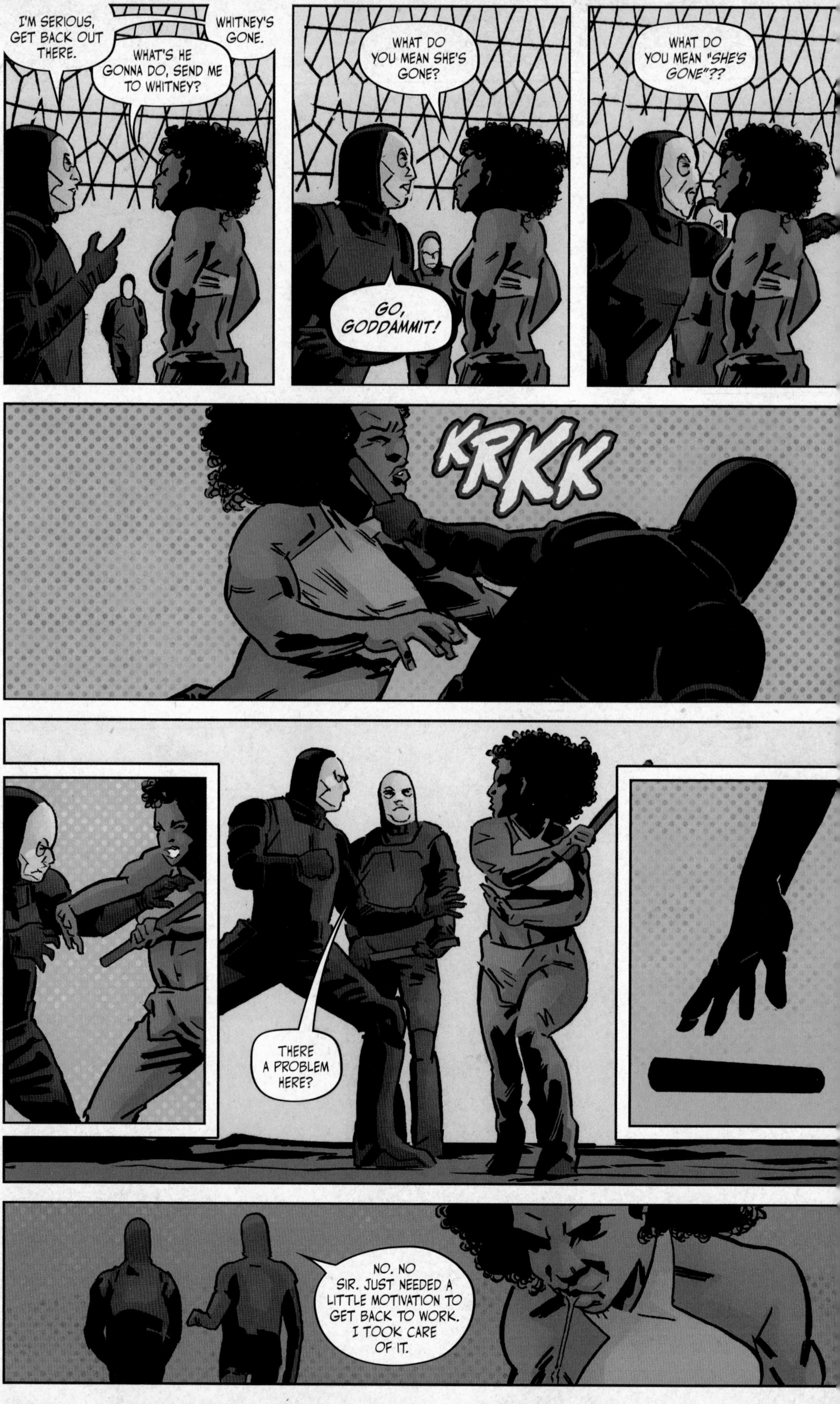
I'M SERIOUS, GET BACK OUT THERE.
WHITNEY'S GONE.
WHAT'S HE GONNA DO, SEND ME TO WHITNEY?
WHAT DO YOU MEAN SHE'S GONE?
GO, GODDAMMIT!
WHAT DO YOU MEAN "SHE'S GONE"??
KRKK
THERE A PROBLEM HERE?
NO. NO SIR. JUST NEEDED A LITTLE MOTIVATION TO GET BACK TO WORK. I TOOK CARE OF IT.

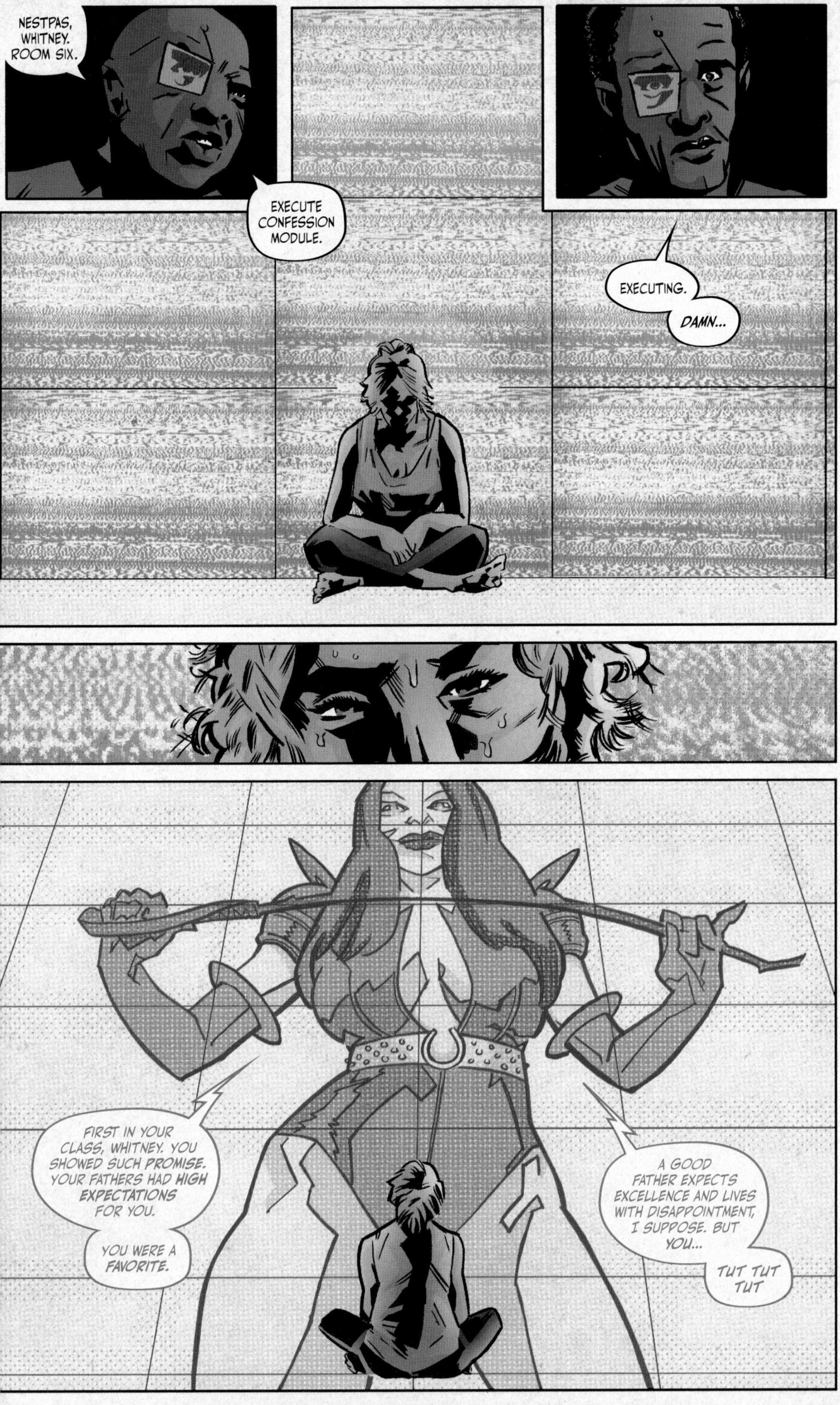
NESTPAS, WHITNEY. ROOM SIX.
EXECUTE CONFESSION MODULE.
EXECUTING.
DAMN...
FIRST IN YOUR CLASS, WHITNEY. YOU SHOWED SUCH PROMISE. YOUR FATHERS HAD HIGH EXPECTATIONS FOR YOU.
YOU WERE A FAVORITE.
A GOOD FATHER EXPECTS EXCELLENCE AND LIVES WITH DISAPPOINTMENT, I SUPPOSE. BUT YOU...
TUT TUT TUT

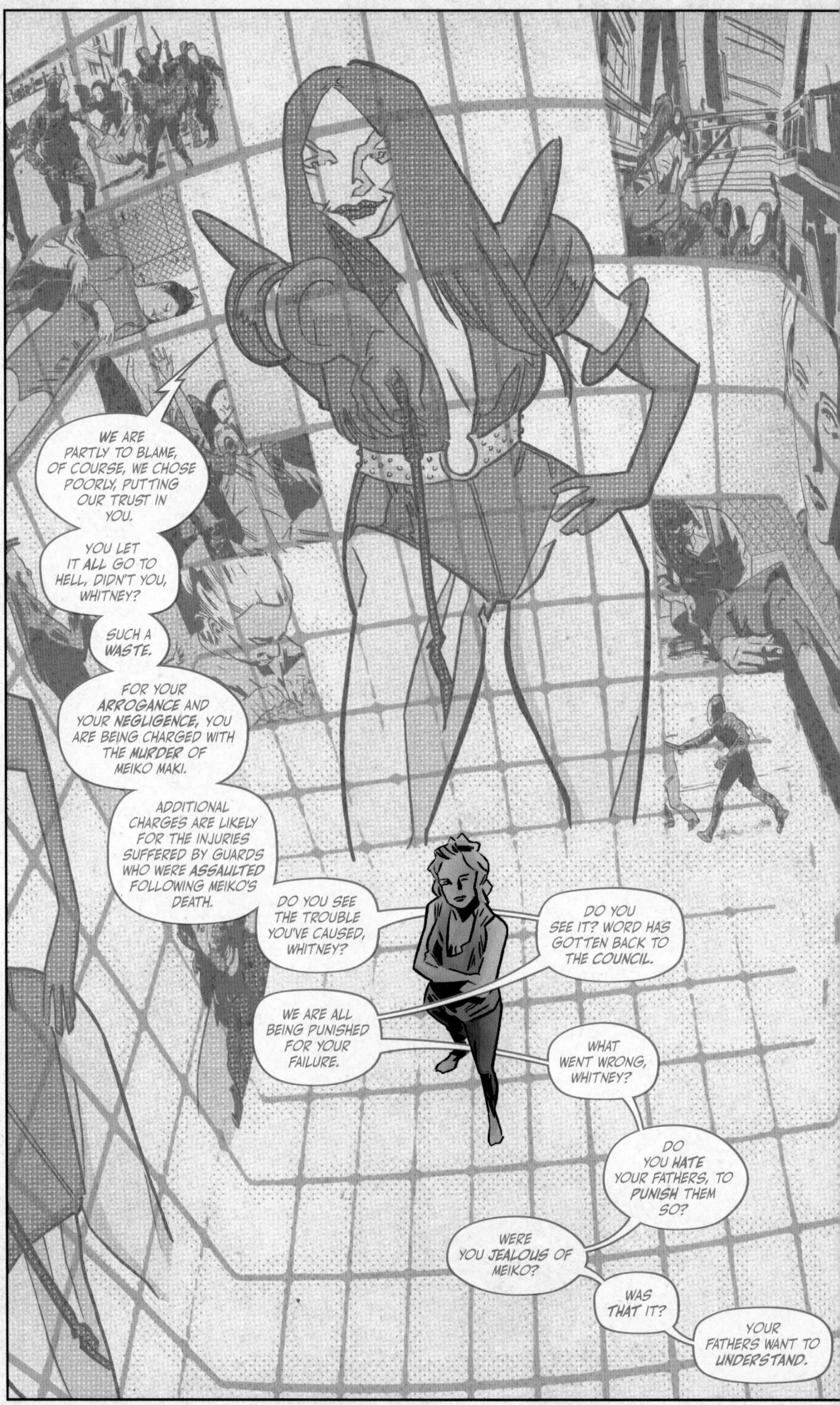

WE ARE PARTLY TO BLAME, OF COURSE. WE CHOSE POORLY, PUTTING OUR TRUST IN YOU.
YOU LET IT ALL GO TO HELL, DIDN'T YOU, WHITNEY?
SUCH A WASTE.
FOR YOUR ARROGANCE AND YOUR NEGLIGENCE, YOU ARE BEING CHARGED WITH THE MURDER OF MEIKO MAKI.
ADDITIONAL CHARGES ARE LIKELY FOR THE INJURIES SUFFERED BY GUARDS WHO WERE ASSAULTED FOLLOWING MEIKO'S DEATH.
DO YOU SEE THE TROUBLE YOU'VE CAUSED, WHITNEY?
DO YOU SEE IT? WORD HAS GOTTEN BACK TO THE COUNCIL.
WE ARE ALL BEING PUNISHED FOR YOUR FAILURE.
WHAT WENT WRONG, WHITNEY?
DO YOU HATE YOUR FATHERS, TO PUNISH THEM SO?
WERE YOU JEALOUS OF MEIKO?
WAS THAT IT?
YOUR FATHERS WANT TO UNDERSTAND.

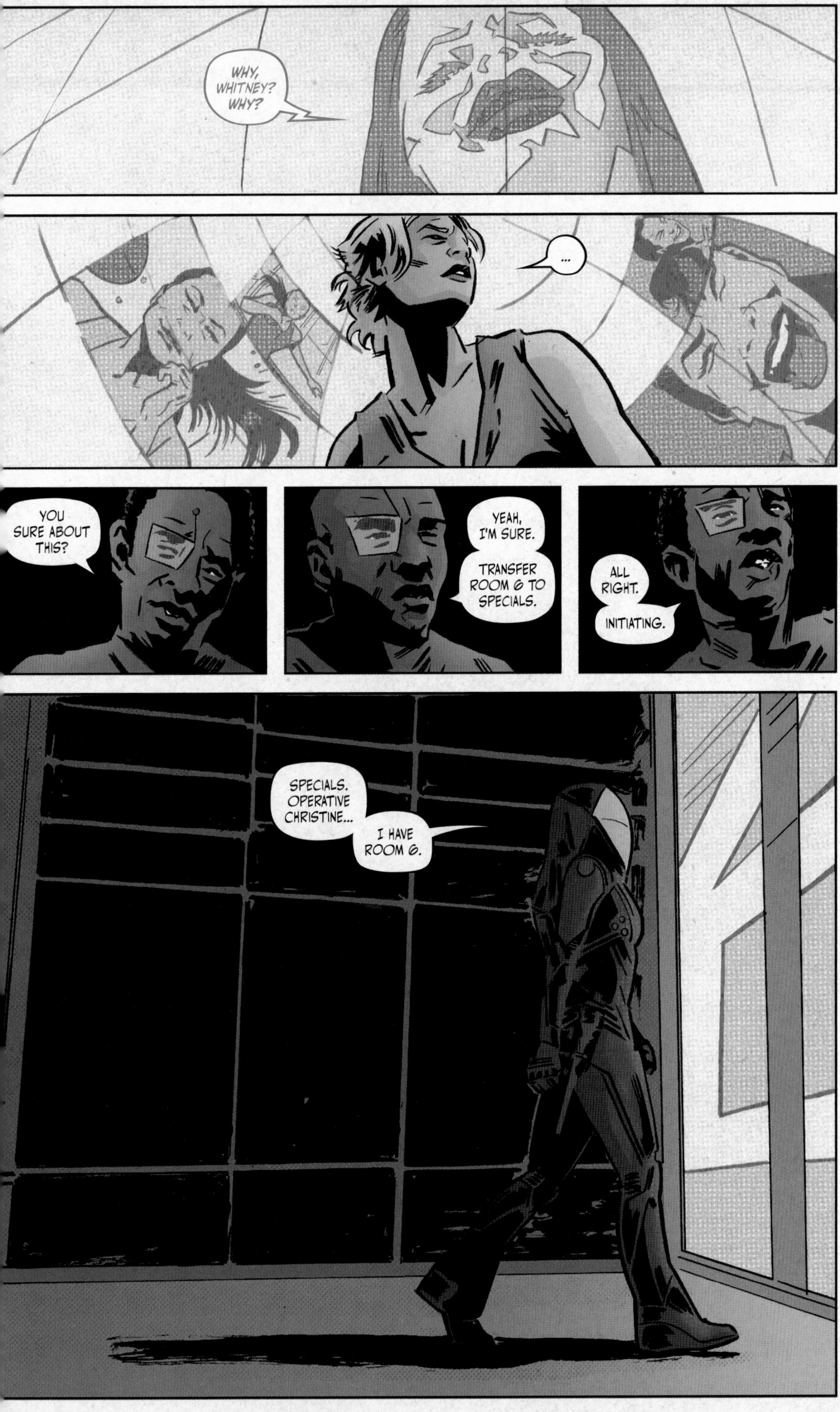
WHY, WHITNEY? WHY?
...
YOU SURE ABOUT THIS?
YEAH, I'M SURE.
TRANSFER ROOM 6 TO SPECIALS.
ALL RIGHT.
INITIATING.
SPECIALS. OPERATIVE CHRISTINE...
I HAVE ROOM 6.

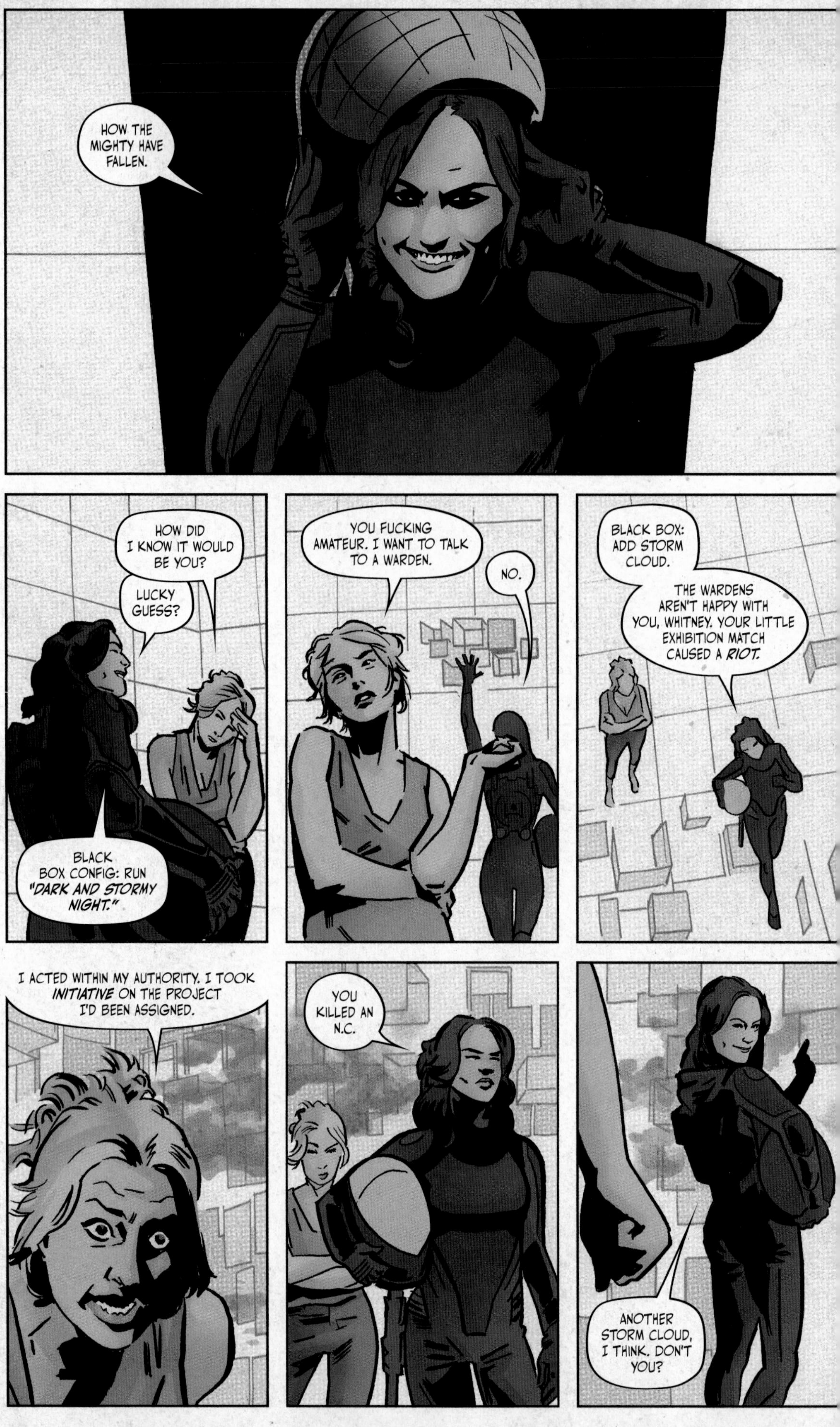
HOW THE MIGHTY HAVE FALLEN.
HOW DID I KNOW IT WOULD BE YOU?
LUCKY GUESS?
BLACK BOX CONFIG: RUN *"DARK AND STORMY NIGHT."*
YOU FUCKING AMATEUR. I WANT TO TALK TO A WARDEN.
NO.
BLACK BOX: ADD STORM CLOUD.
THE WARDENS AREN'T HAPPY WITH YOU, WHITNEY. YOUR LITTLE EXHIBITION MATCH CAUSED A *RIOT.*
I ACTED WITHIN MY AUTHORITY. I TOOK *INITIATIVE* ON THE PROJECT I'D BEEN ASSIGNED.
YOU KILLED AN N.C.
ANOTHER STORM CLOUD, I THINK. DON'T YOU?

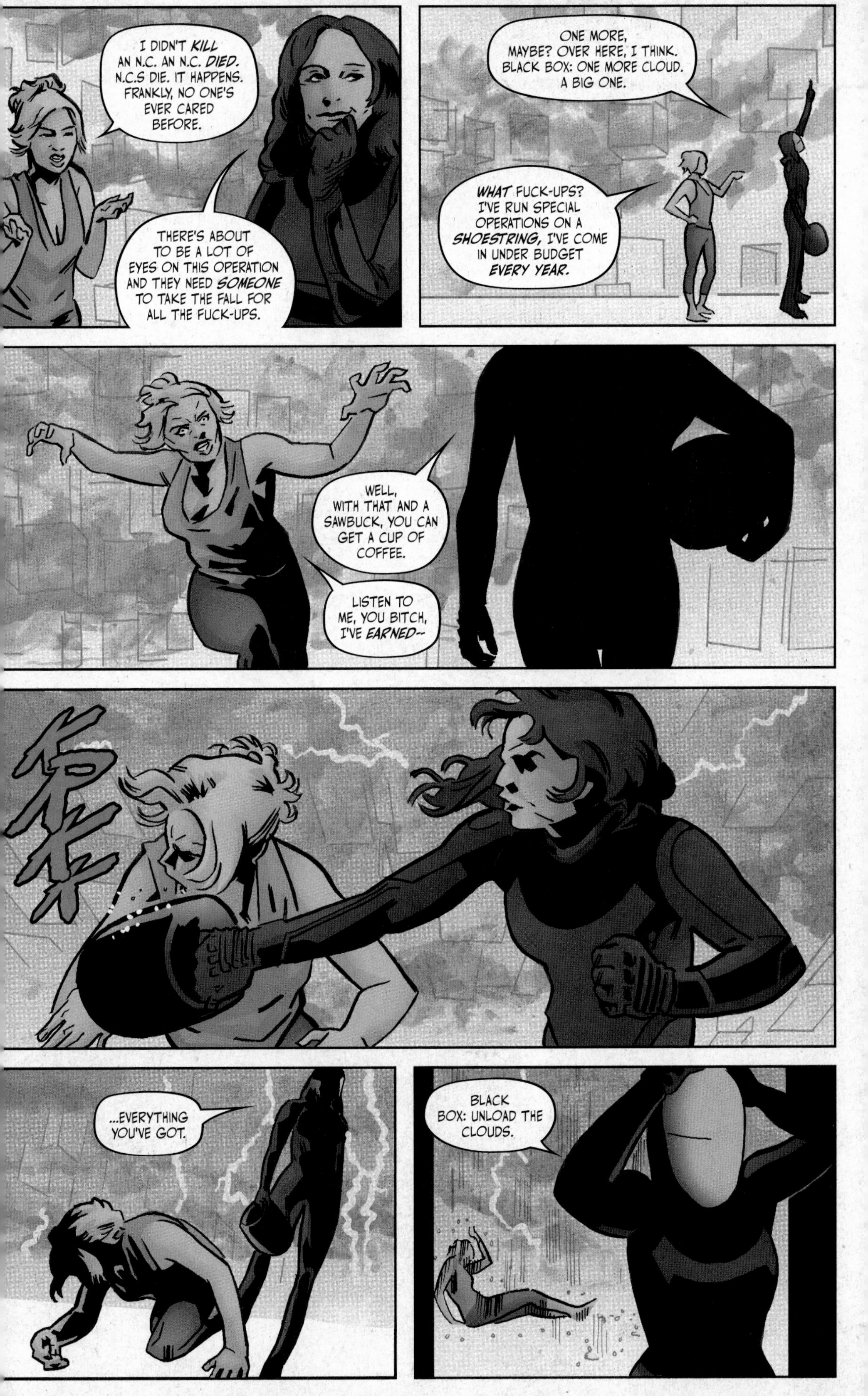
I DIDN'T *KILL* AN N.C. AN N.C. *DIED.* N.C.S DIE. IT HAPPENS. FRANKLY, NO ONE'S EVER CARED BEFORE.
THERE'S ABOUT TO BE A LOT OF EYES ON THIS OPERATION AND THEY NEED *SOMEONE* TO TAKE THE FALL FOR ALL THE FUCK-UPS.
ONE MORE, MAYBE? OVER HERE, I THINK. BLACK BOX: ONE MORE CLOUD. A BIG ONE.
WHAT FUCK-UPS? I'VE RUN SPECIAL OPERATIONS ON A *SHOESTRING,* I'VE COME IN UNDER BUDGET *EVERY YEAR.*
WELL, WITH THAT AND A SAWBUCK, YOU CAN GET A CUP OF COFFEE.
LISTEN TO ME, YOU BITCH, I'VE *EARNED--*
...EVERYTHING YOU'VE GOT.
BLACK BOX: UNLOAD THE CLOUDS.

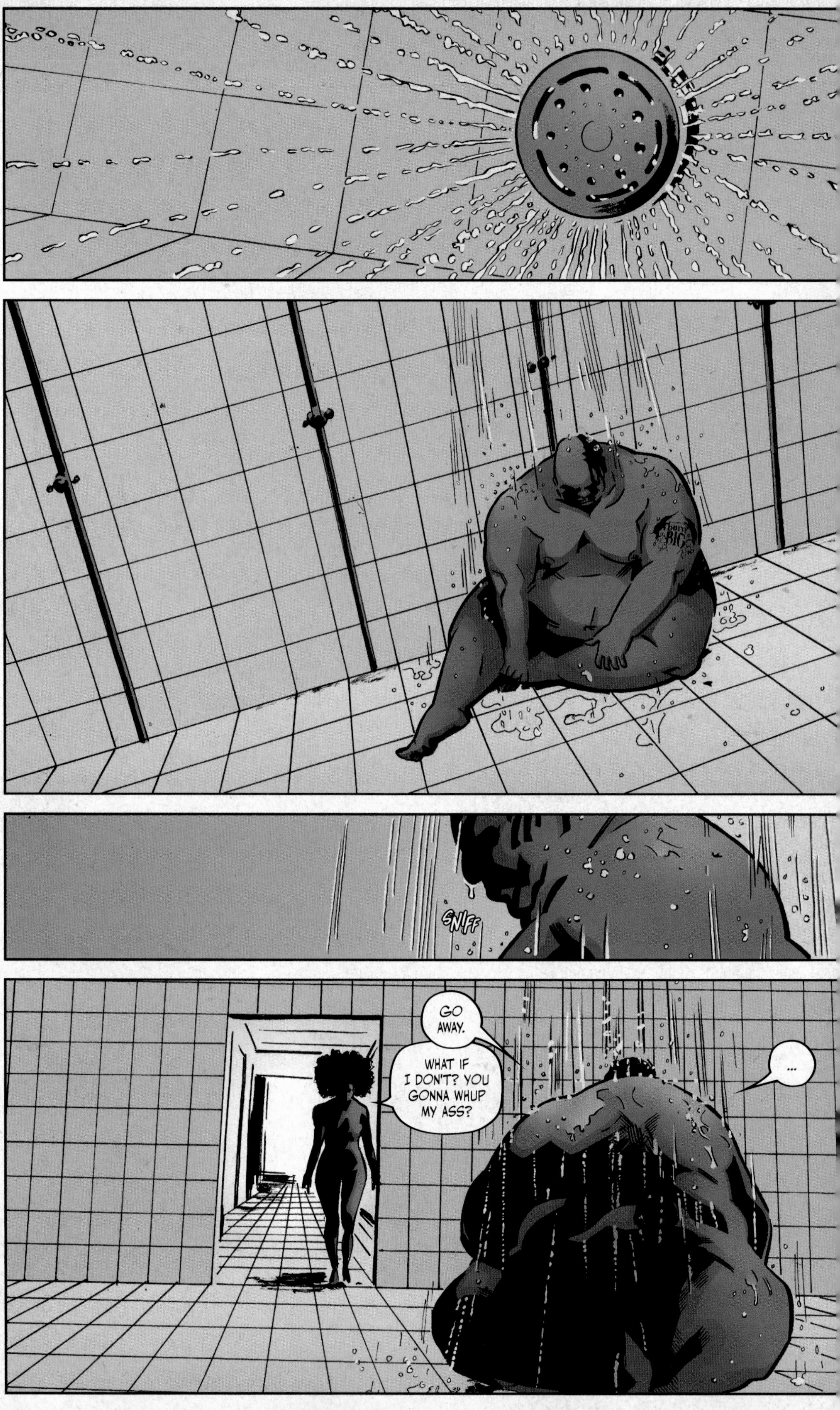
SNIFF
GO AWAY.
WHAT IF I DON'T? YOU GONNA WHUP MY ASS?
...

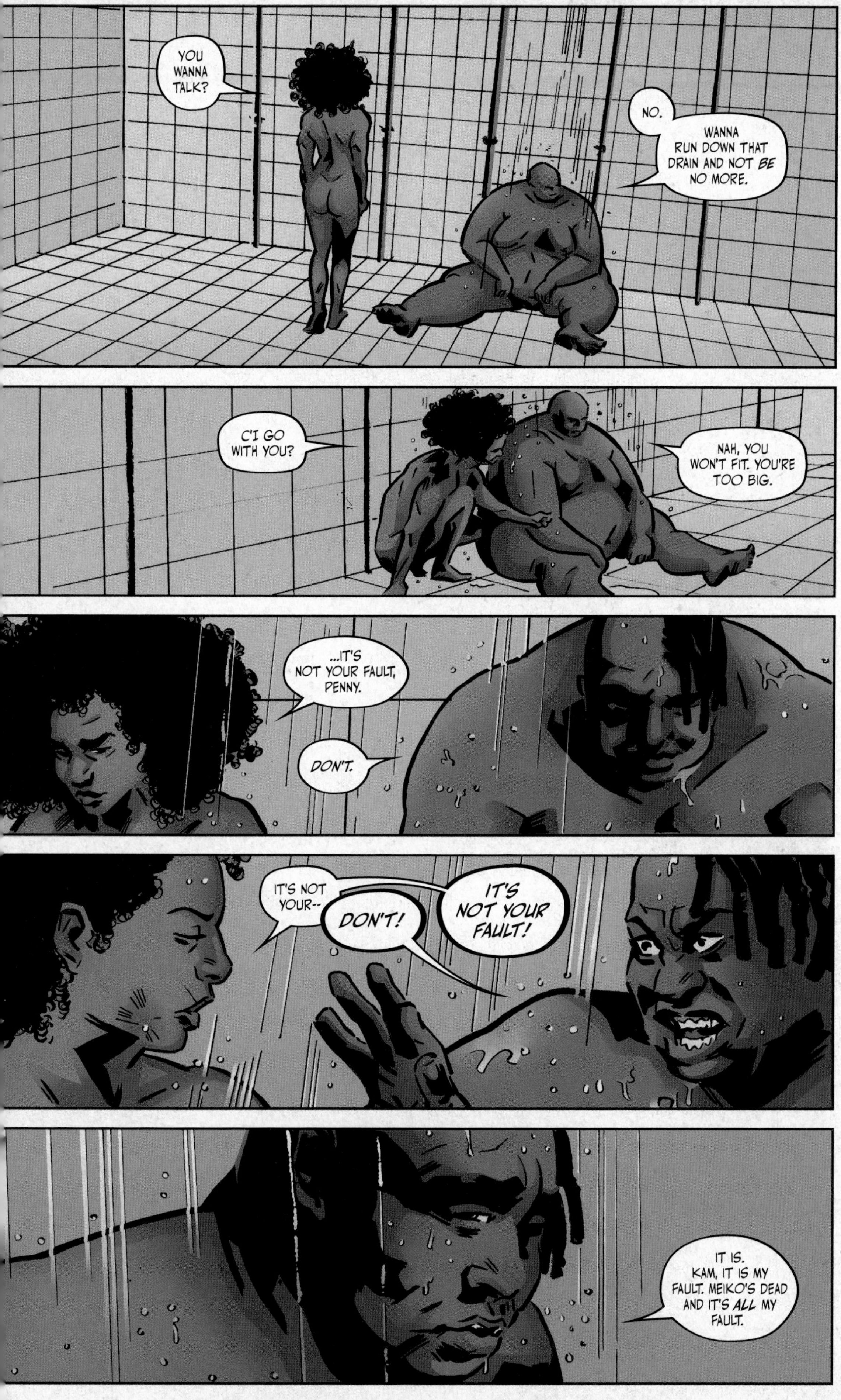
YOU WANNA TALK?
NO.
WANNA RUN DOWN THAT DRAIN AND NOT *BE* NO MORE.
C'I GO WITH YOU?
NAH, YOU WON'T FIT. YOU'RE TOO BIG.
...IT'S NOT YOUR FAULT, PENNY.
DON'T.
IT'S NOT YOUR--
DON'T!
IT'S NOT YOUR FAULT!
IT IS. KAM, IT IS MY FAULT. MEIKO'S DEAD AND IT'S *ALL* MY FAULT.

YOU COULDA GOT THERE, YOU COULDA BEEN RIGHT UP *ON* HER AND MAYBE SHE'D STILL BE IN THE GROUND.

WE'RE NEVER GONNA KNOW CAUSE WE DIDN'T LIVE *THAT* LIFE. WE'RE LIVING THIS ONE, PENNY. *THIS ONE.*

WE'RE STRONG, RIGHT? YOU AND ME. WE SPEND OUR WHOLE LIVES BEING STRONG, AND THEN...

ONE DAY YOU REALIZE *STRONG* AIN'T *STRONG ENOUGH.*

CLEAR THE SHOWERS.

YOU IN HERE BLAMING YOURSELF...

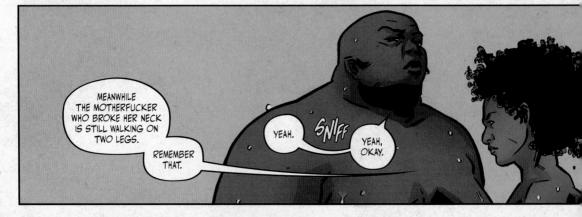

MEANWHILE THE MOTHERFUCKER WHO BROKE HER NECK IS STILL WALKING ON TWO LEGS. REMEMBER THAT.

YEAH.

SNIFF

YEAH, OKAY.

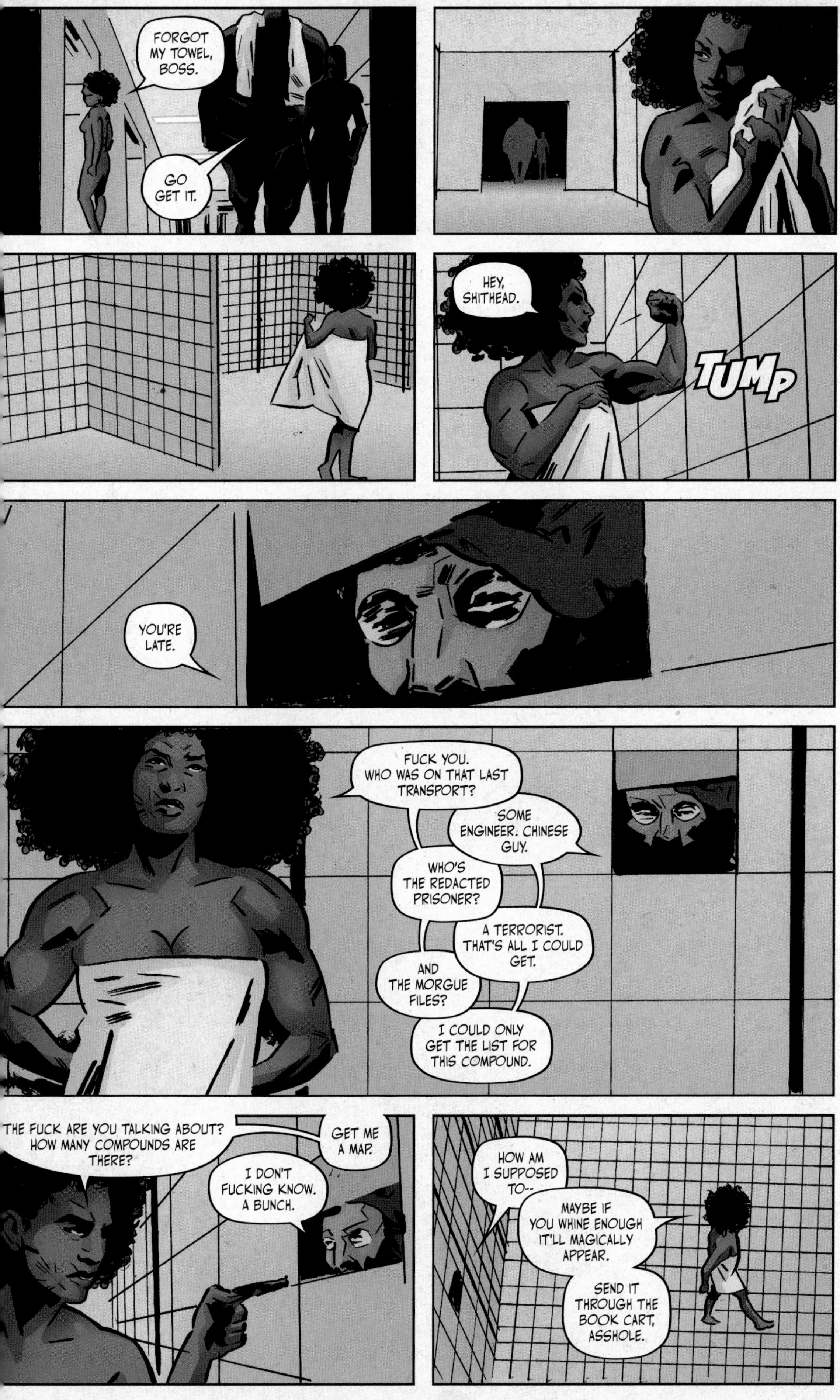
FORGOT MY TOWEL, BOSS.
GO GET IT.
HEY, SHITHEAD.
TUMP
YOU'RE LATE.
FUCK YOU. WHO WAS ON THAT LAST TRANSPORT?
SOME ENGINEER. CHINESE GUY.
WHO'S THE REDACTED PRISONER?
A TERRORIST. THAT'S ALL I COULD GET.
AND THE MORGUE FILES?
I COULD ONLY GET THE LIST FOR THIS COMPOUND.
THE FUCK ARE YOU TALKING ABOUT? HOW MANY COMPOUNDS ARE THERE?
I DON'T FUCKING KNOW. A BUNCH.
GET ME A MAP.
HOW AM I SUPPOSED TO--
MAYBE IF YOU WHINE ENOUGH IT'LL MAGICALLY APPEAR.
SEND IT THROUGH THE BOOK CART, ASSHOLE.

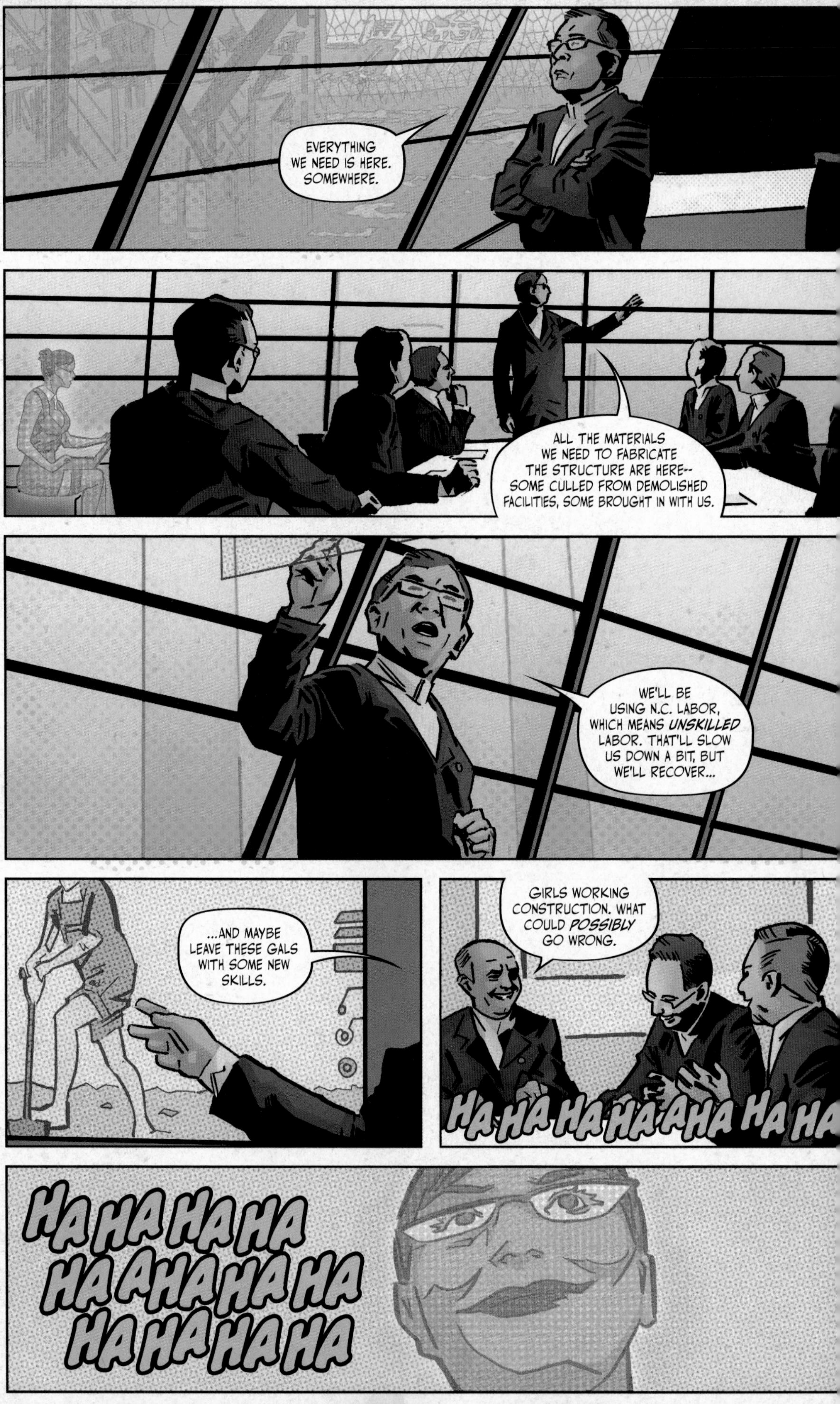
EVERYTHING WE NEED IS HERE. SOMEWHERE.
ALL THE MATERIALS WE NEED TO FABRICATE THE STRUCTURE ARE HERE-- SOME CULLED FROM DEMOLISHED FACILITIES, SOME BROUGHT IN WITH US.
WE'LL BE USING N.C. LABOR, WHICH MEANS UNSKILLED LABOR. THAT'LL SLOW US DOWN A BIT, BUT WE'LL RECOVER...
...AND MAYBE LEAVE THESE GALS WITH SOME NEW SKILLS.
GIRLS WORKING CONSTRUCTION. WHAT COULD POSSIBLY GO WRONG.
HA HA HA HA HA AHA HA HA HA
HA HA HA HA
HA AHA HA HA HA
HA HA HA HA

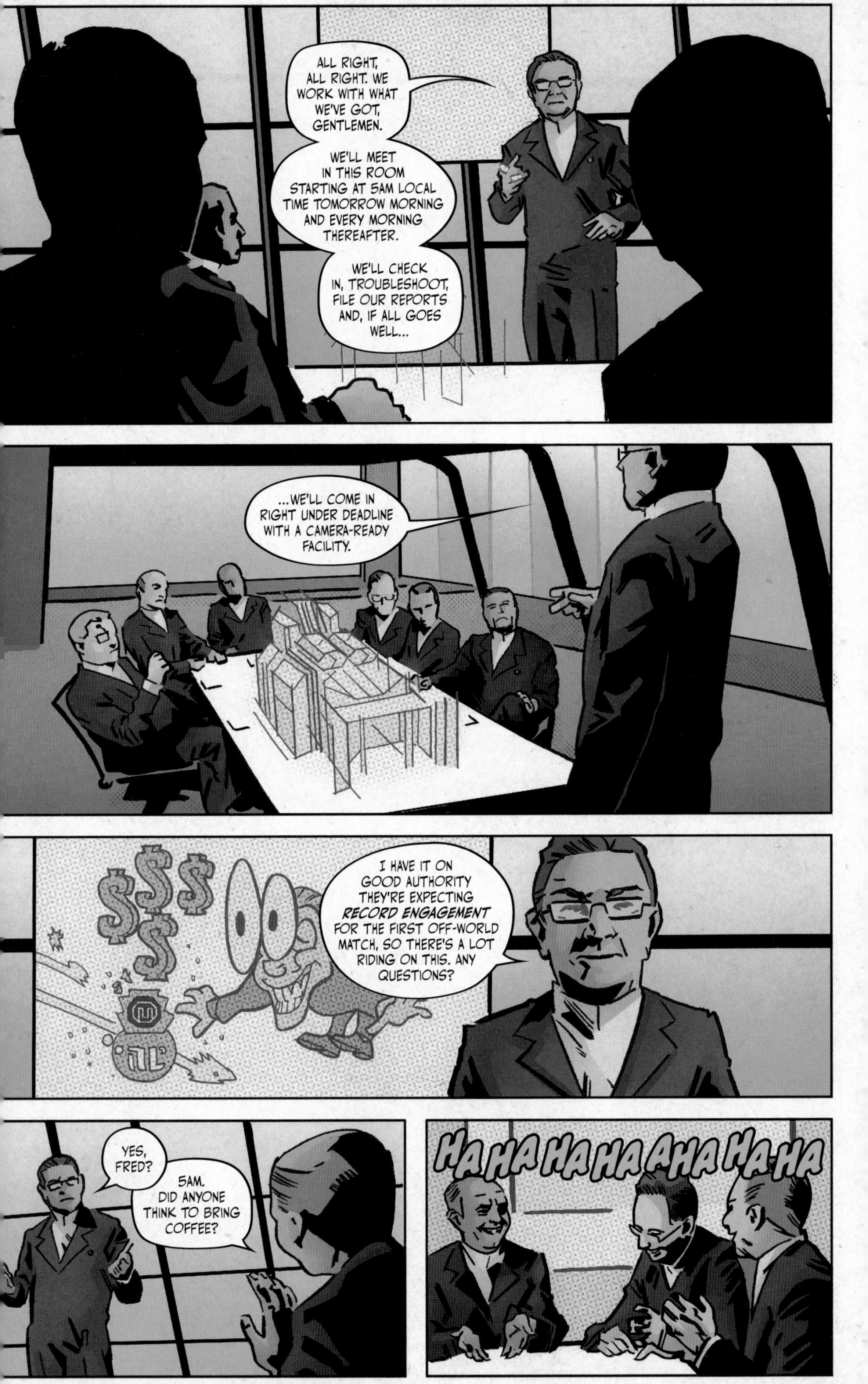
ALL RIGHT, ALL RIGHT. WE WORK WITH WHAT WE'VE GOT, GENTLEMEN.
WE'LL MEET IN THIS ROOM STARTING AT 5AM LOCAL TIME TOMORROW MORNING AND EVERY MORNING THEREAFTER.
WE'LL CHECK IN, TROUBLESHOOT, FILE OUR REPORTS AND, IF ALL GOES WELL...
...WE'LL COME IN RIGHT UNDER DEADLINE WITH A CAMERA-READY FACILITY.
I HAVE IT ON GOOD AUTHORITY THEY'RE EXPECTING *RECORD ENGAGEMENT* FOR THE FIRST OFF-WORLD MATCH, SO THERE'S A LOT RIDING ON THIS. ANY QUESTIONS?
YES, FRED?
5AM. DID ANYONE THINK TO BRING COFFEE?
HA HA HA HA HA AHA HA HA-HA

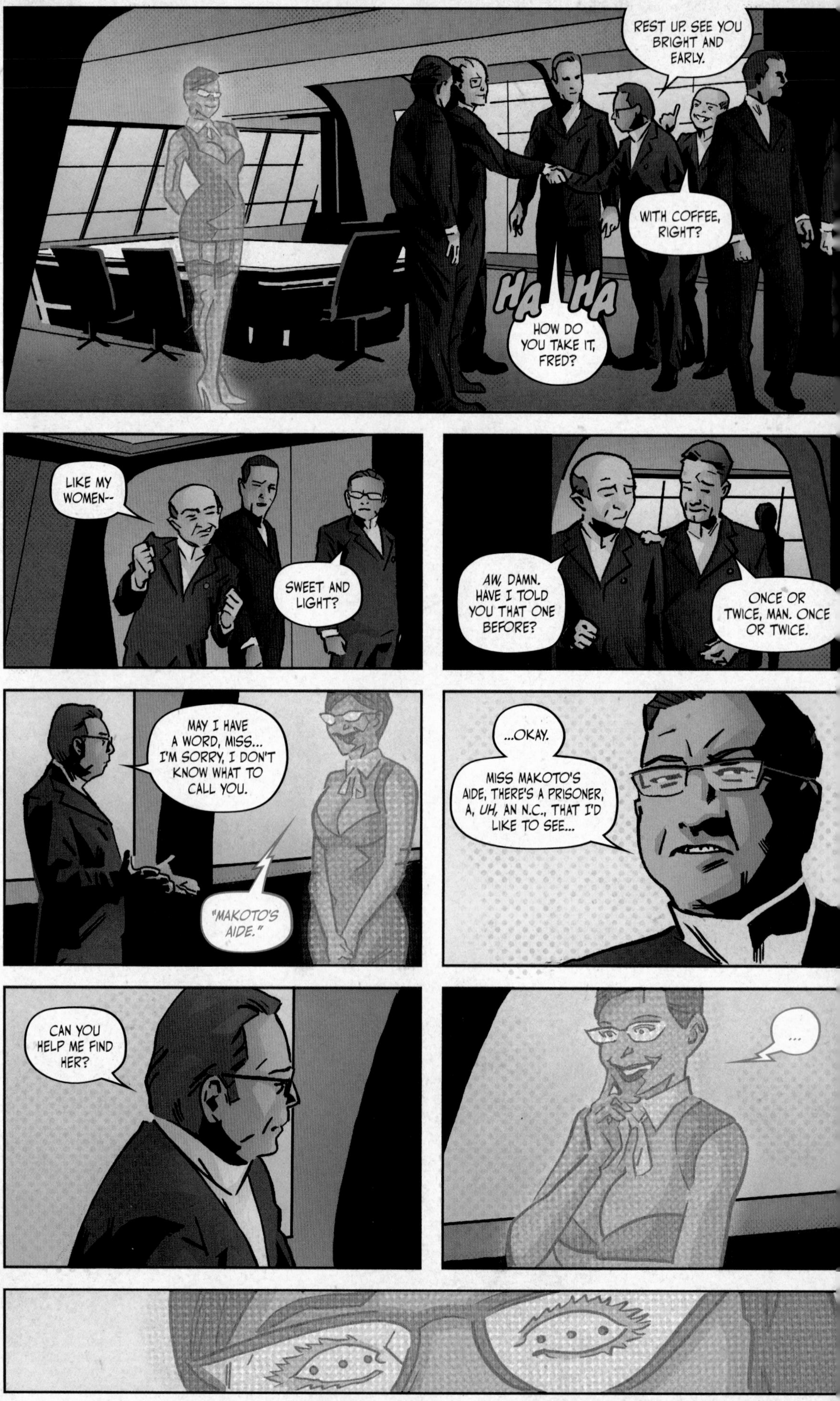
REST UP. SEE YOU BRIGHT AND EARLY.
WITH COFFEE, RIGHT?
HA HA
HOW DO YOU TAKE IT, FRED?
LIKE MY WOMEN--
SWEET AND LIGHT?
AW, DAMN. HAVE I TOLD YOU THAT ONE BEFORE?
ONCE OR TWICE, MAN. ONCE OR TWICE.
MAY I HAVE A WORD, MISS... I'M SORRY, I DON'T KNOW WHAT TO CALL YOU.
"MAKOTO'S AIDE."
...OKAY.
MISS MAKOTO'S AIDE, THERE'S A PRISONER, A, UH, AN N.C., THAT I'D LIKE TO SEE...
CAN YOU HELP ME FIND HER?
...

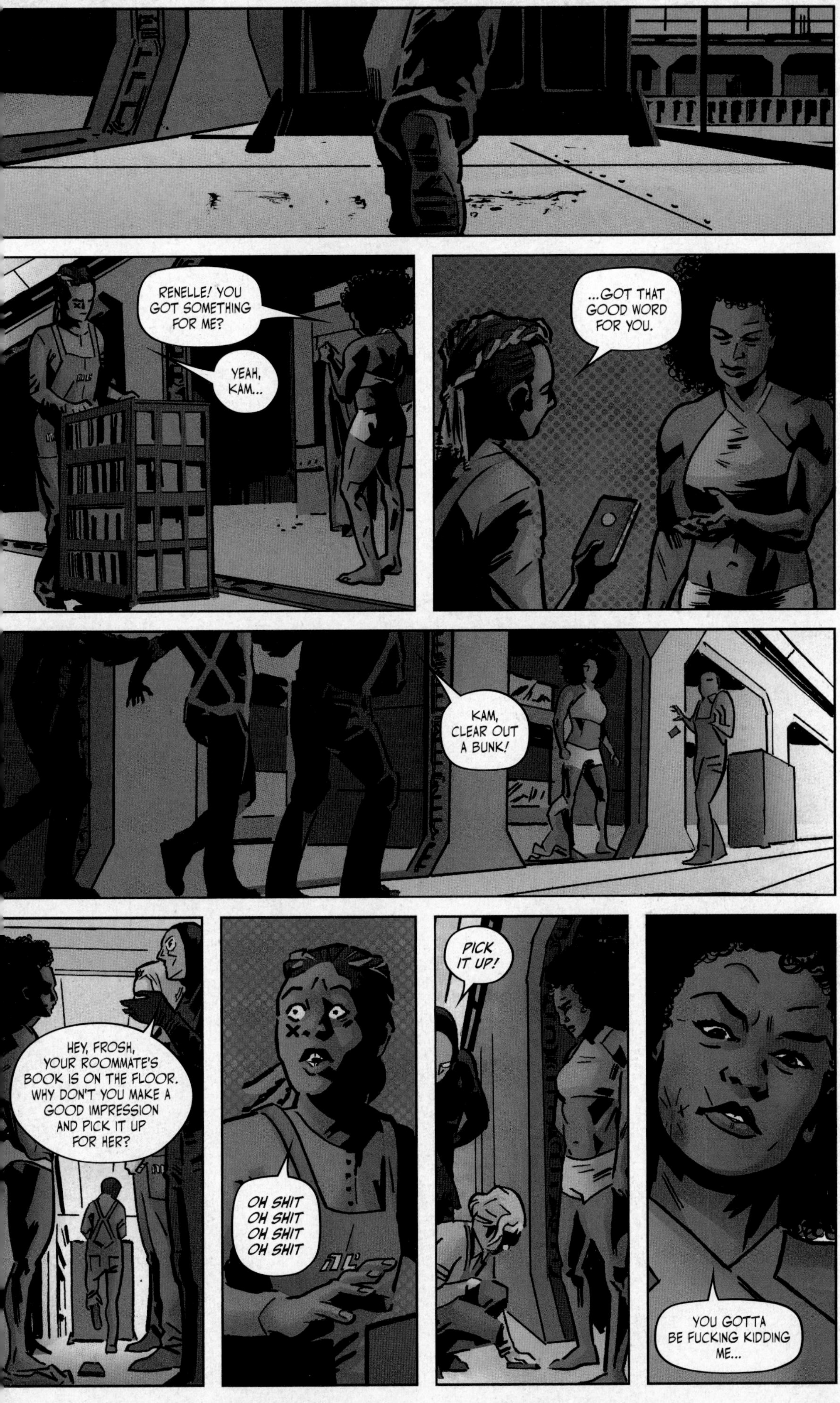
RENELLE! YOU GOT SOMETHING FOR ME?
YEAH, KAM...
...GOT THAT GOOD WORD FOR YOU.
KAM, CLEAR OUT A BUNK!
HEY, FROSH, YOUR ROOMMATE'S BOOK IS ON THE FLOOR. WHY DON'T YOU MAKE A GOOD IMPRESSION AND PICK IT UP FOR HER?
OH SHIT OH SHIT OH SHIT OH SHIT
PICK IT UP!
YOU GOTTA BE FUCKING KIDDING ME...

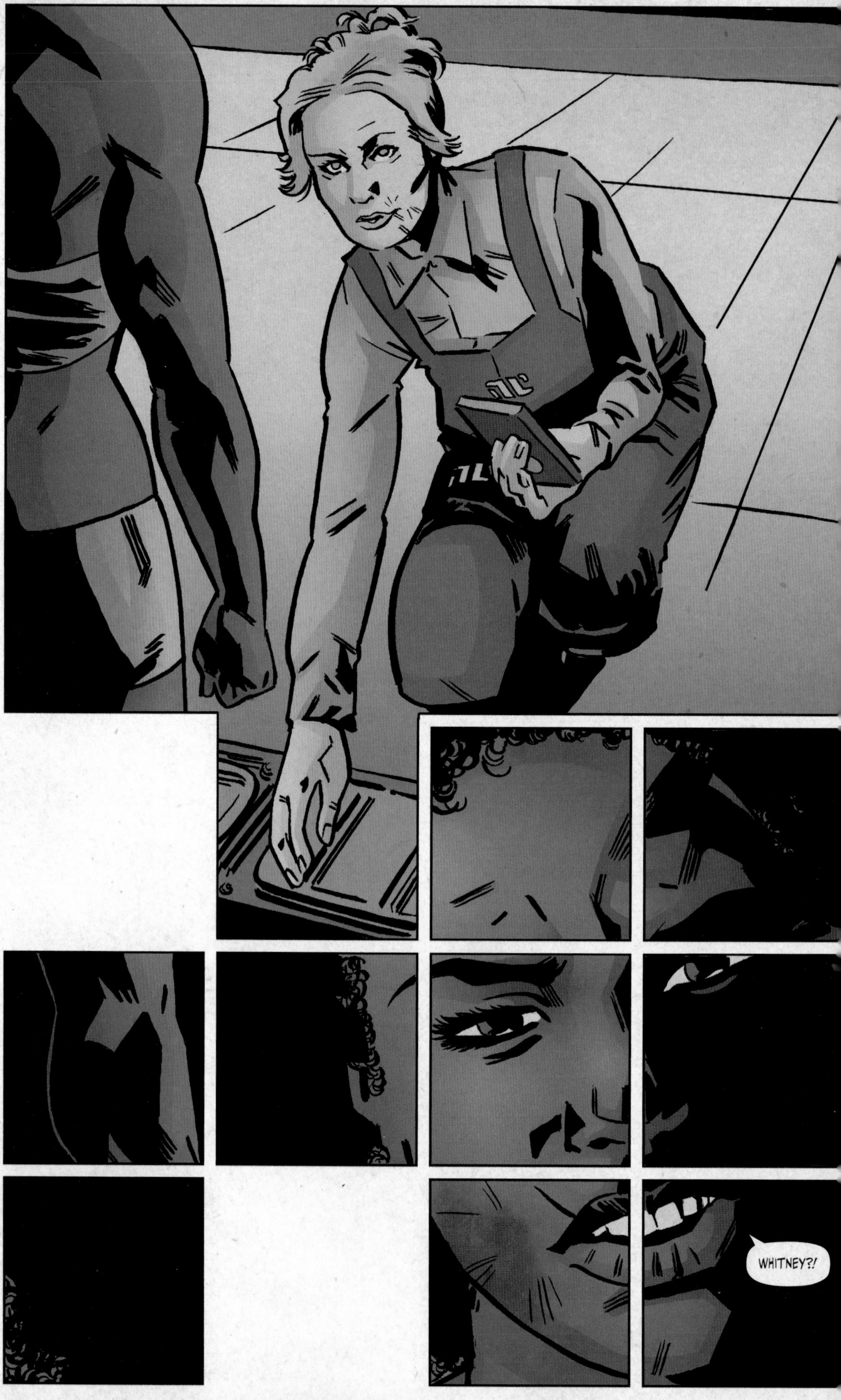
WHITNEY?!

"Women are *naturally* more self-conscious than men when it comes to their appearance."

NATURALLY. it's not conditioning or systematic oppression, ladies. It's just nature. And really, the weight of responsibility for aesthetic crimes does lie on the shoulders of all women, so do your part to hide your heinousness! BUT! Wait! Makeup is also a LIE! You ugly cow, he thought you really did have cheekbones that were cut with a laser. You tricked him! You're damned if you do and damned if you don't, you lying strumpet. Might as well *steer in*...

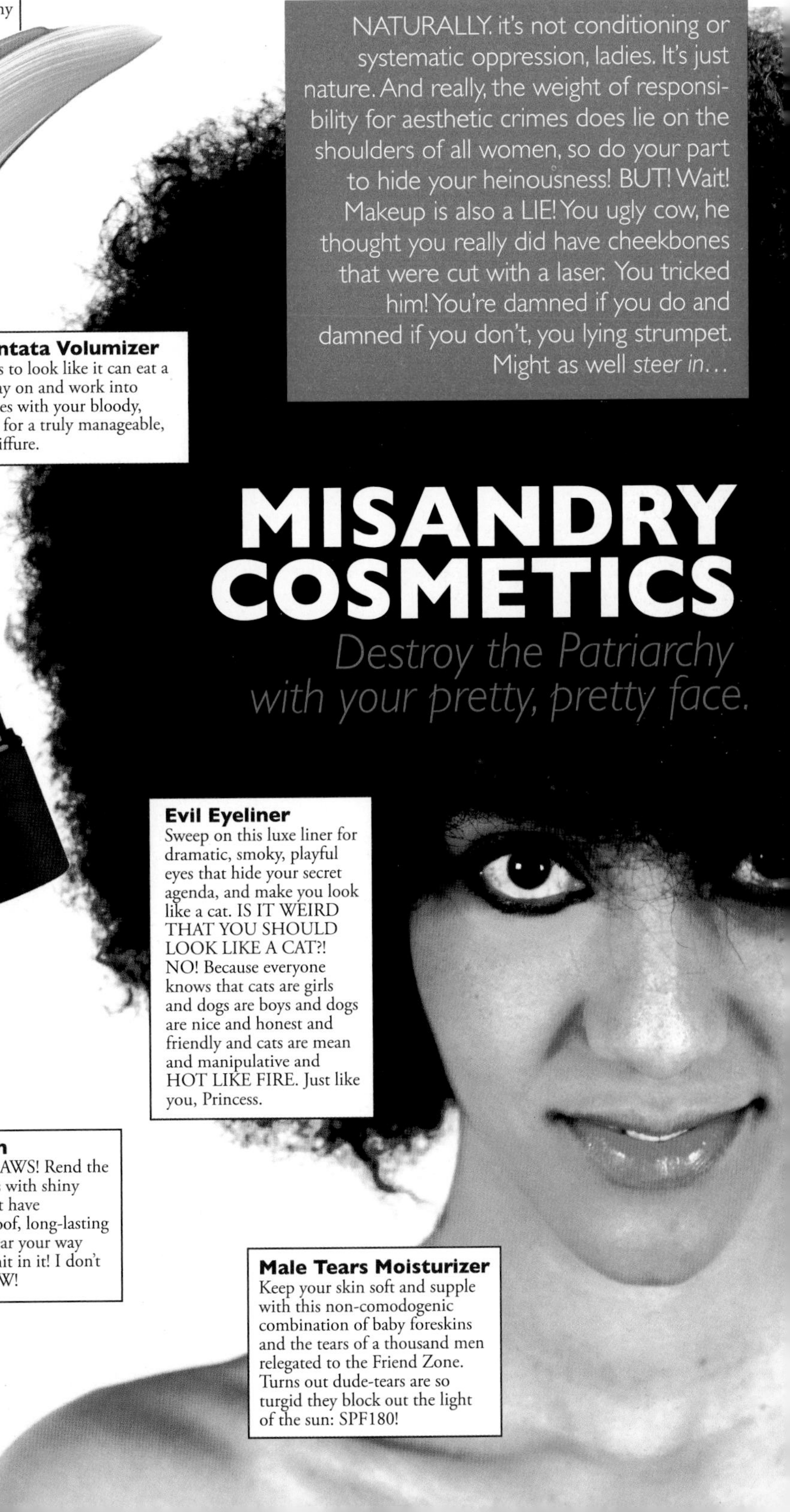

MISANDRY COSMETICS

Destroy the Patriarchy with your pretty, pretty face.

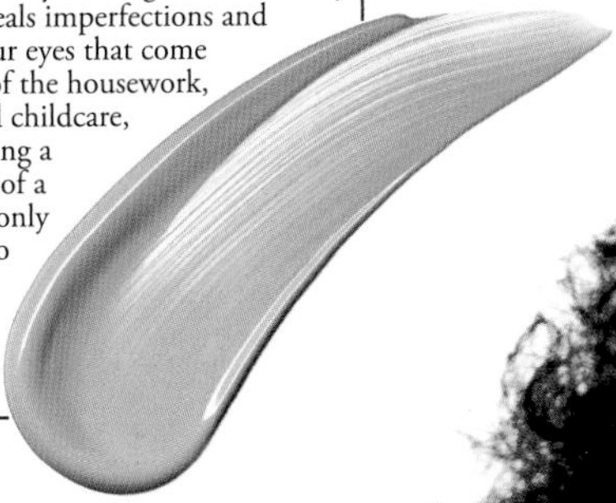

Crafty Concealer
Light-refracting all-day coverage with a creamy formula that conceals imperfections and the bags under your eyes that come from doing 80% of the housework, meal planning and childcare, all while still holding a full-time job! Part of a daily routine that only takes a half hour to apply—because what do we have if not loads of free time??

Vagina Dentata Volumizer
Your hair needs to look like it can eat a man alive. Spray on and work into your limp tresses with your bloody, taloned fingers for a truly manageable, man-killing coiffure.

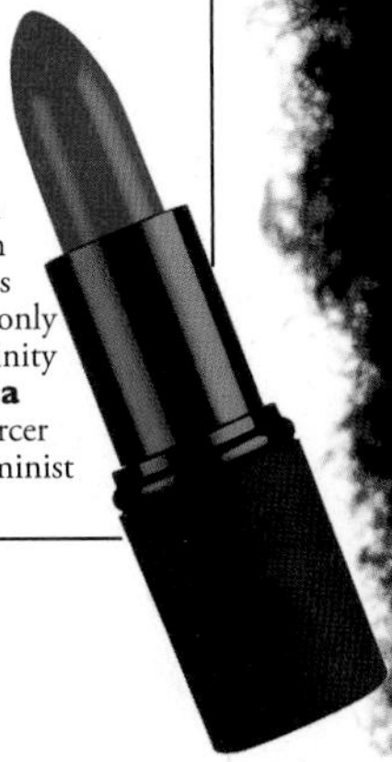

Lipstick of Lies
Red like the bleeding wounds of the dying men at your feet, this luminous shade highlights your mouth as you screech a stream of invective in the faces of innocent men who only want to explain femininity to you. Pair with **Labia Lipliner** for fuller, fiercer and more furiously feminist engorgement.

Evil Eyeliner
Sweep on this luxe liner for dramatic, smoky, playful eyes that hide your secret agenda, and make you look like a cat. IS IT WEIRD THAT YOU SHOULD LOOK LIKE A CAT?! NO! Because everyone knows that cats are girls and dogs are boys and dogs are nice and honest and friendly and cats are mean and manipulative and HOT LIKE FIRE. Just like you, Princess.

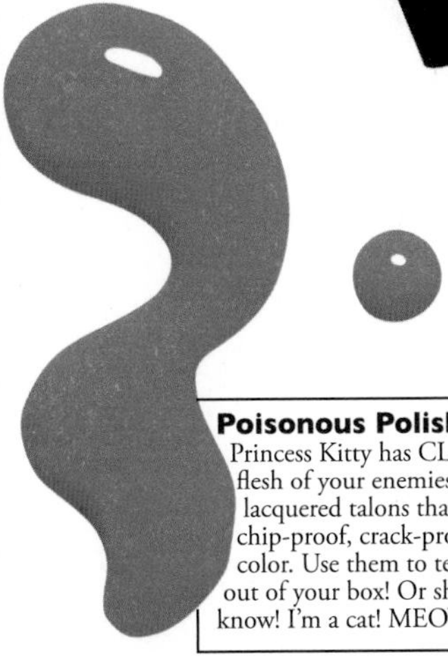

Poisonous Polish
Princess Kitty has CLAWS! Rend the flesh of your enemies with shiny lacquered talons that have chip-proof, crack-proof, long-lasting color. Use them to tear your way out of your box! Or shit in it! I don't know! I'm a cat! MEOW!

Male Tears Moisturizer
Keep your skin soft and supple with this non-comodogenic combination of baby foreskins and the tears of a thousand men relegated to the Friend Zone. Turns out dude-tears are so turgid they block out the light of the sun: SPF180!

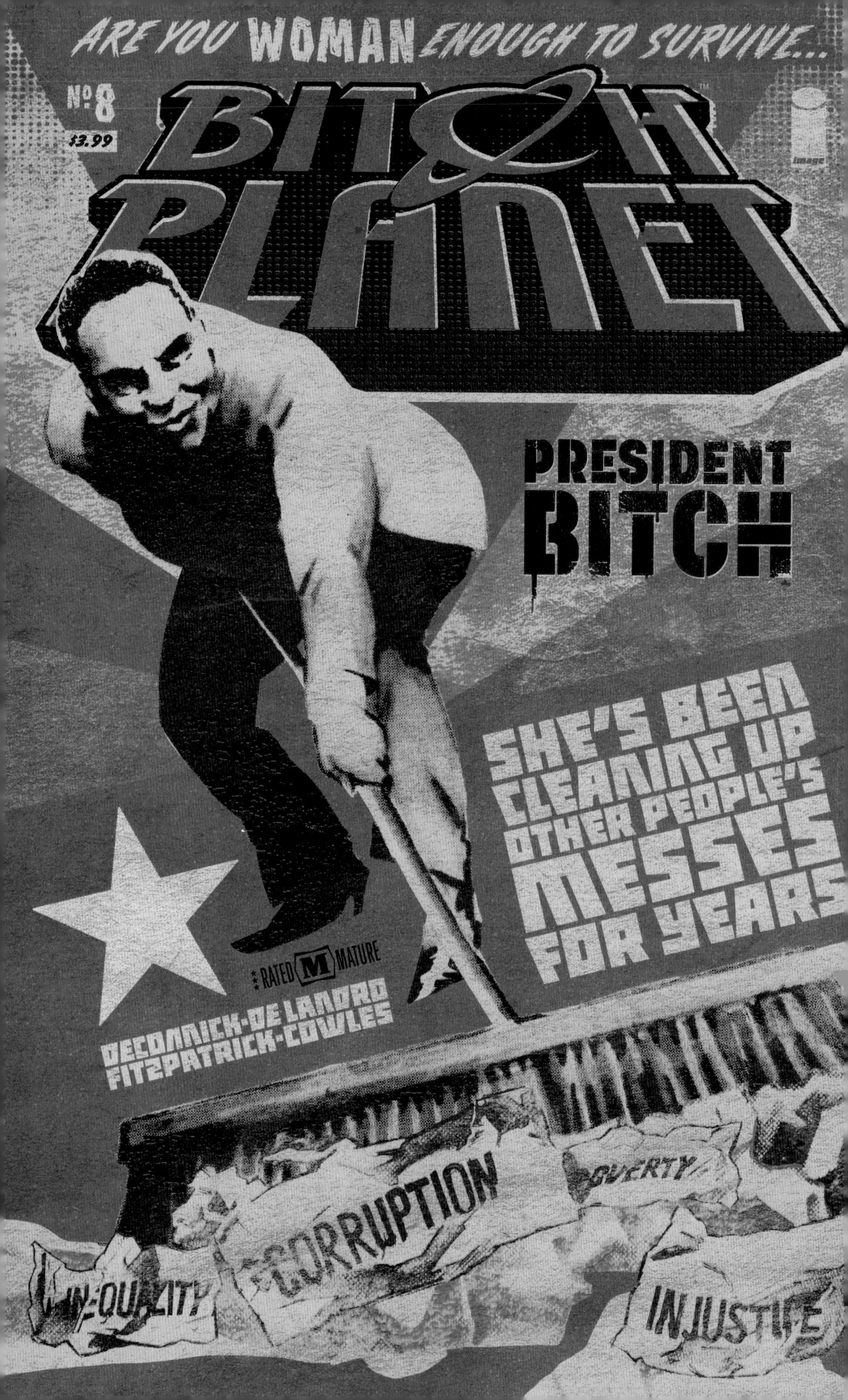

ARE YOU WOMAN ENOUGH TO SURVIVE...
Nº8
$3.99
BITCH PLANET
PRESIDENT BITCH
SHE'S BEEN CLEANING UP OTHER PEOPLE'S MESSES FOR YEARS
RATED M MATURE
DECONNICK·DE LANDRO
FITZPATRICK·COWLES
CORRUPTION
OVERTY
IN-EQUALITY
INJUSTICE

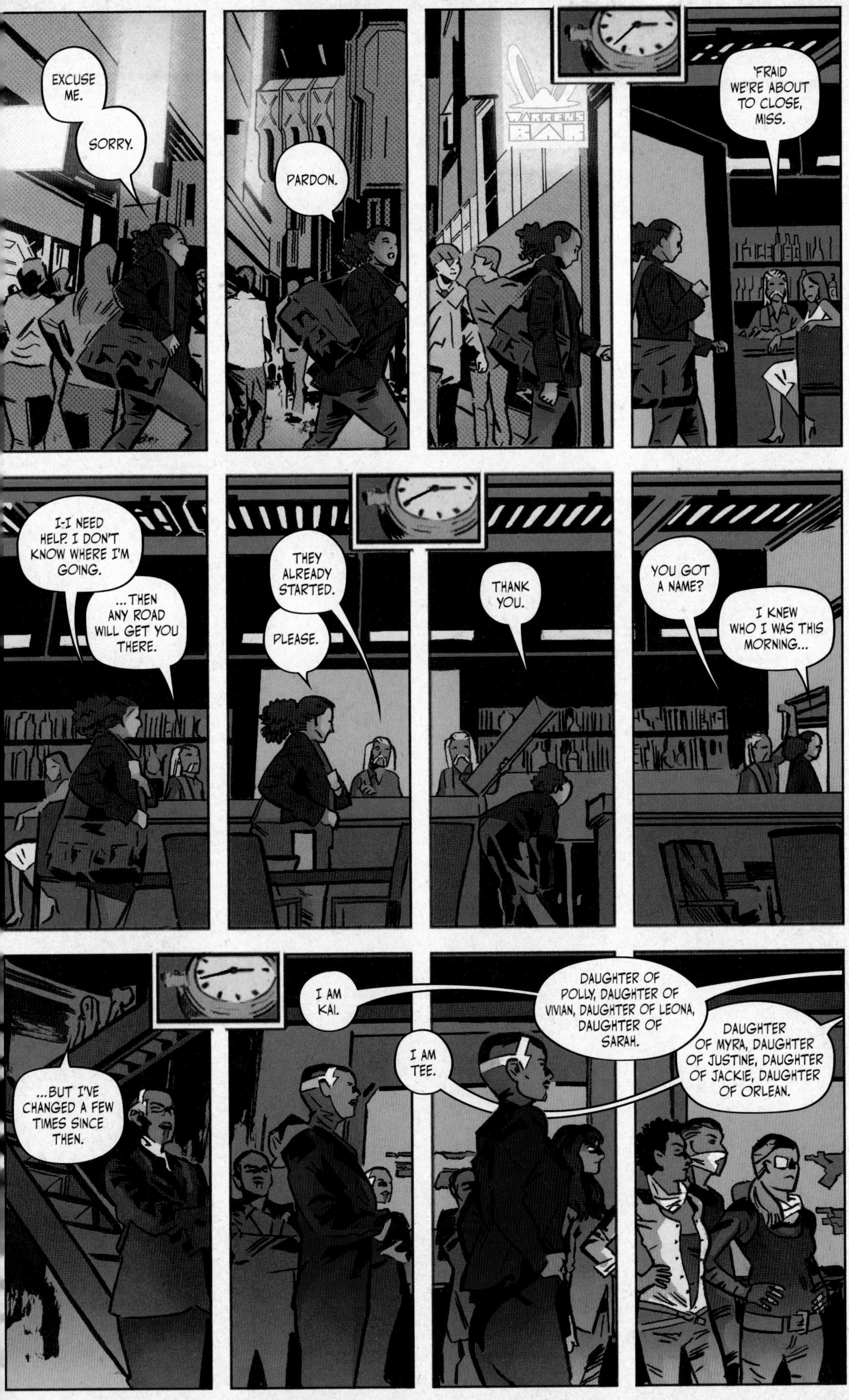
EXCUSE ME.
SORRY.
PARDON.
WARRENS BAR
'FRAID WE'RE ABOUT TO CLOSE, MISS.
I-I NEED HELP. I DON'T KNOW WHERE I'M GOING.
...THEN ANY ROAD WILL GET YOU THERE.
THEY ALREADY STARTED.
PLEASE.
THANK YOU.
YOU GOT A NAME?
I KNEW WHO I WAS THIS MORNING...
...BUT I'VE CHANGED A FEW TIMES SINCE THEN.
I AM KAI.
I AM TEE.
DAUGHTER OF POLLY, DAUGHTER OF VIVIAN, DAUGHTER OF LEONA, DAUGHTER OF SARAH.
DAUGHTER OF MYRA, DAUGHTER OF JUSTINE, DAUGHTER OF JACKIE, DAUGHTER OF ORLEAN.

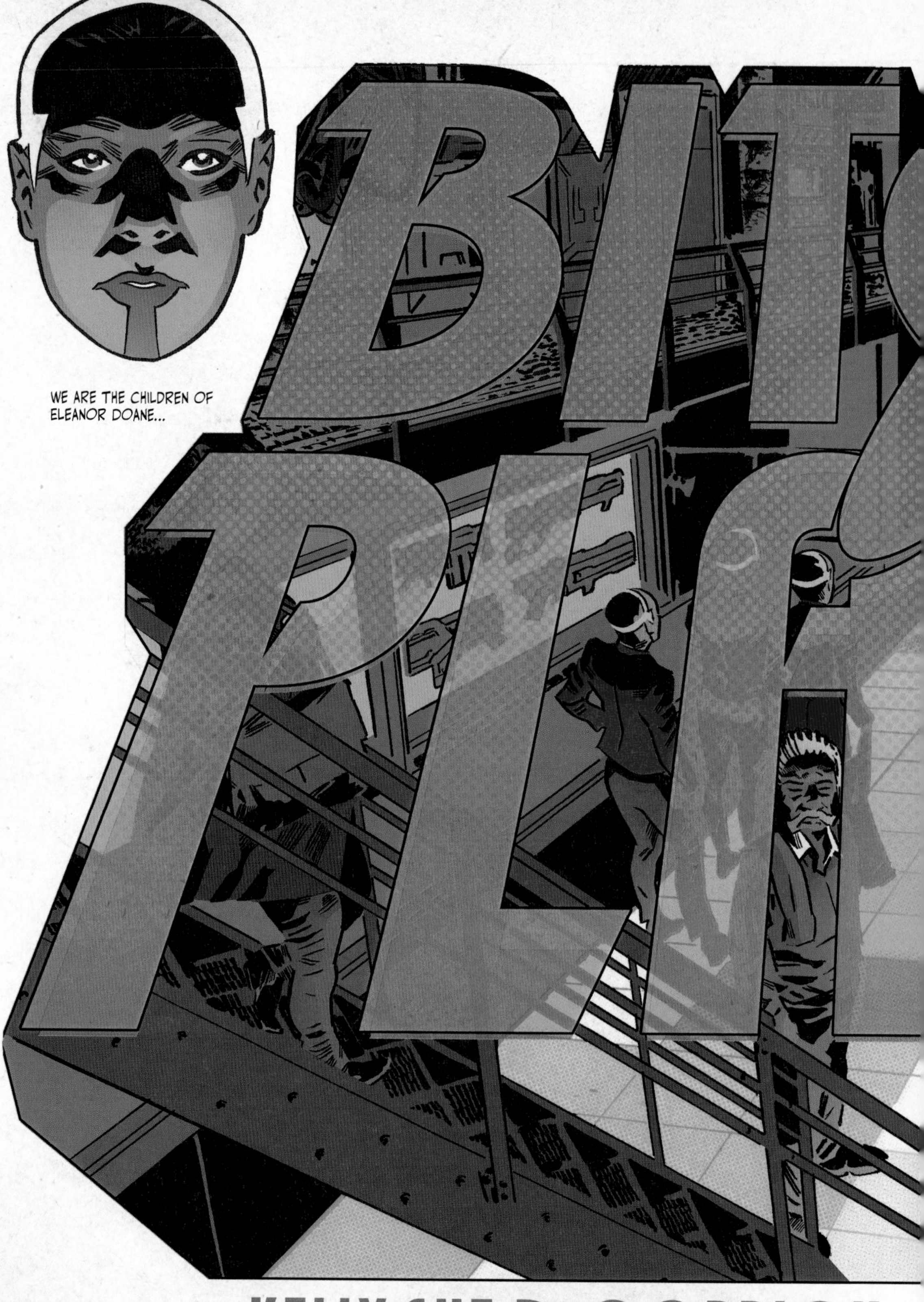
WE ARE THE CHILDREN OF
ELEANOR DOANE...

KELLY SUE DeCONNICK
SCRIPT

KELLY FITZPATRICK
COLORS

CLAYTON COWLES
LETTERS

RIAN HUGHES
COVER DESIGN & LOGO DESIGN

LAURENN McCUBBIN
BACKMATTER DESIGN

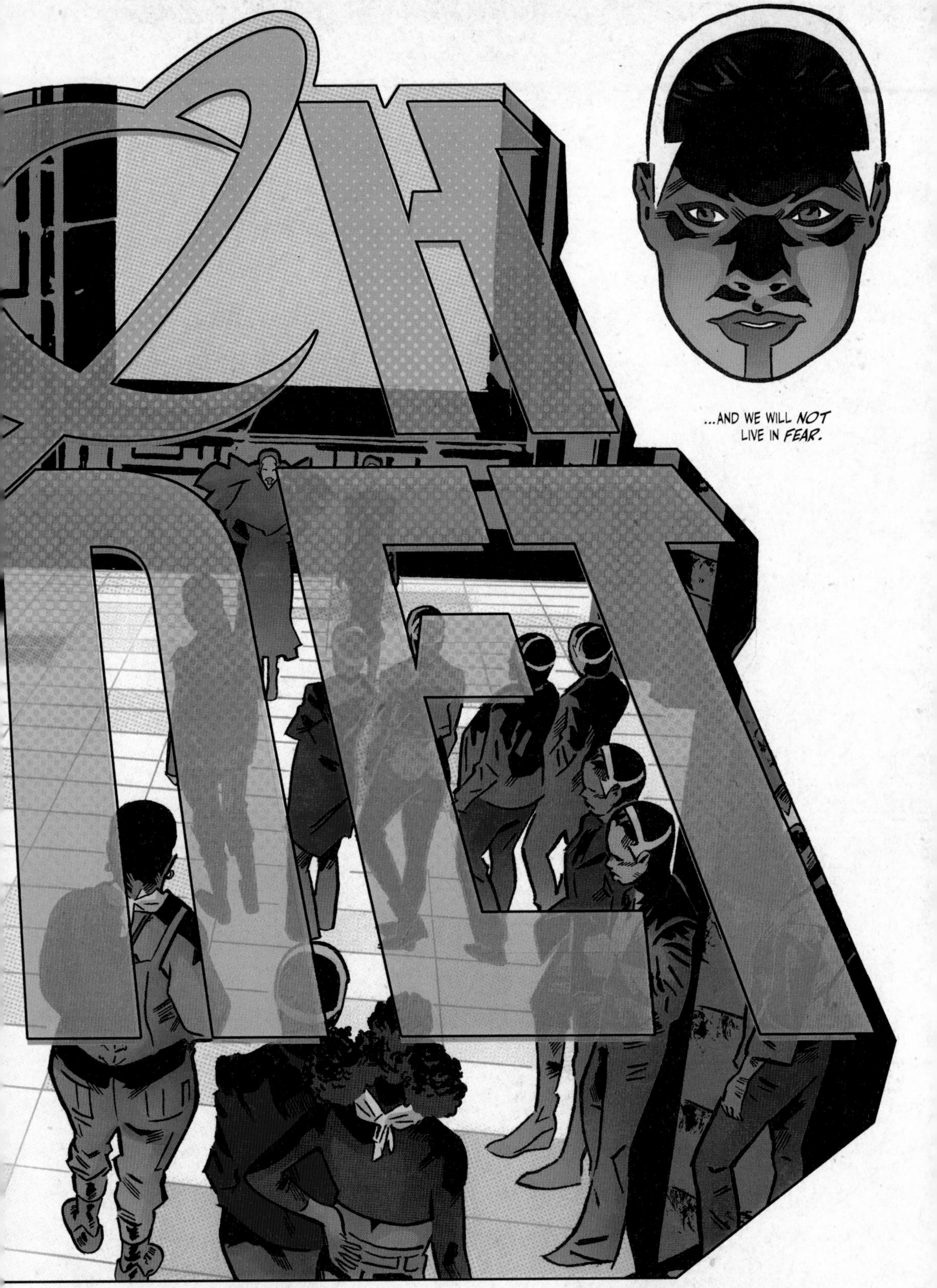
...AND WE WILL NOT LIVE IN FEAR.

VALENTINE DE LANDRO
ART/COVERS

LAUREN SANKOVITCH
EDITOR

SPECIAL THANKS TO
ARIA EHREN, EMMA HOUXBOIS, MEY VALDIVIA RUDE & NICK SHADOW

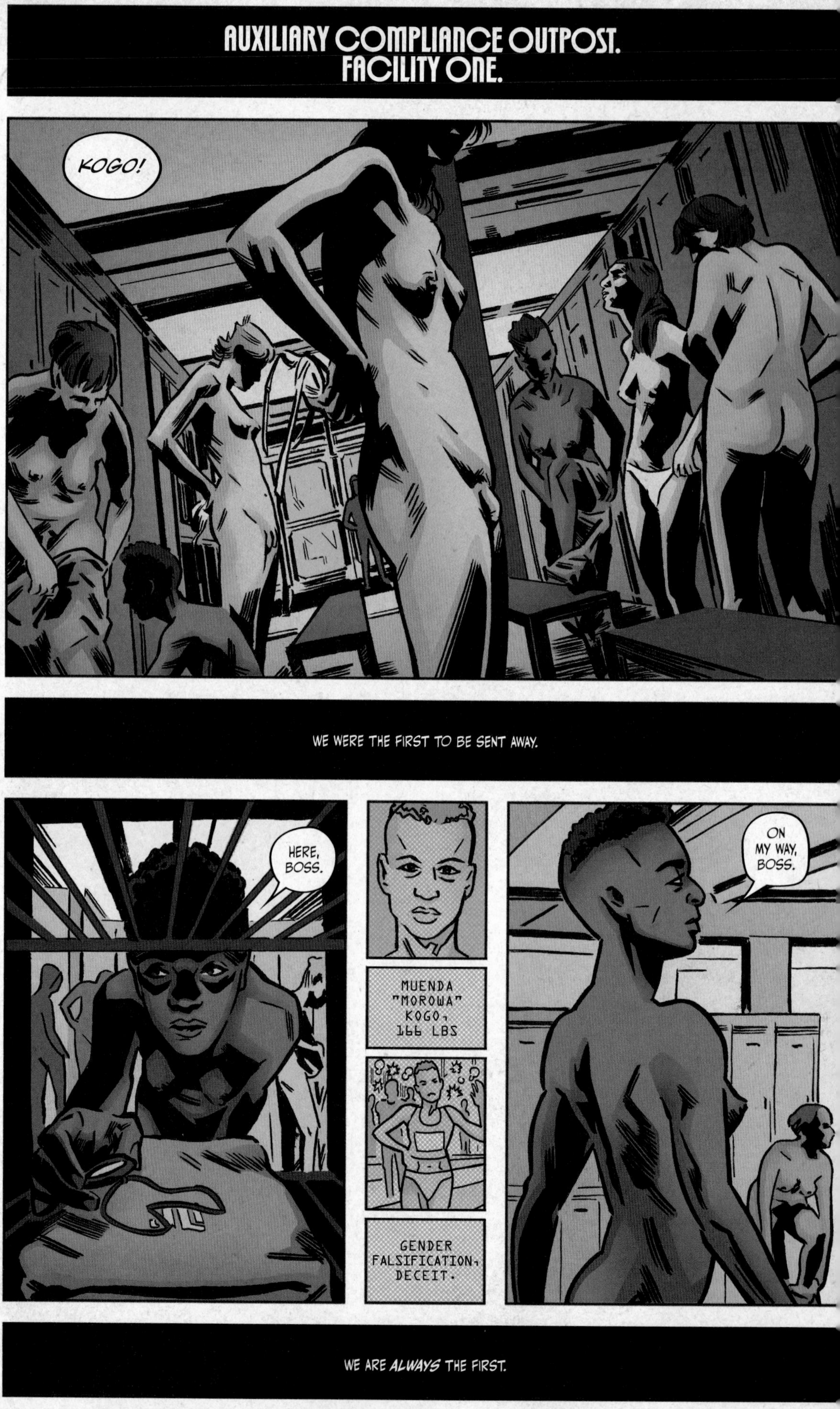
AUXILIARY COMPLIANCE OUTPOST.
FACILITY ONE.
KOGO!
WE WERE THE FIRST TO BE SENT AWAY.
HERE, BOSS.
MUENDA "MOROWA" KOGO, 166 LBS
GENDER FALSIFICATION, DECEIT.
ON MY WAY, BOSS.
WE ARE *ALWAYS* THE FIRST.

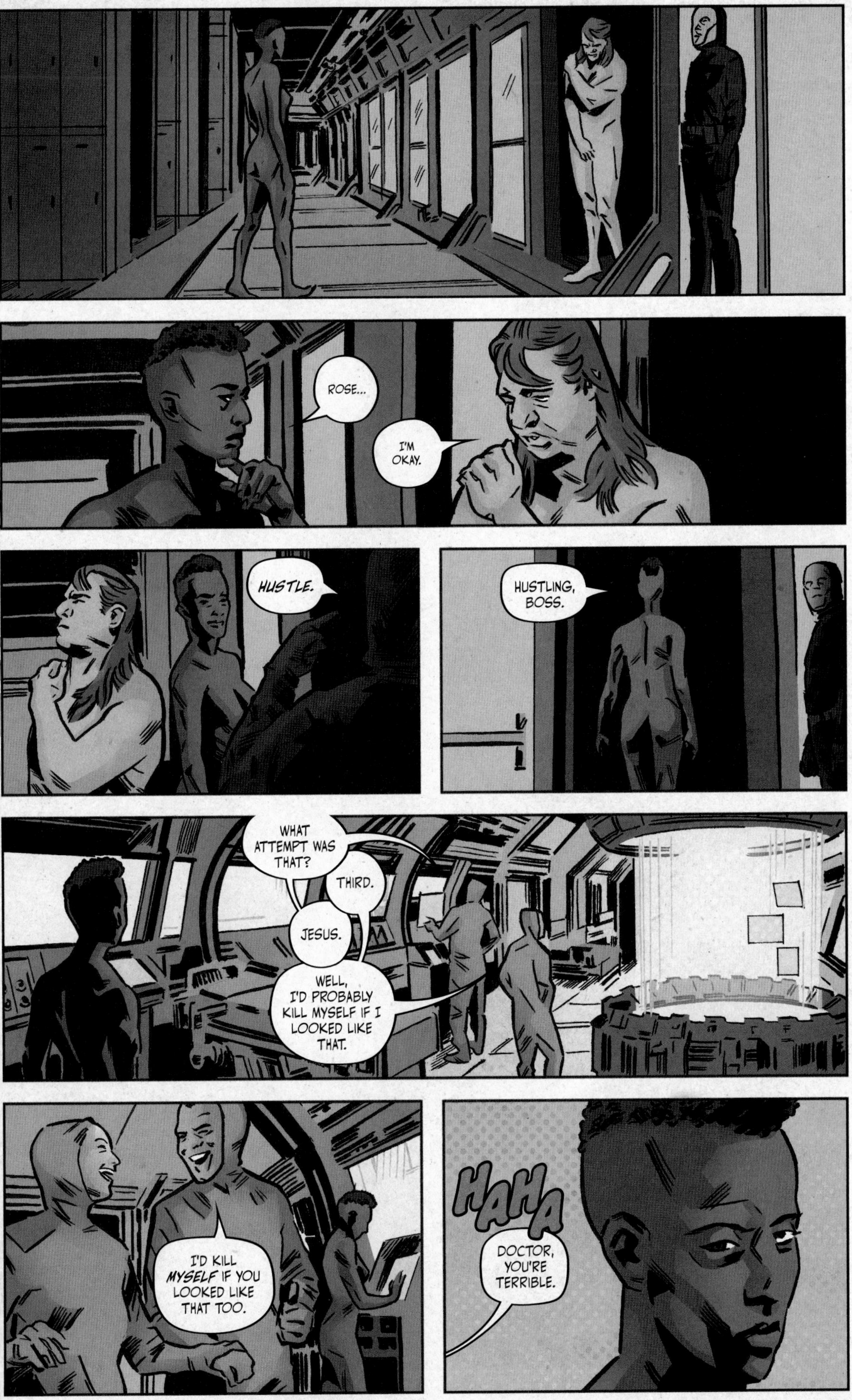
ROSE...
I'M OKAY.
HUSTLE.
HUSTLING, BOSS.
WHAT ATTEMPT WAS THAT?
THIRD.
JESUS.
WELL, I'D PROBABLY KILL MYSELF IF I LOOKED LIKE THAT.
I'D KILL MYSELF IF YOU LOOKED LIKE THAT TOO.
HAHA
DOCTOR, YOU'RE TERRIBLE.

WE GOT ALL THE LABS ON THIS ONE?

STOOL... CHECK. BLOOD... CHECK. SALIVA... OH, WE NEED HAIR.

HAIR.

WHY DO YOU DO THIS?

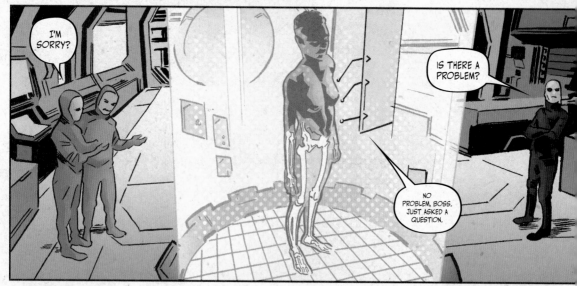

I'M SORRY?

IS THERE A PROBLEM?

NO PROBLEM, BOSS. JUST ASKED A QUESTION.

WHY DO WE TAKE SAMPLES? TO MONITOR YOUR HEALTH.

YOU SEND US HERE TO DIE. WHAT DO YOU CARE HOW IT HAPPENS?

I DIDN'T SEND YOU HERE, ALL RIGHT? YOU MADE *CHOICES* WITH CONSEQUENCES.

I COME HERE ONCE A YEAR AT GREAT PERSONAL RISK TO MYSELF BECAUSE I TOOK AN *OATH*--

HERE I THOUGHT IT WAS 'CAUSE YOU *CARED*.

AAHHH!

EHREN, YOU'RE NEXT.

YES, BOSS.

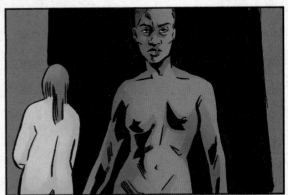

ARE YOU OKAY, MOROWA?

I'M FINE, ROSE.

AND NOW WE'RE BOTH PRETTY.

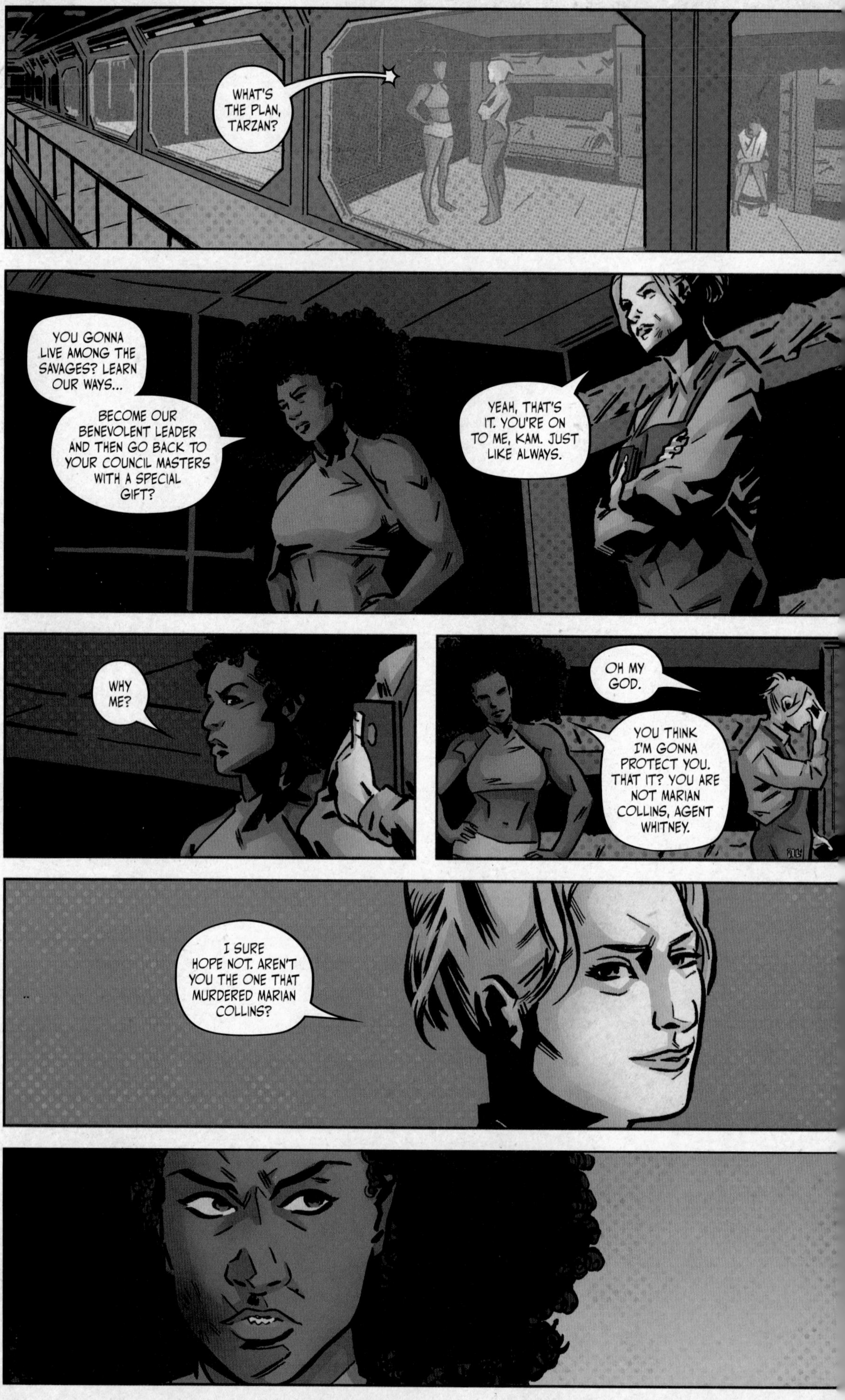
WHAT'S THE PLAN, TARZAN?
YOU GONNA LIVE AMONG THE SAVAGES? LEARN OUR WAYS...
BECOME OUR BENEVOLENT LEADER AND THEN GO BACK TO YOUR COUNCIL MASTERS WITH A SPECIAL GIFT?
YEAH, THAT'S IT. YOU'RE ON TO ME, KAM. JUST LIKE ALWAYS.
WHY ME?
OH MY GOD.
YOU THINK I'M GONNA PROTECT YOU. THAT IT? YOU ARE NOT MARIAN COLLINS, AGENT WHITNEY.
I SURE HOPE NOT. AREN'T YOU THE ONE THAT MURDERED MARIAN COLLINS?

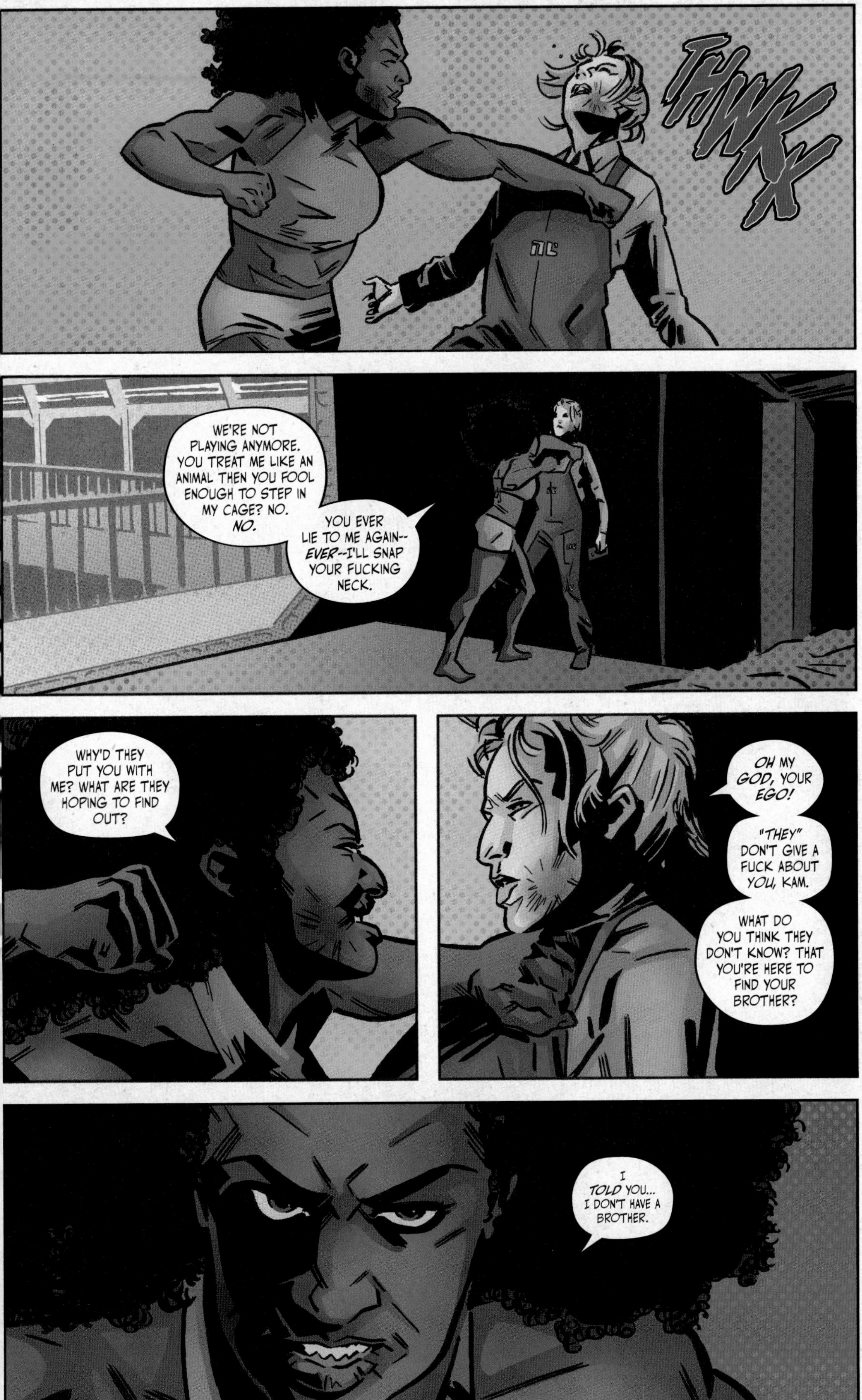
THWKK
WE'RE NOT PLAYING ANYMORE. YOU TREAT ME LIKE AN ANIMAL THEN YOU FOOL ENOUGH TO STEP IN MY CAGE? NO. NO.
YOU EVER LIE TO ME AGAIN-- EVER--I'LL SNAP YOUR FUCKING NECK.
WHY'D THEY PUT YOU WITH ME? WHAT ARE THEY HOPING TO FIND OUT?
OH MY GOD, YOUR EGO!
"THEY" DON'T GIVE A FUCK ABOUT YOU, KAM.
WHAT DO YOU THINK THEY DON'T KNOW? THAT YOU'RE HERE TO FIND YOUR BROTHER?
I TOLD YOU... I DON'T HAVE A BROTHER.

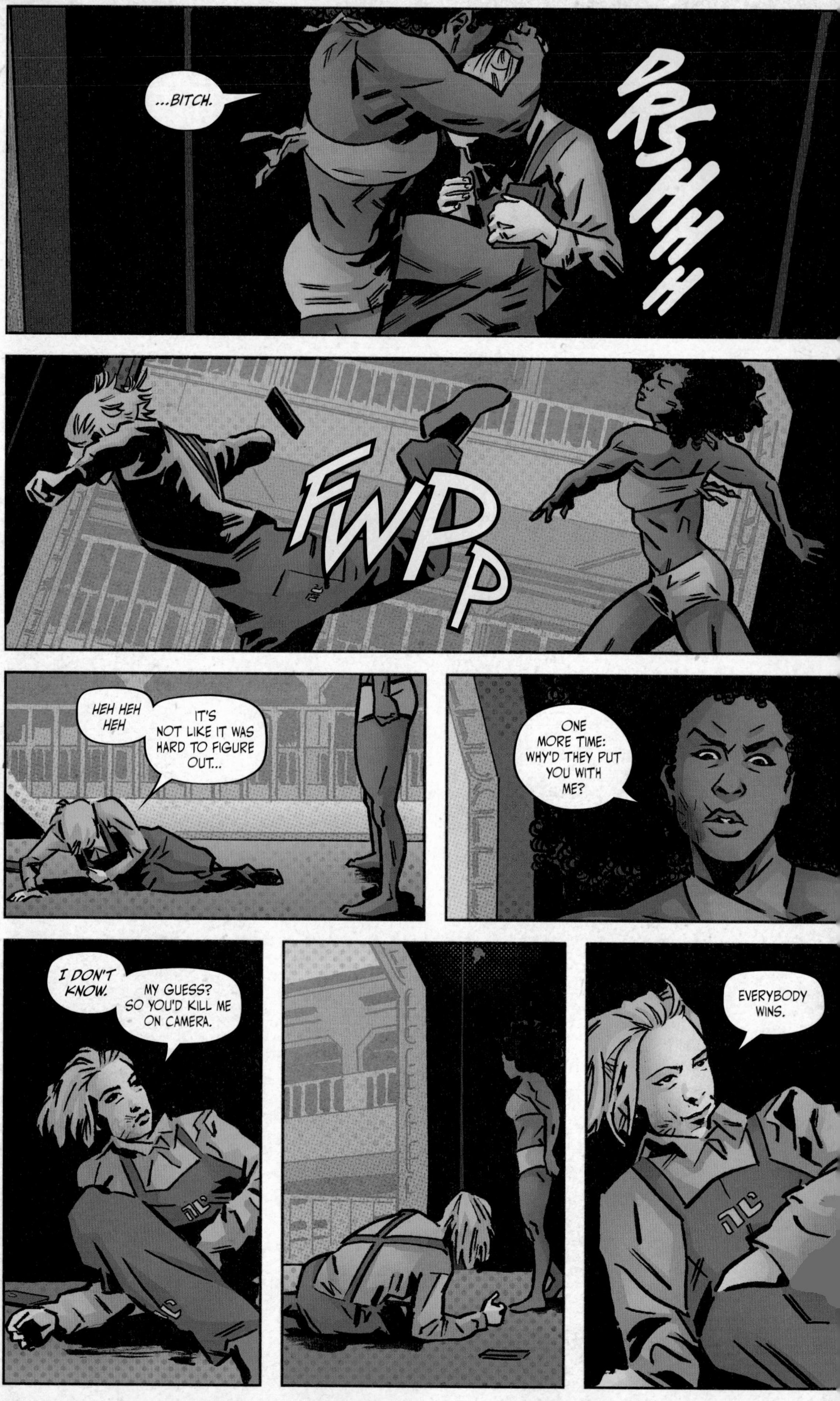
...BITCH.
DRSHHHH
FWPP
HEH HEH HEH
IT'S NOT LIKE IT WAS HARD TO FIGURE OUT...
ONE MORE TIME: WHY'D THEY PUT YOU WITH ME?
I DON'T KNOW.
MY GUESS? SO YOU'D KILL ME ON CAMERA.
EVERYBODY WINS.

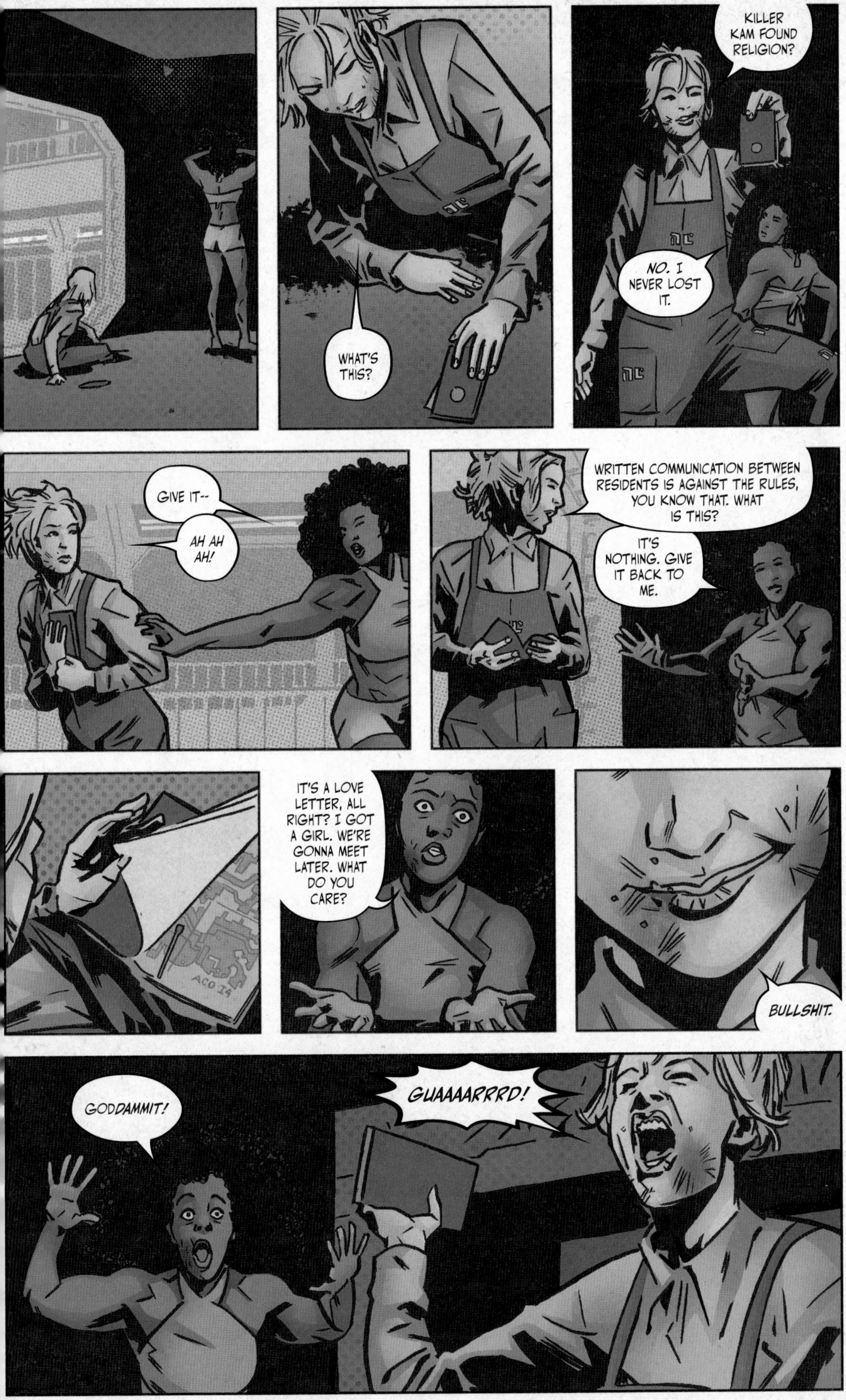
WHAT'S THIS?
KILLER KAM FOUND RELIGION?
NO. I NEVER LOST IT.
GIVE IT--
AH AH AH!
WRITTEN COMMUNICATION BETWEEN RESIDENTS IS AGAINST THE RULES, YOU KNOW THAT. WHAT IS THIS?
IT'S NOTHING. GIVE IT BACK TO ME.
ACO 19
IT'S A LOVE LETTER, ALL RIGHT? I GOT A GIRL. WE'RE GONNA MEET LATER. WHAT DO YOU CARE?
BULLSHIT.
GODDAMMIT!
GUAAAARRRD!

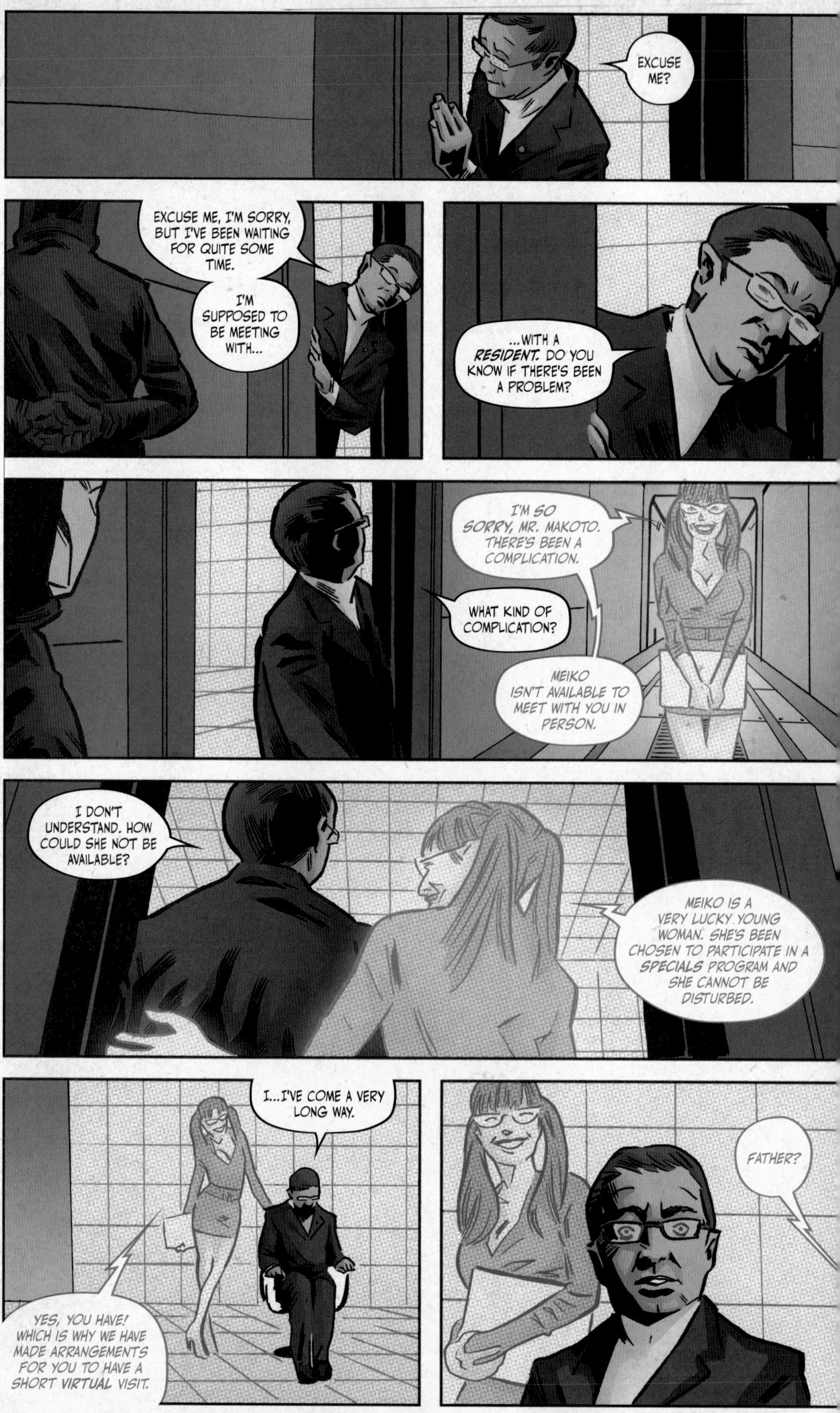
EXCUSE ME?
EXCUSE ME, I'M SORRY, BUT I'VE BEEN WAITING FOR QUITE SOME TIME.
I'M SUPPOSED TO BE MEETING WITH...
...WITH A *RESIDENT.* DO YOU KNOW IF THERE'S BEEN A PROBLEM?
I'M SO *SORRY,* MR. MAKOTO. THERE'S BEEN A COMPLICATION.
WHAT KIND OF COMPLICATION?
MEIKO ISN'T AVAILABLE TO MEET WITH YOU IN PERSON.
I DON'T UNDERSTAND. HOW COULD SHE NOT BE AVAILABLE?
MEIKO IS A VERY LUCKY YOUNG WOMAN. SHE'S BEEN CHOSEN TO PARTICIPATE IN A *SPECIALS* PROGRAM AND SHE CANNOT BE DISTURBED.
I...I'VE COME A VERY LONG WAY.
YES, YOU HAVE! WHICH IS WHY WE HAVE MADE ARRANGEMENTS FOR YOU TO HAVE A SHORT *VIRTUAL* VISIT.
FATHER?

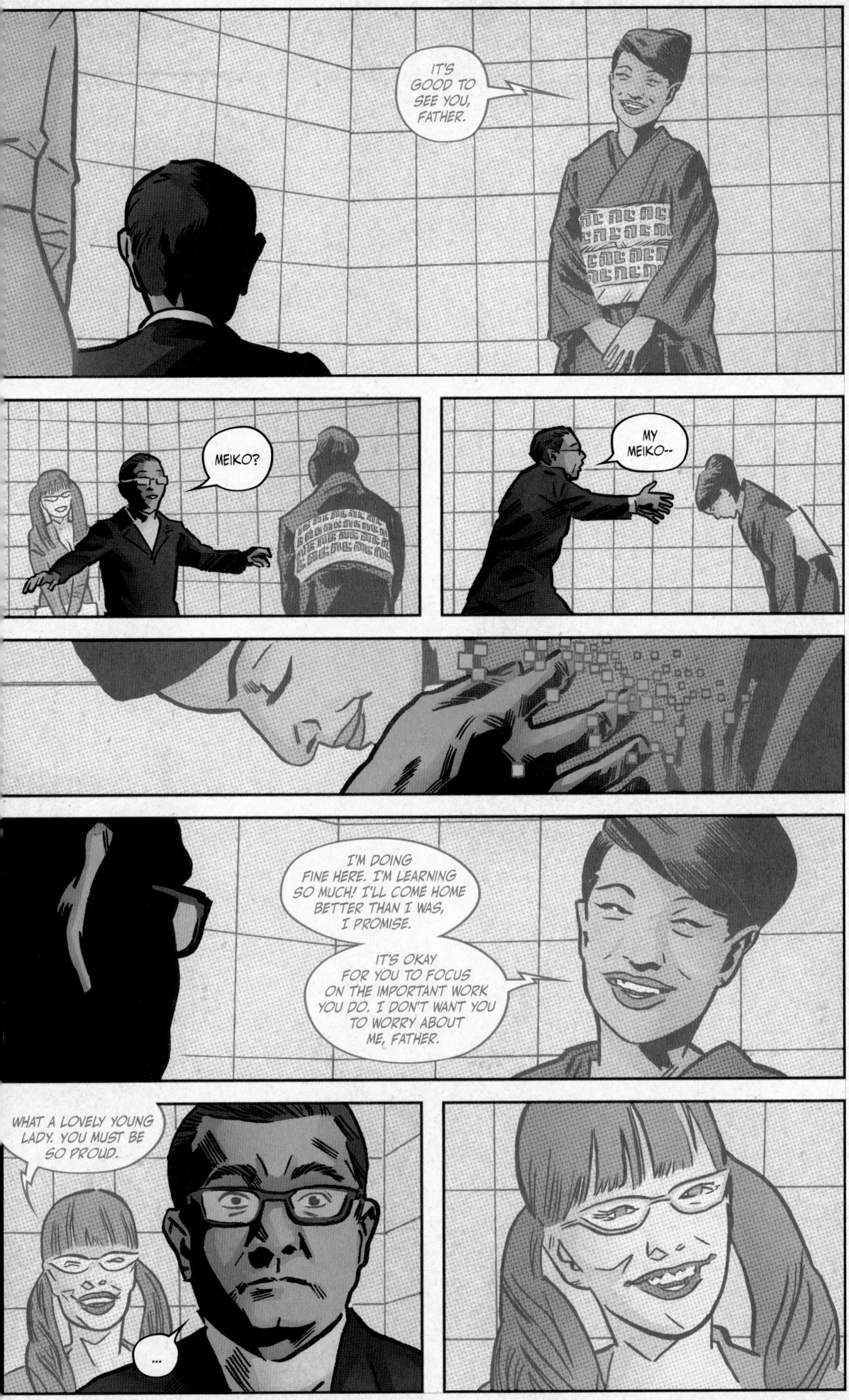

IT'S GOOD TO SEE YOU, FATHER.
MEIKO?
MY MEIKO--
I'M DOING FINE HERE. I'M LEARNING SO MUCH! I'LL COME HOME BETTER THAN I WAS, I PROMISE.
IT'S OKAY FOR YOU TO FOCUS ON THE IMPORTANT WORK YOU DO. I DON'T WANT YOU TO WORRY ABOUT ME, FATHER.
WHAT A LOVELY YOUNG LADY. YOU MUST BE SO PROUD.
...

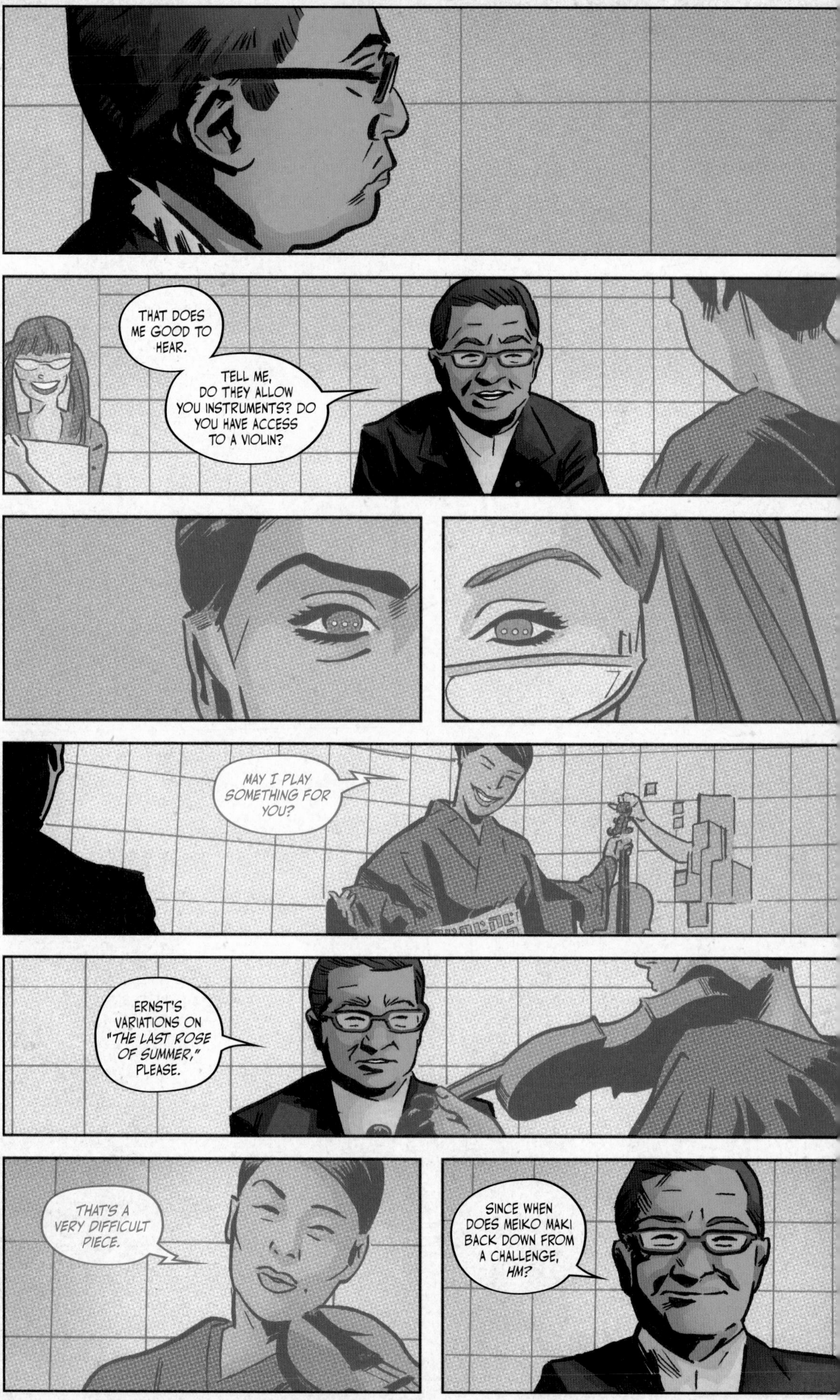
THAT DOES ME GOOD TO HEAR.
TELL ME, DO THEY ALLOW YOU INSTRUMENTS? DO YOU HAVE ACCESS TO A VIOLIN?
MAY I PLAY SOMETHING FOR YOU?
ERNST'S VARIATIONS ON "THE LAST ROSE OF SUMMER," PLEASE.
THAT'S A VERY DIFFICULT PIECE.
SINCE WHEN DOES MEIKO MAKI BACK DOWN FROM A CHALLENGE, HM?

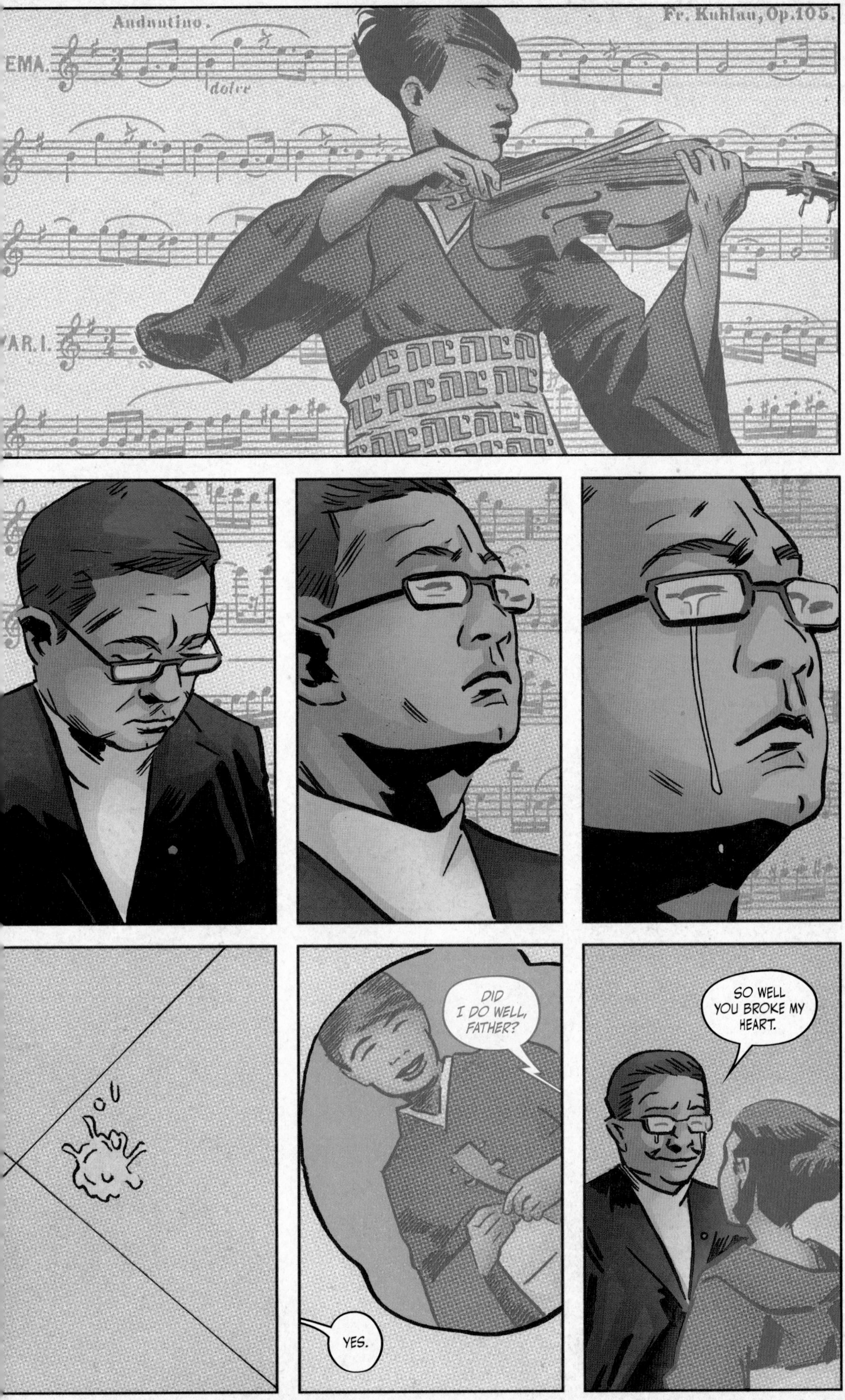
Andantino.
Fr. Kuhlau, Op.105.
EMA.
dolce
VAR. I.
DID I DO WELL, FATHER?
YES.
SO WELL YOU BROKE MY HEART.

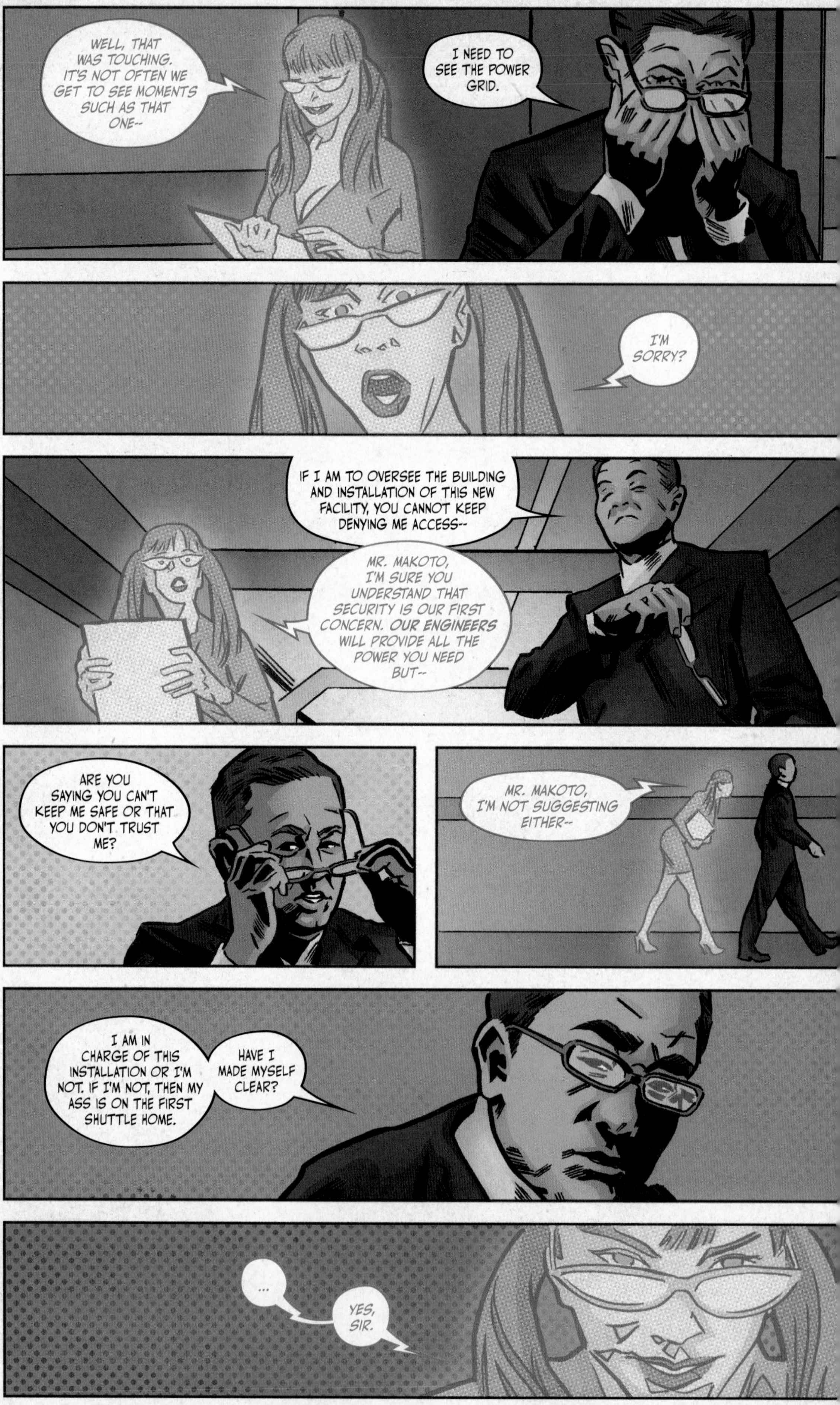
WELL, THAT WAS TOUCHING. IT'S NOT OFTEN WE GET TO SEE MOMENTS SUCH AS THAT ONE--
I NEED TO SEE THE POWER GRID.
I'M SORRY?
IF I AM TO OVERSEE THE BUILDING AND INSTALLATION OF THIS NEW FACILITY, YOU CANNOT KEEP DENYING ME ACCESS--
MR. MAKOTO, I'M SURE YOU UNDERSTAND THAT SECURITY IS OUR FIRST CONCERN. OUR ENGINEERS WILL PROVIDE ALL THE POWER YOU NEED BUT--
ARE YOU SAYING YOU CAN'T KEEP ME SAFE OR THAT YOU DON'T TRUST ME?
MR. MAKOTO, I'M NOT SUGGESTING EITHER--
I AM IN CHARGE OF THIS INSTALLATION OR I'M NOT. IF I'M NOT, THEN MY ASS IS ON THE FIRST SHUTTLE HOME.
HAVE I MADE MYSELF CLEAR?
...
YES, SIR.

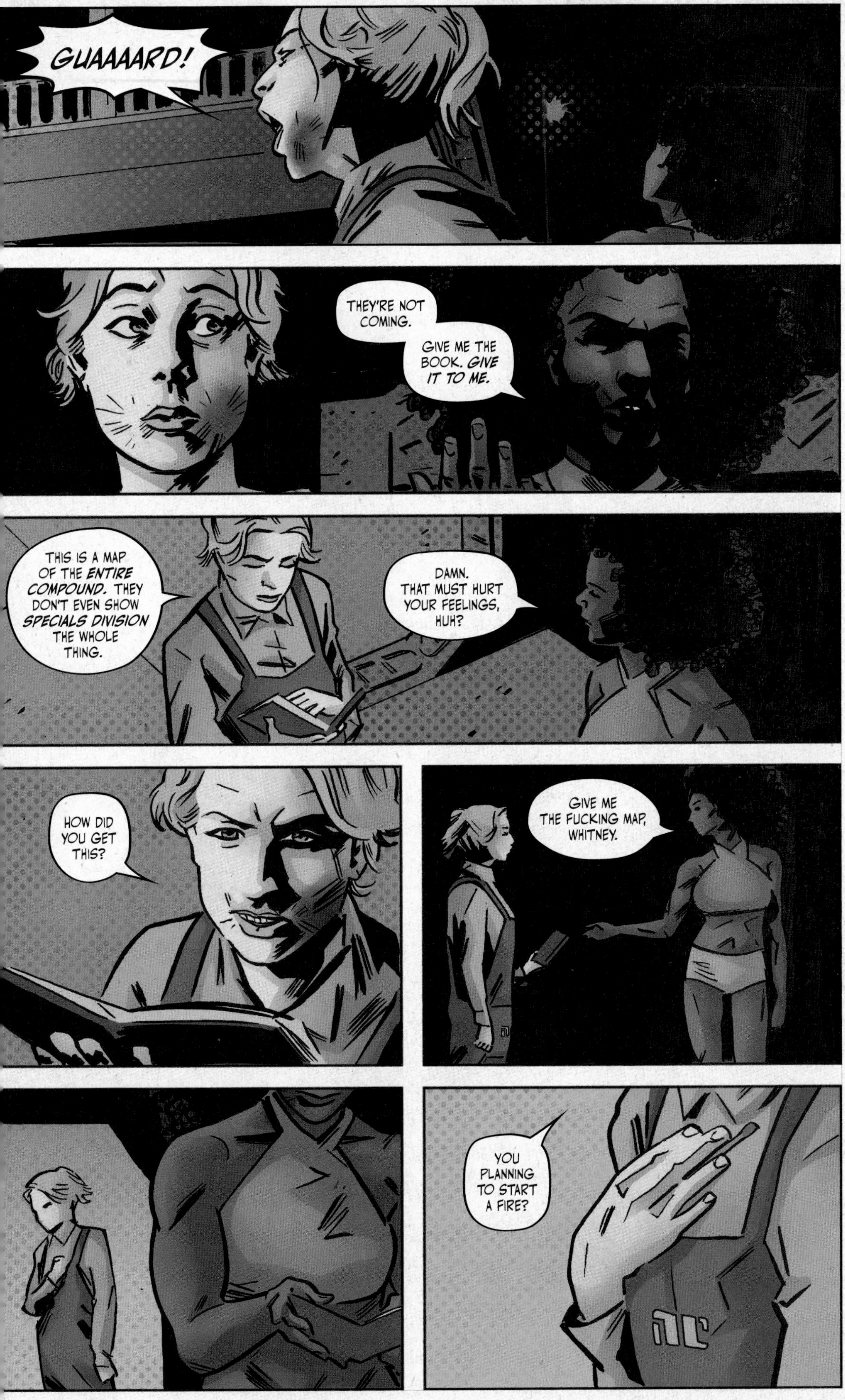
GUAAAARD!
THEY'RE NOT COMING.
GIVE ME THE BOOK. GIVE IT TO ME.
THIS IS A MAP OF THE ENTIRE COMPOUND. THEY DON'T EVEN SHOW SPECIALS DIVISION THE WHOLE THING.
DAMN. THAT MUST HURT YOUR FEELINGS, HUH?
HOW DID YOU GET THIS?
GIVE ME THE FUCKING MAP, WHITNEY.
YOU PLANNING TO START A FIRE?

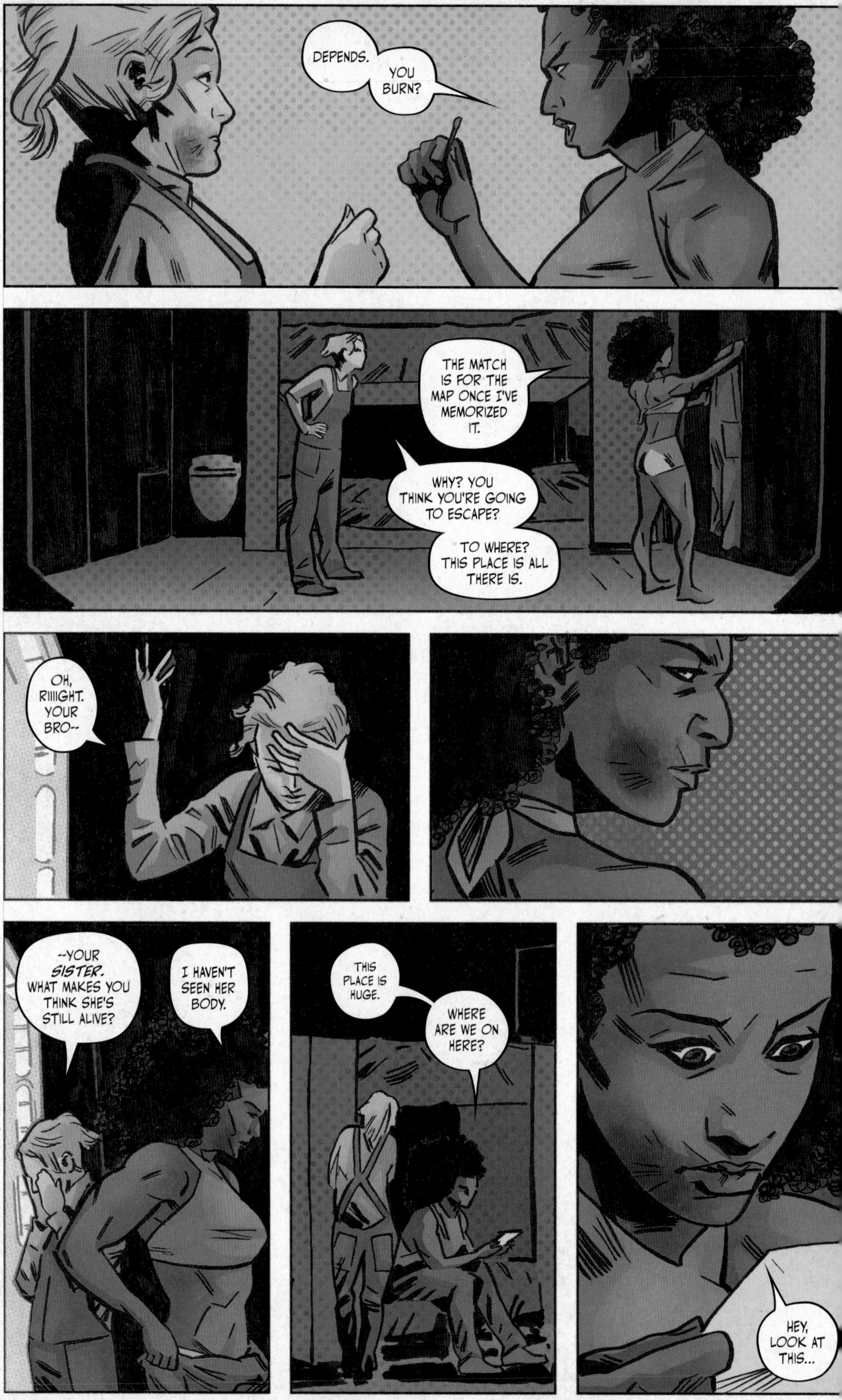
DEPENDS.
YOU BURN?
THE MATCH IS FOR THE MAP ONCE I'VE MEMORIZED IT.
WHY? YOU THINK YOU'RE GOING TO ESCAPE?
TO WHERE? THIS PLACE IS ALL THERE IS.
OH, RIIIIGHT. YOUR BRO--
--YOUR SISTER. WHAT MAKES YOU THINK SHE'S STILL ALIVE?
I HAVEN'T SEEN HER BODY.
THIS PLACE IS HUGE.
WHERE ARE WE ON HERE?
HEY, LOOK AT THIS...

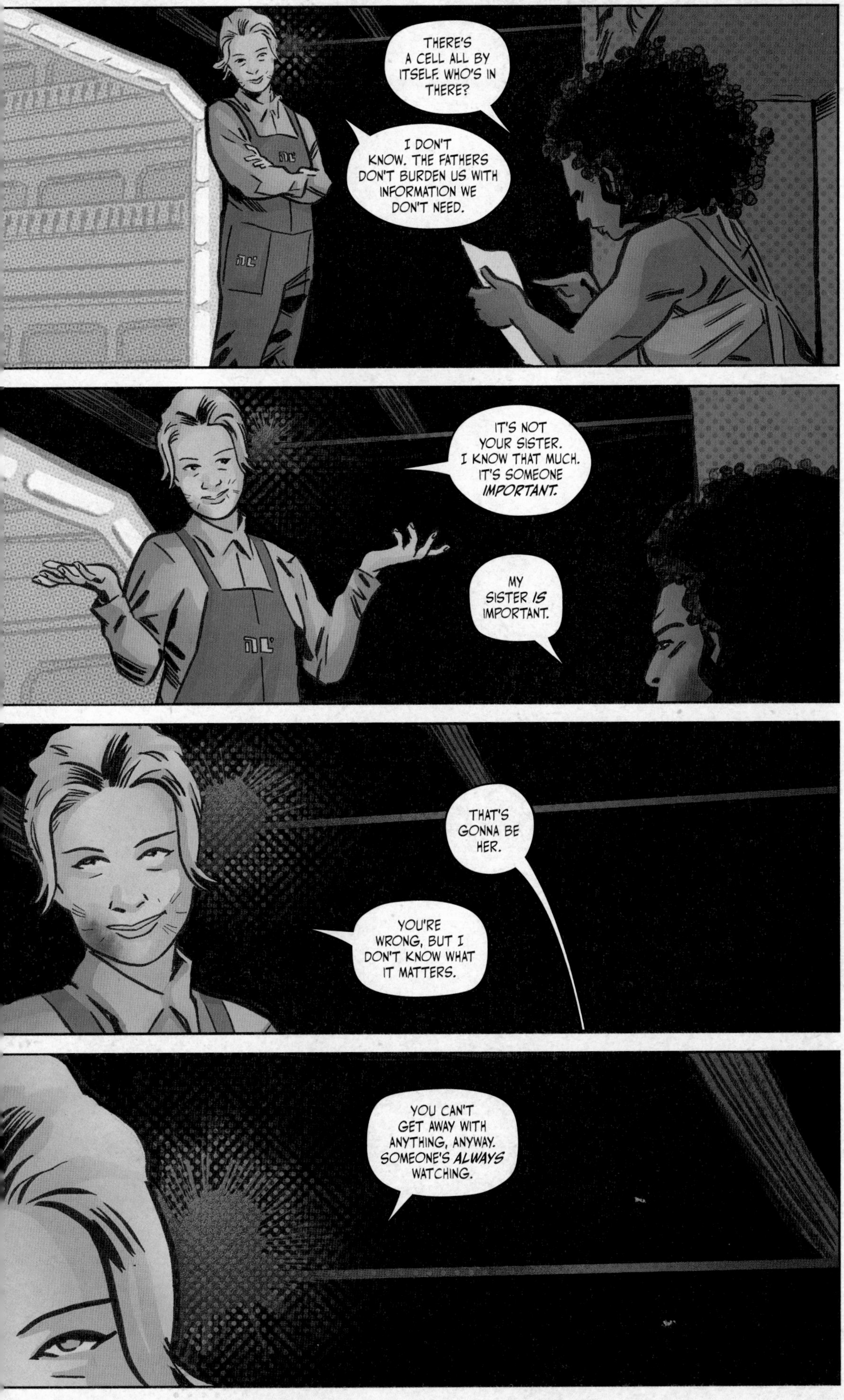

THERE'S A CELL ALL BY ITSELF. WHO'S IN THERE?
I DON'T KNOW. THE FATHERS DON'T BURDEN US WITH INFORMATION WE DON'T NEED.
IT'S NOT YOUR SISTER. I KNOW THAT MUCH. IT'S SOMEONE *IMPORTANT.*
MY SISTER *IS* IMPORTANT.
THAT'S GONNA BE HER.
YOU'RE WRONG, BUT I DON'T KNOW WHAT IT MATTERS.
YOU CAN'T GET AWAY WITH ANYTHING, ANYWAY. SOMEONE'S *ALWAYS* WATCHING.

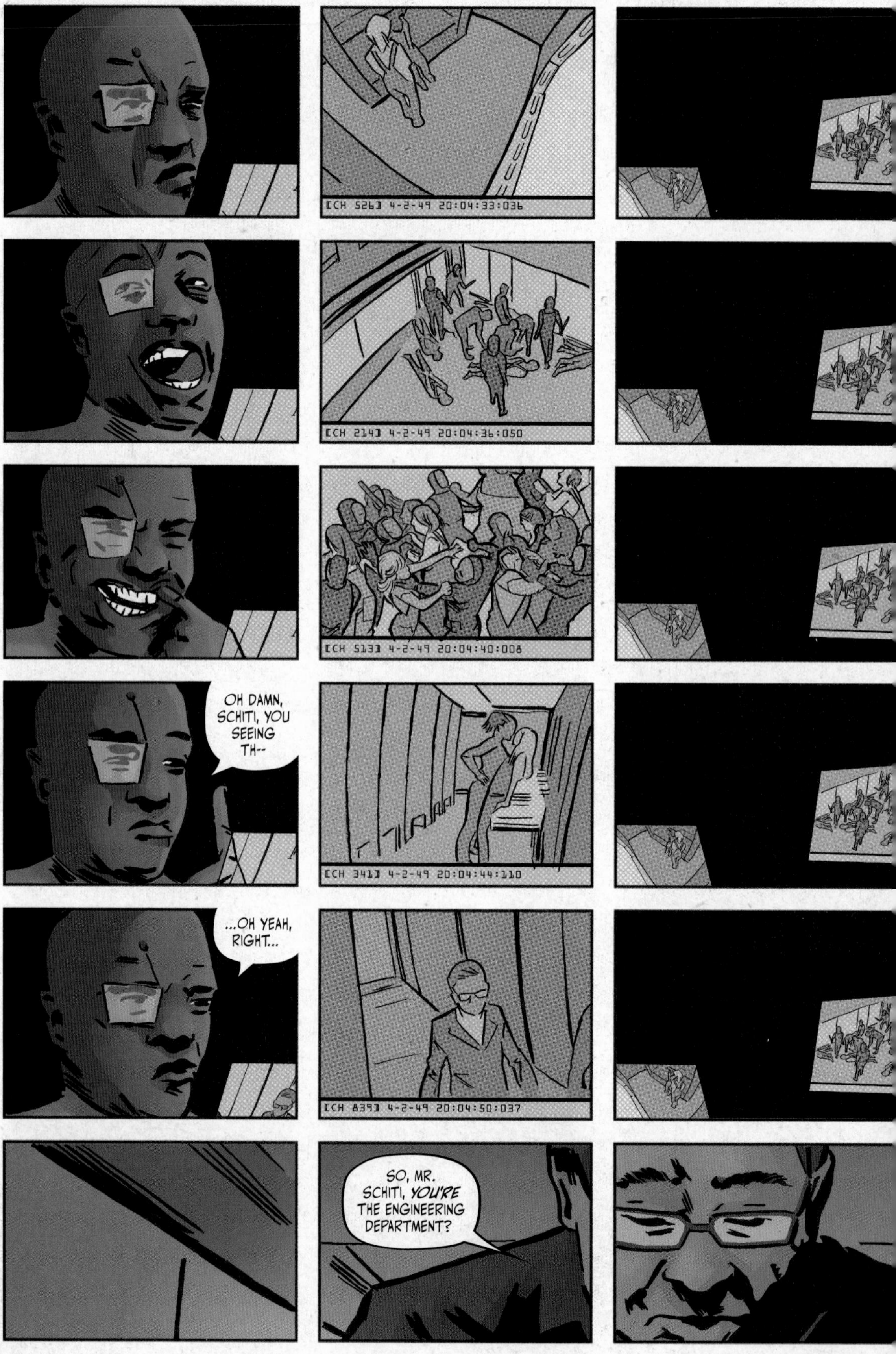
[CH 526] 4-2-49 20:04:33:036
[CH 214] 4-2-49 20:04:36:050
[CH 513] 4-2-49 20:04:40:008
OH DAMN, SCHITI, YOU SEEING TH--
[CH 341] 4-2-49 20:04:44:110
...OH YEAH, RIGHT...
[CH 839] 4-2-49 20:04:50:037
SO, MR. SCHITI, *YOU'RE* THE ENGINEERING DEPARTMENT?

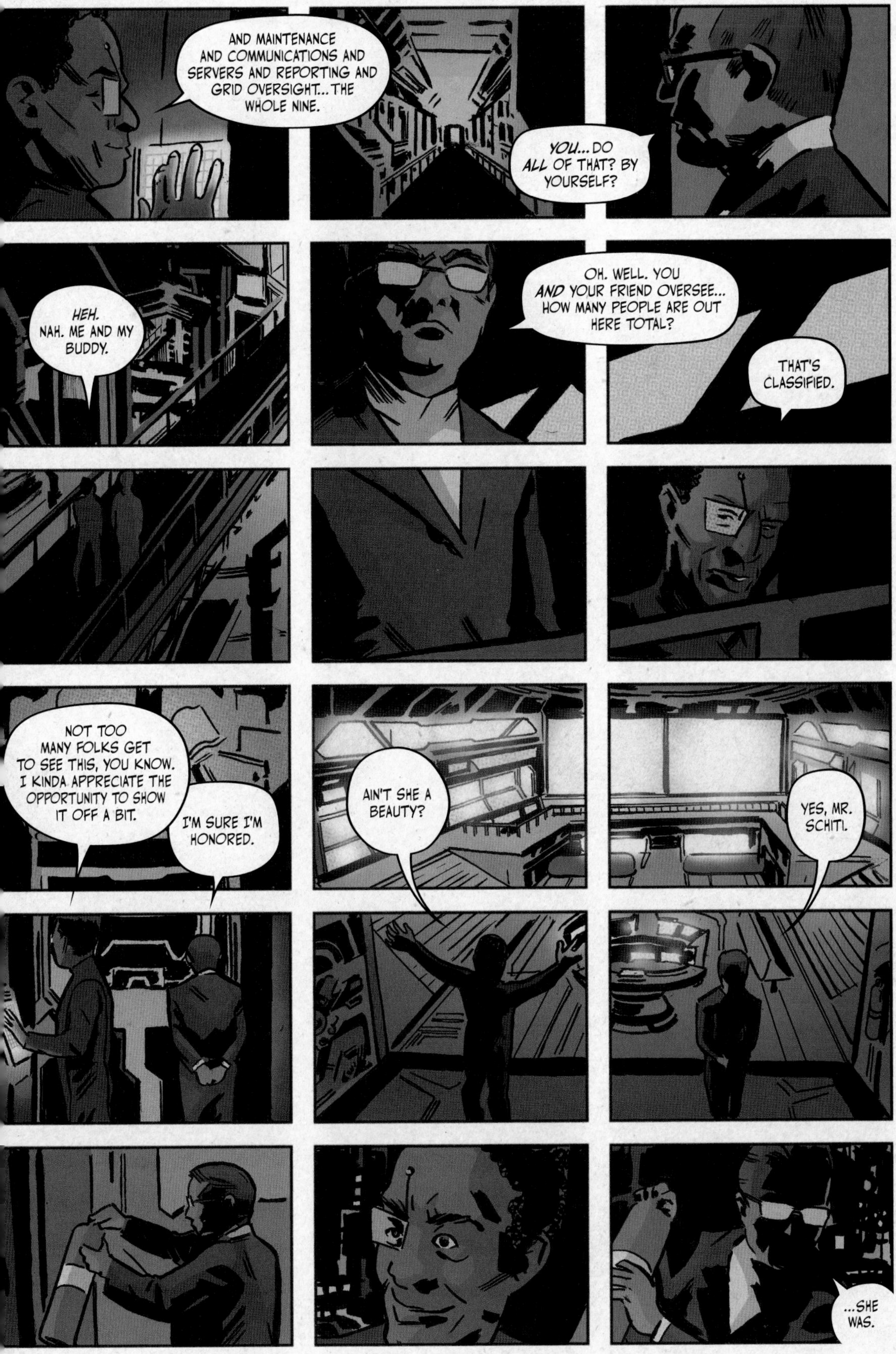
AND MAINTENANCE AND COMMUNICATIONS AND SERVERS AND REPORTING AND GRID OVERSIGHT... THE WHOLE NINE.
YOU... DO *ALL* OF THAT? BY YOURSELF?
HEH. NAH. ME AND MY BUDDY.
OH. WELL. YOU *AND* YOUR FRIEND OVERSEE... HOW MANY PEOPLE ARE OUT HERE TOTAL?
THAT'S CLASSIFIED.
NOT TOO MANY FOLKS GET TO SEE THIS, YOU KNOW. I KINDA APPRECIATE THE OPPORTUNITY TO SHOW IT OFF A BIT.
I'M SURE I'M HONORED.
AIN'T SHE A BEAUTY?
YES, MR. SCHITI.
...SHE WAS.

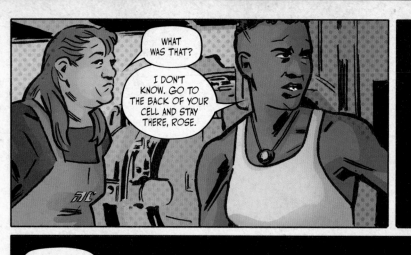

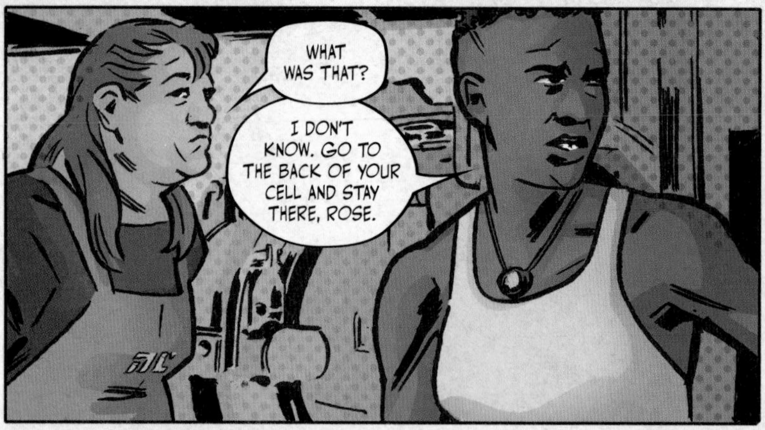
WHAT WAS THAT?
I DON'T KNOW. GO TO THE BACK OF YOUR CELL AND STAY THERE, ROSE.

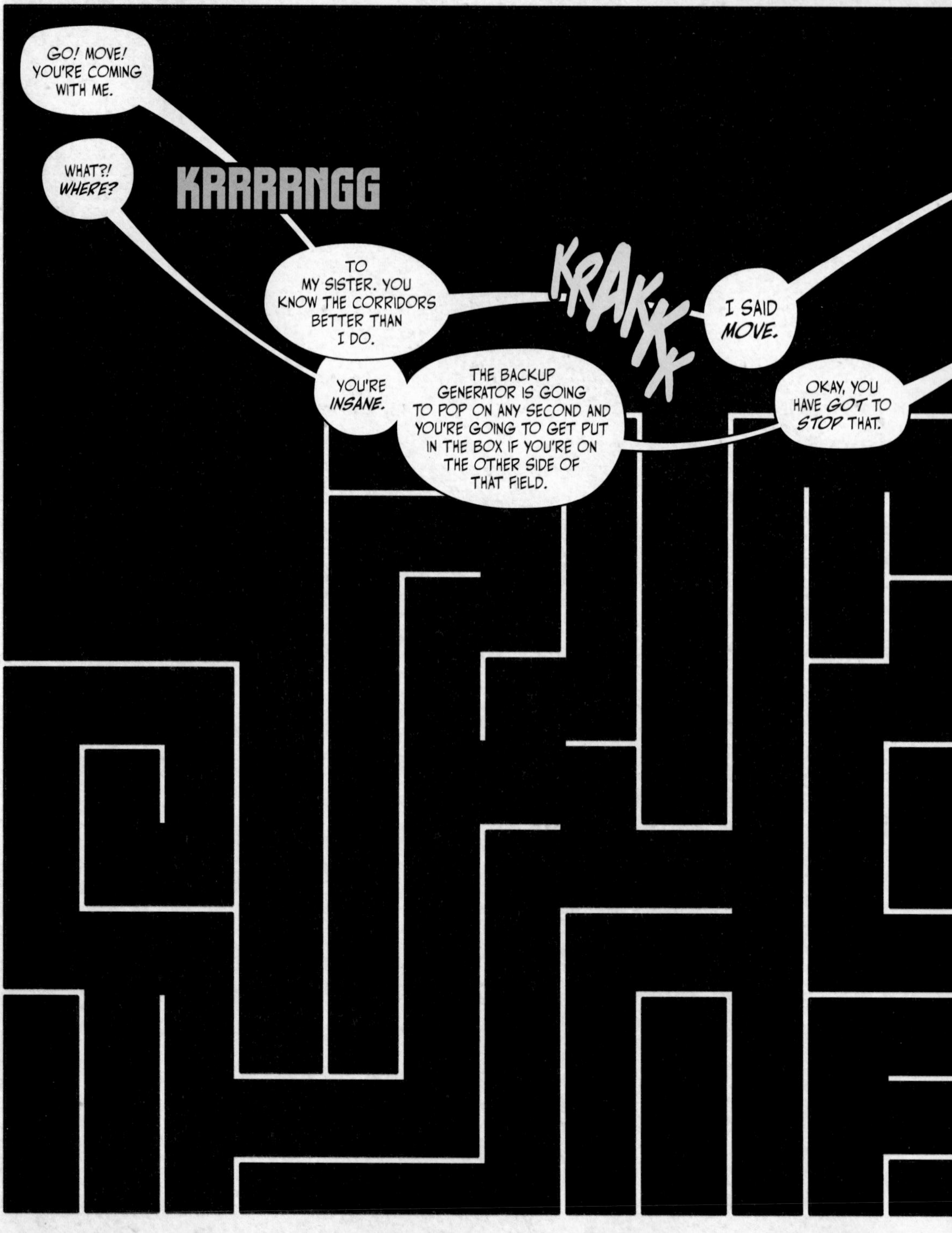
GO! MOVE! YOU'RE COMING WITH ME.
WHAT?! WHERE?
KRRRRNGG
TO MY SISTER. YOU KNOW THE CORRIDORS BETTER THAN I DO.
KRAKKK
I SAID MOVE.
YOU'RE INSANE.
THE BACKUP GENERATOR IS GOING TO POP ON ANY SECOND AND YOU'RE GOING TO GET PUT IN THE BOX IF YOU'RE ON THE OTHER SIDE OF THAT FIELD.
OKAY, YOU HAVE GOT TO STOP THAT.

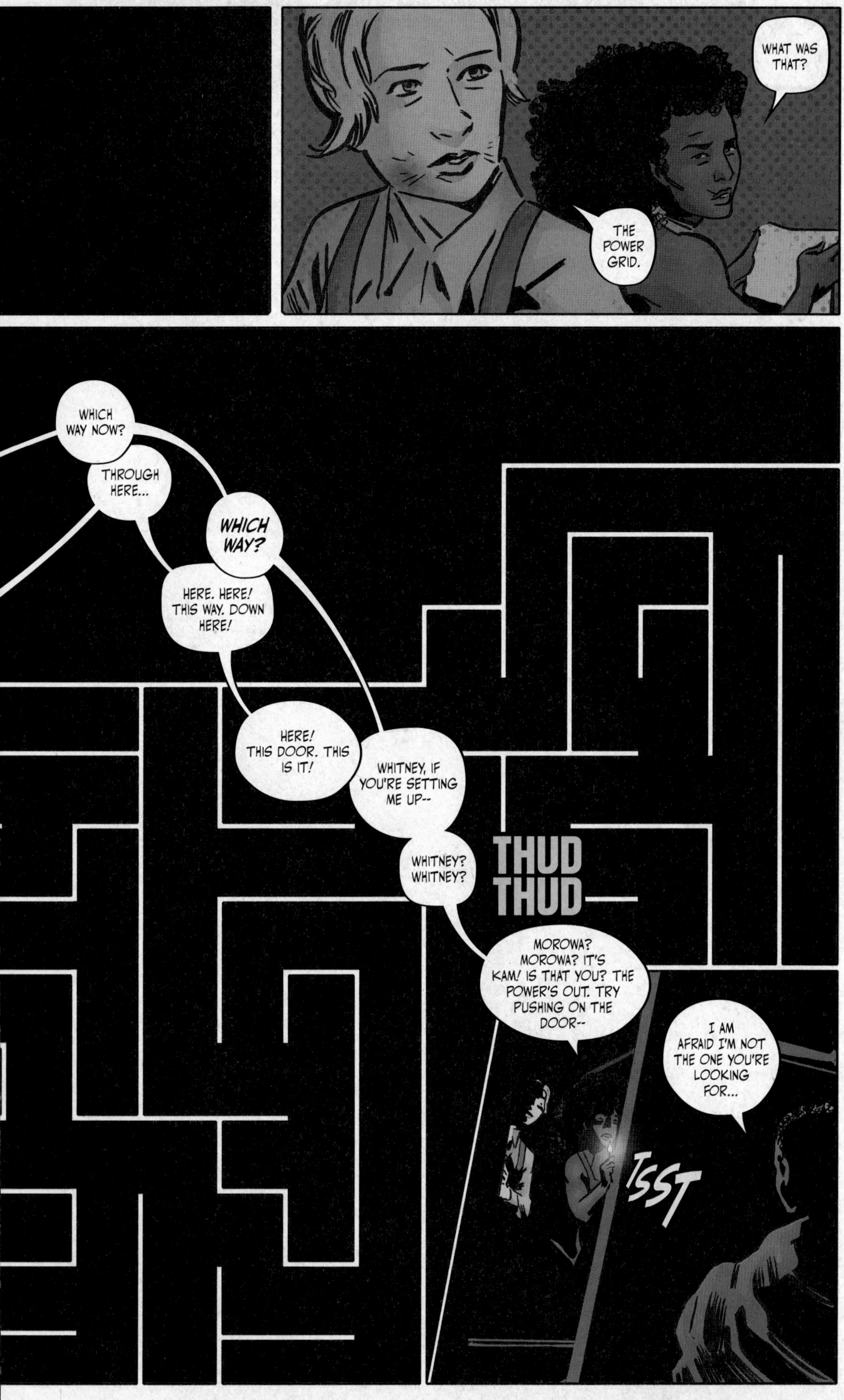
WHAT WAS THAT?
THE POWER GRID.
WHICH WAY NOW?
THROUGH HERE...
WHICH WAY?
HERE. HERE! THIS WAY. DOWN HERE!
HERE! THIS DOOR. THIS IS IT!
WHITNEY, IF YOU'RE SETTING ME UP--
WHITNEY? WHITNEY?
THUD THUD
MOROWA? MOROWA? IT'S KAM! IS THAT YOU? THE POWER'S OUT. TRY PUSHING ON THE DOOR--
I AM AFRAID I'M NOT THE ONE YOU'RE LOOKING FOR...
TSST

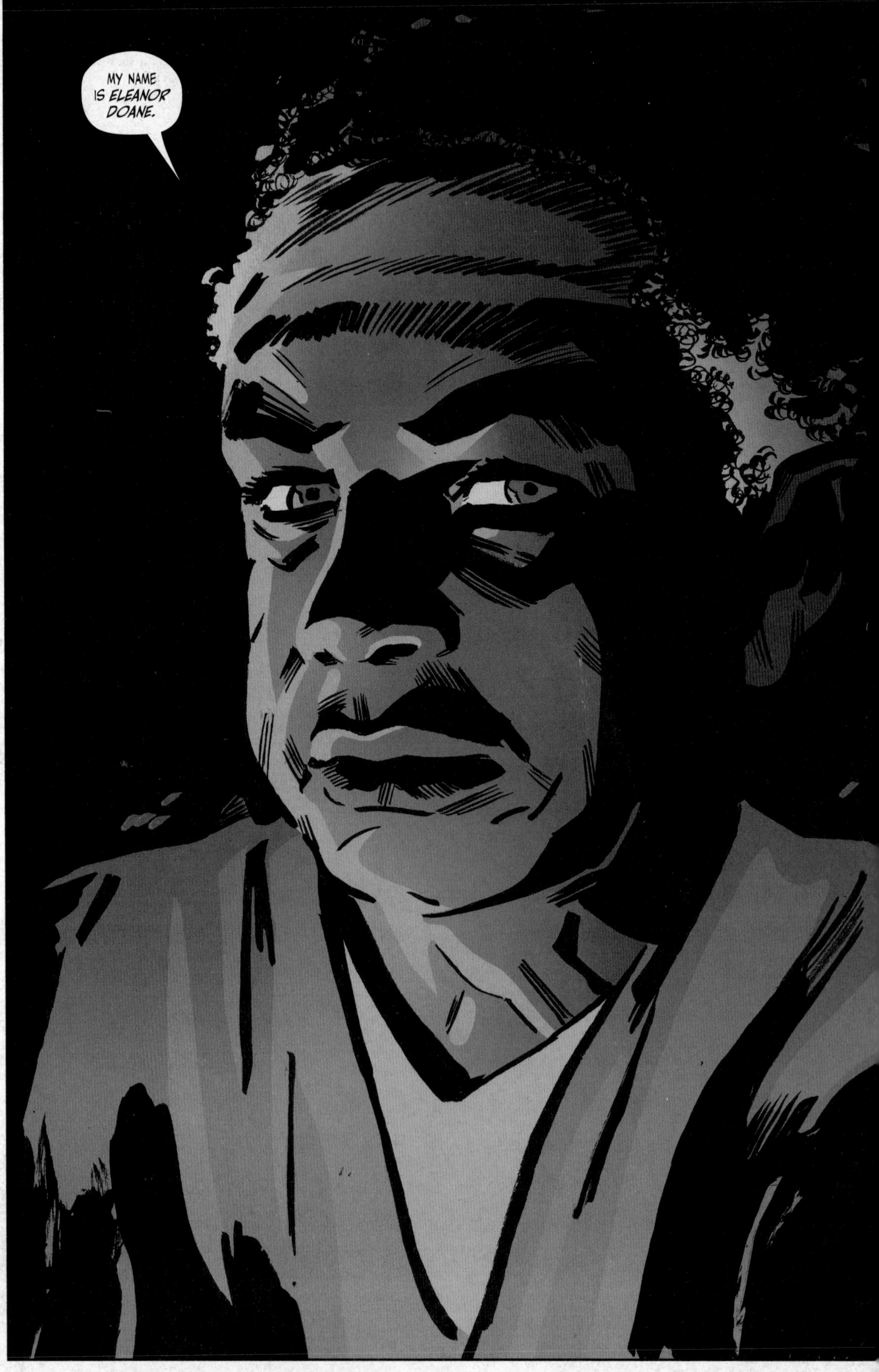
MY NAME IS ELEANOR DOANE.

The B. Compliant Company

Non-Compliant Overalls

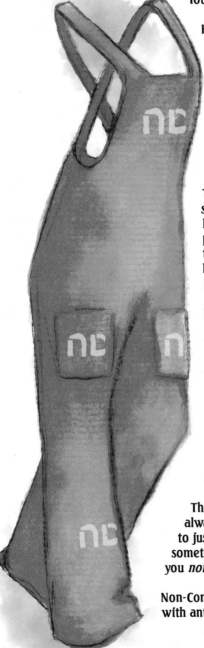

You're trouble.

He can see it from across the room.

It's your posture. The world presses down on you, plants your feet on the ground, it means to plant you *in* the ground, but still you hold your head high. It's an effort. Standing upright, forcing the edges of your mouth up, up, up, up into something like a smile. The effect is more like a growl.

Rrrrun, boy. Rrrrrun fast.

The strain of keeping your head aloft, keeping conscious, causes you to sweat. He thinks it's him. He thinks he makes you nervous. He is titillated by his imaginary power. The loose cotton wicks the saline from your flesh, the antimicrobial coating perfumes your stench. You look like the ass-end of a ox, but you smell like shopping mall. In the rain.

He laughs. You're cute when you're suffering.

You don't respond. Probably you didn't notice.

You've made him angry now.

He doesn't know why exactly. It's something about the way you're not asking for his attention. It's maddening. Do you think you're better than him? You do, don't you? Deep down? Admit it.

Bitch.

There's something wrong with you. Something broken. You always have to do things the hard way. Would it kill you to just play the game? To fold yourself up, up, up, up into something small, something pretty. Would it kill you? It's killing you *not* to.

Non-Compliant Dungarees. 100% indigenous, breathable cotton, with antimicrobial coating and no protection at all.

Color: Red
Price: Your Freedom

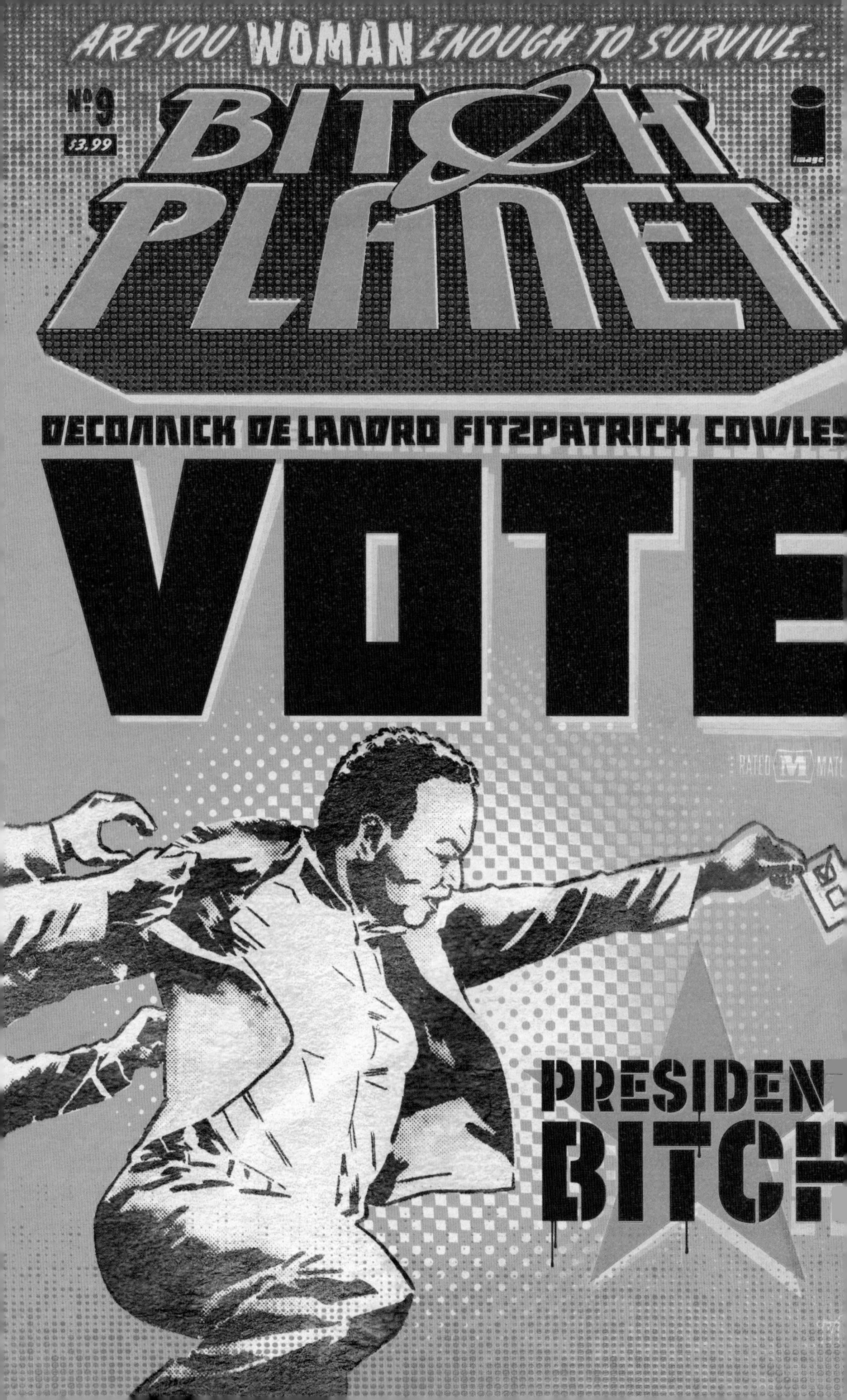
ARE YOU WOMAN ENOUGH TO SURVIVE..
Nº9
$3.99
BITCH PLANET
DECONNICK DE LANDRO FITZPATRICK COWLES
VOTE
PRESIDEN
BITC

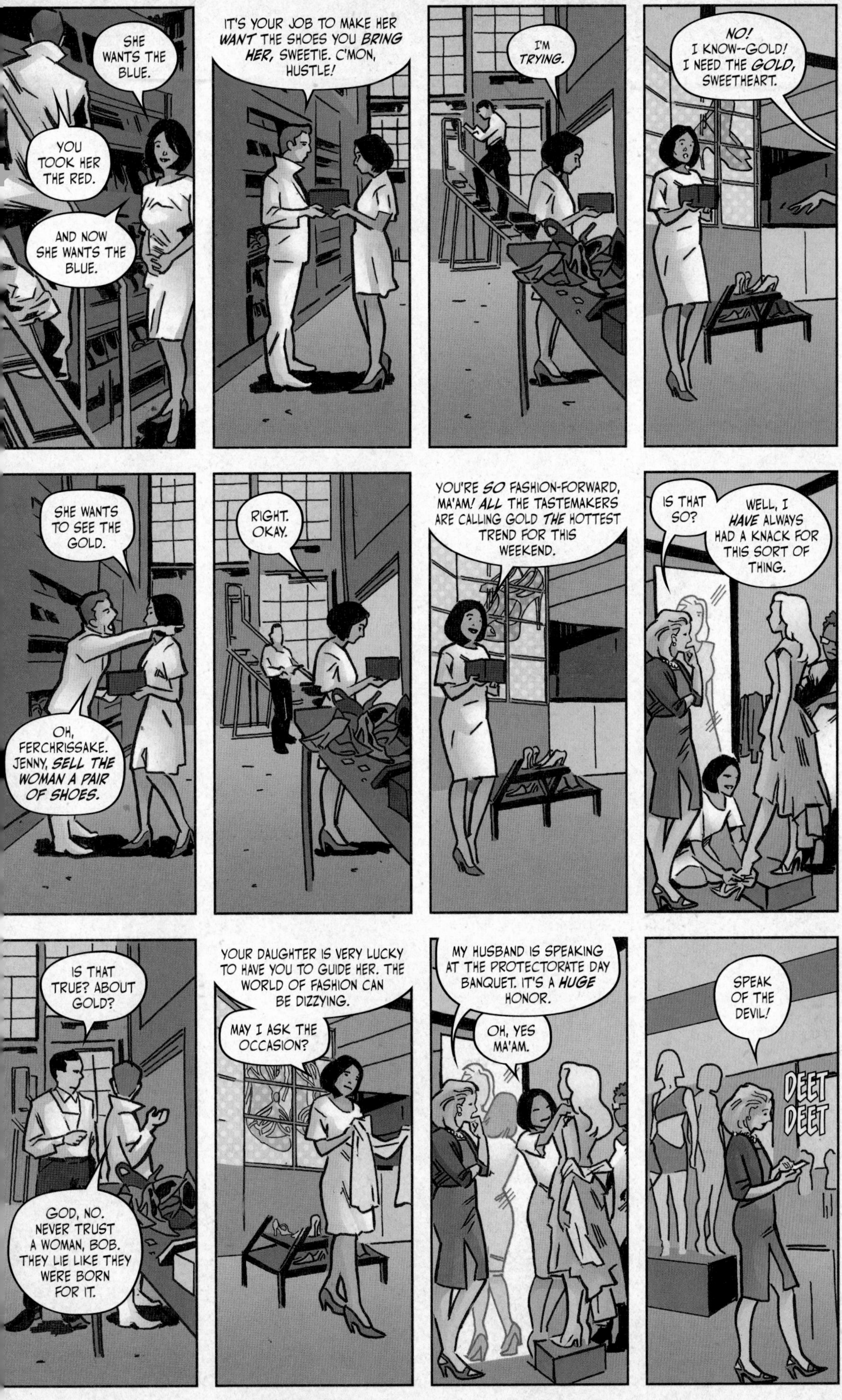
SHE WANTS THE BLUE.
YOU TOOK HER THE RED.
AND NOW SHE WANTS THE BLUE.
IT'S YOUR JOB TO MAKE HER *WANT* THE SHOES YOU *BRING HER,* SWEETIE. C'MON, HUSTLE!
I'M *TRYING.*
NO! I KNOW--GOLD! I NEED THE *GOLD,* SWEETHEART.
SHE WANTS TO SEE THE GOLD.
OH, FERCHRISSAKE. JENNY, *SELL THE WOMAN A PAIR OF SHOES.*
RIGHT. OKAY.
YOU'RE *SO* FASHION-FORWARD, MA'AM! *ALL* THE TASTEMAKERS ARE CALLING GOLD *THE* HOTTEST TREND FOR THIS WEEKEND.
IS THAT SO?
WELL, I *HAVE* ALWAYS HAD A KNACK FOR THIS SORT OF THING.
IS THAT TRUE? ABOUT GOLD?
GOD, NO. NEVER TRUST A WOMAN, BOB. THEY LIE LIKE THEY WERE BORN FOR IT.
YOUR DAUGHTER IS VERY LUCKY TO HAVE YOU TO GUIDE HER. THE WORLD OF FASHION CAN BE DIZZYING.
MAY I ASK THE OCCASION?
MY HUSBAND IS SPEAKING AT THE PROTECTORATE DAY BANQUET. IT'S A *HUGE* HONOR.
OH, YES MA'AM.
SPEAK OF THE DEVIL!
DEET DEET

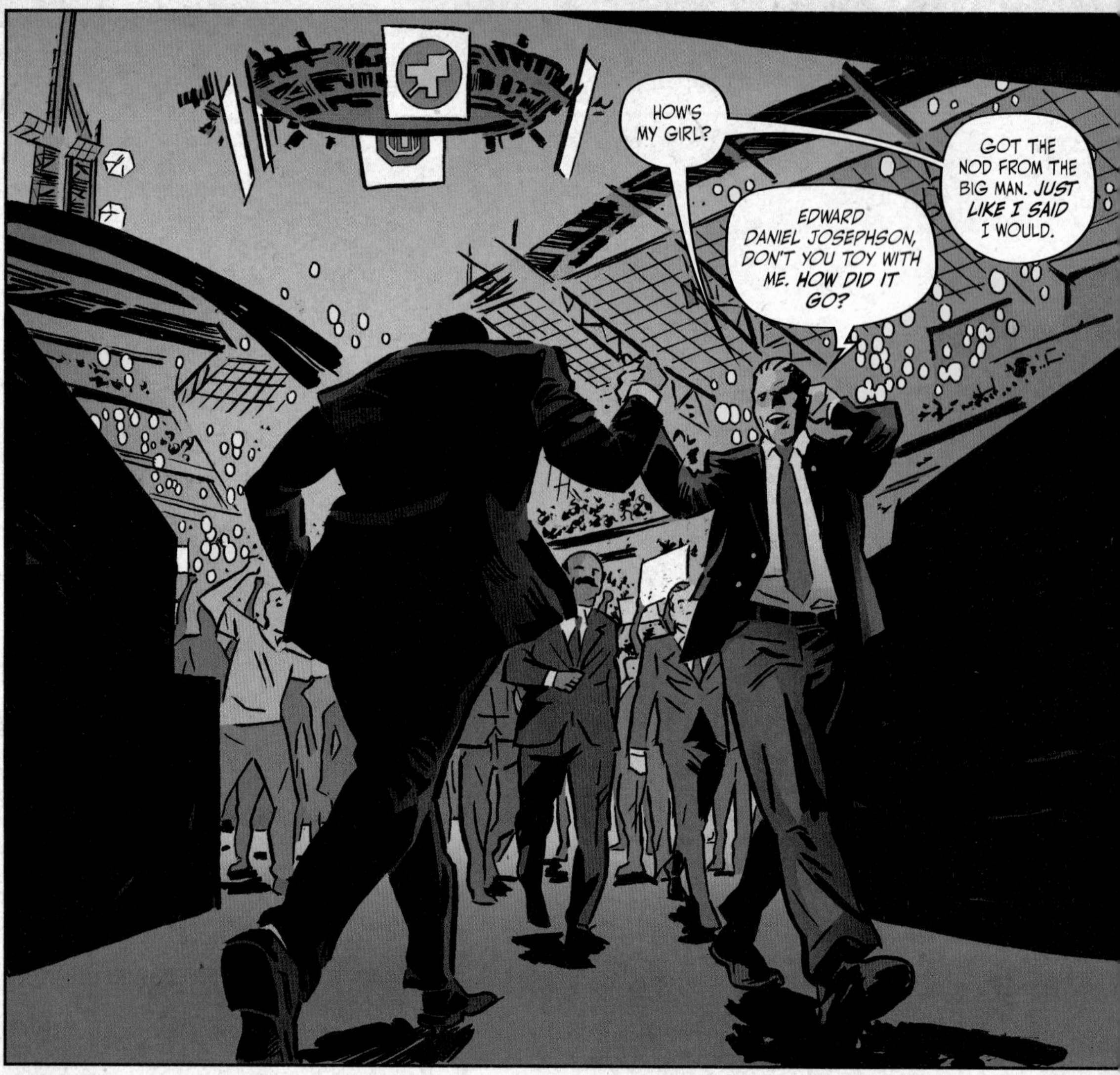
HOW'S MY GIRL?
EDWARD DANIEL JOSEPHSON, DON'T YOU TOY WITH ME. HOW DID IT GO?
GOT THE NOD FROM THE BIG MAN. JUST LIKE I SAID I WOULD.

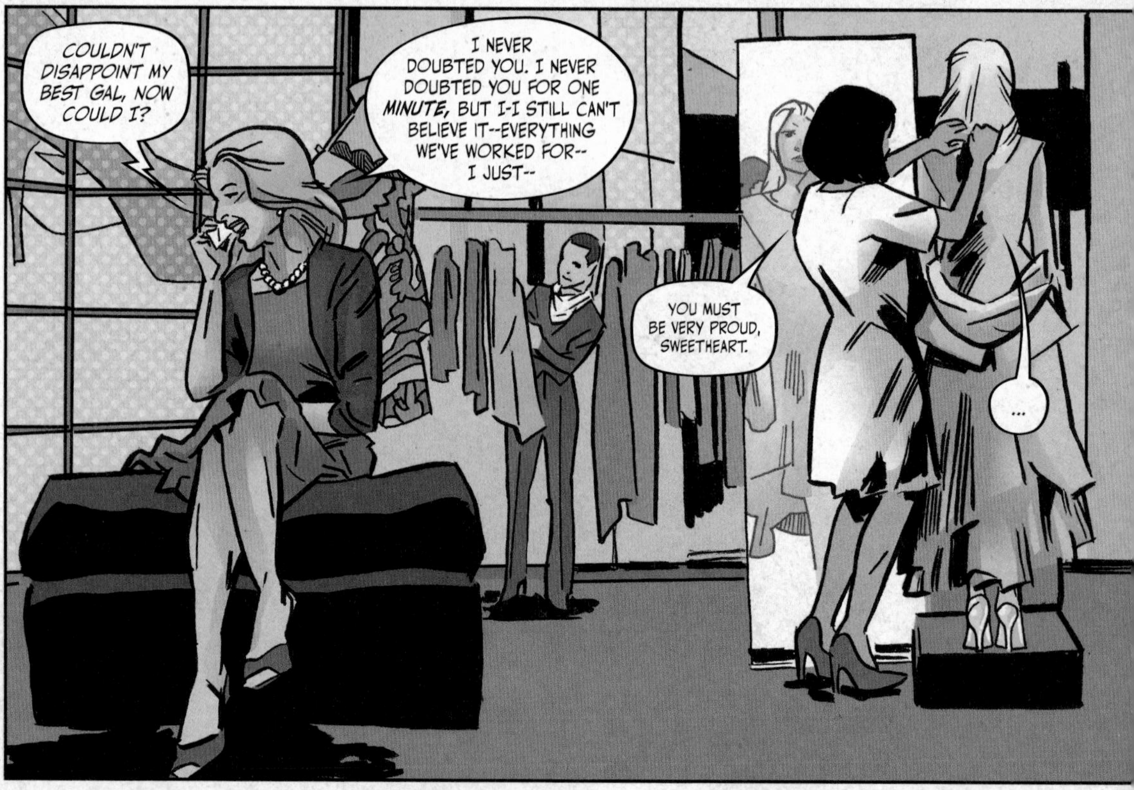
COULDN'T DISAPPOINT MY BEST GAL, NOW COULD I?
I NEVER DOUBTED YOU. I NEVER DOUBTED YOU FOR ONE MINUTE, BUT I-I STILL CAN'T BELIEVE IT--EVERYTHING WE'VE WORKED FOR-- I JUST--
YOU MUST BE VERY PROUD, SWEETHEART.
...

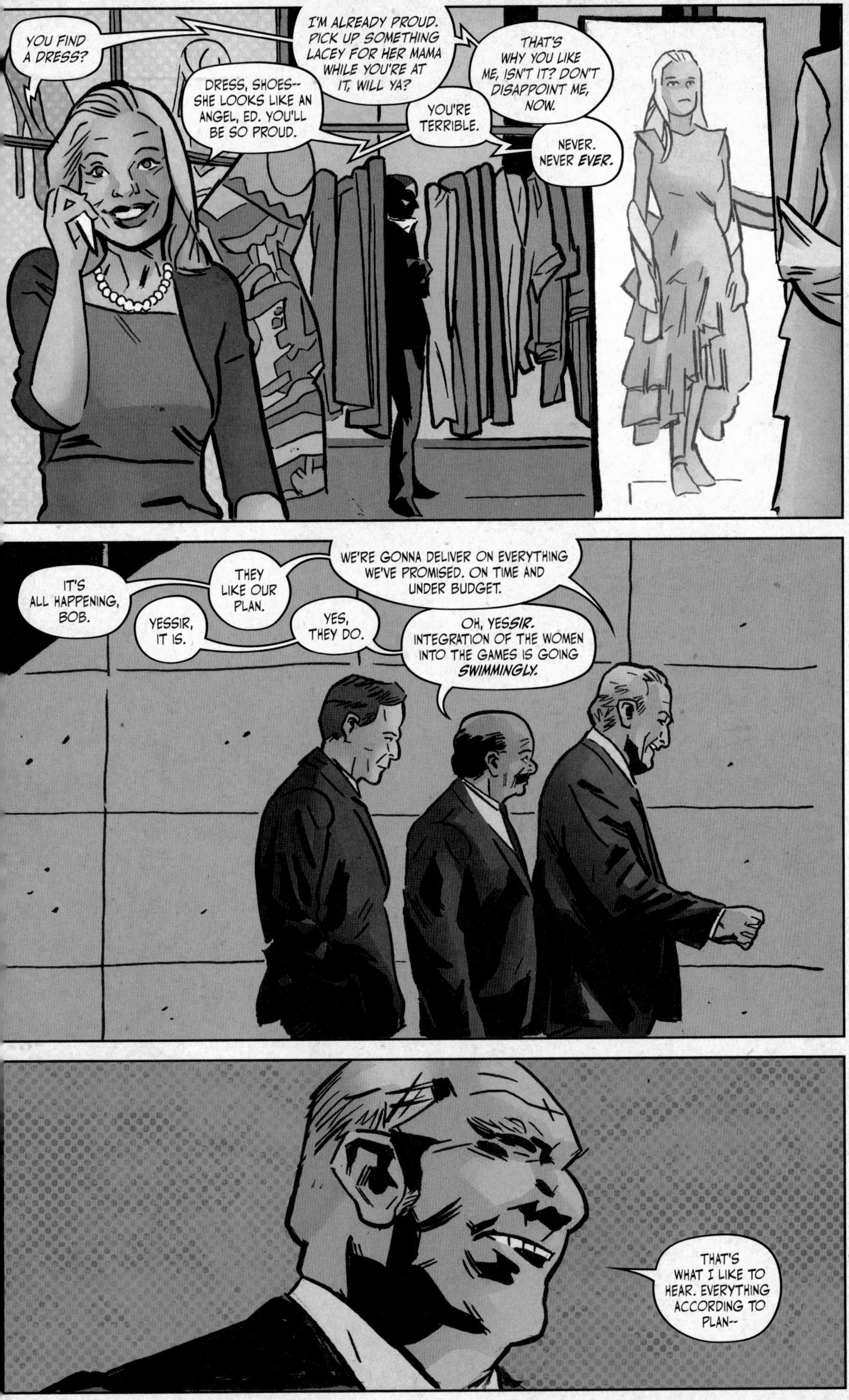
YOU FIND A DRESS?
DRESS, SHOES-- SHE LOOKS LIKE AN ANGEL, ED. YOU'LL BE SO PROUD.
I'M ALREADY PROUD. PICK UP SOMETHING LACEY FOR HER MAMA WHILE YOU'RE AT IT, WILL YA?
YOU'RE TERRIBLE.
THAT'S WHY YOU LIKE ME, ISN'T IT? DON'T DISAPPOINT ME, NOW.
NEVER. NEVER EVER.
IT'S ALL HAPPENING, BOB.
YESSIR, IT IS.
THEY LIKE OUR PLAN.
YES, THEY DO.
WE'RE GONNA DELIVER ON EVERYTHING WE'VE PROMISED. ON TIME AND UNDER BUDGET.
OH, YESSIR. INTEGRATION OF THE WOMEN INTO THE GAMES IS GOING SWIMMINGLY.
THAT'S WHAT I LIKE TO HEAR. EVERYTHING ACCORDING TO PLAN--

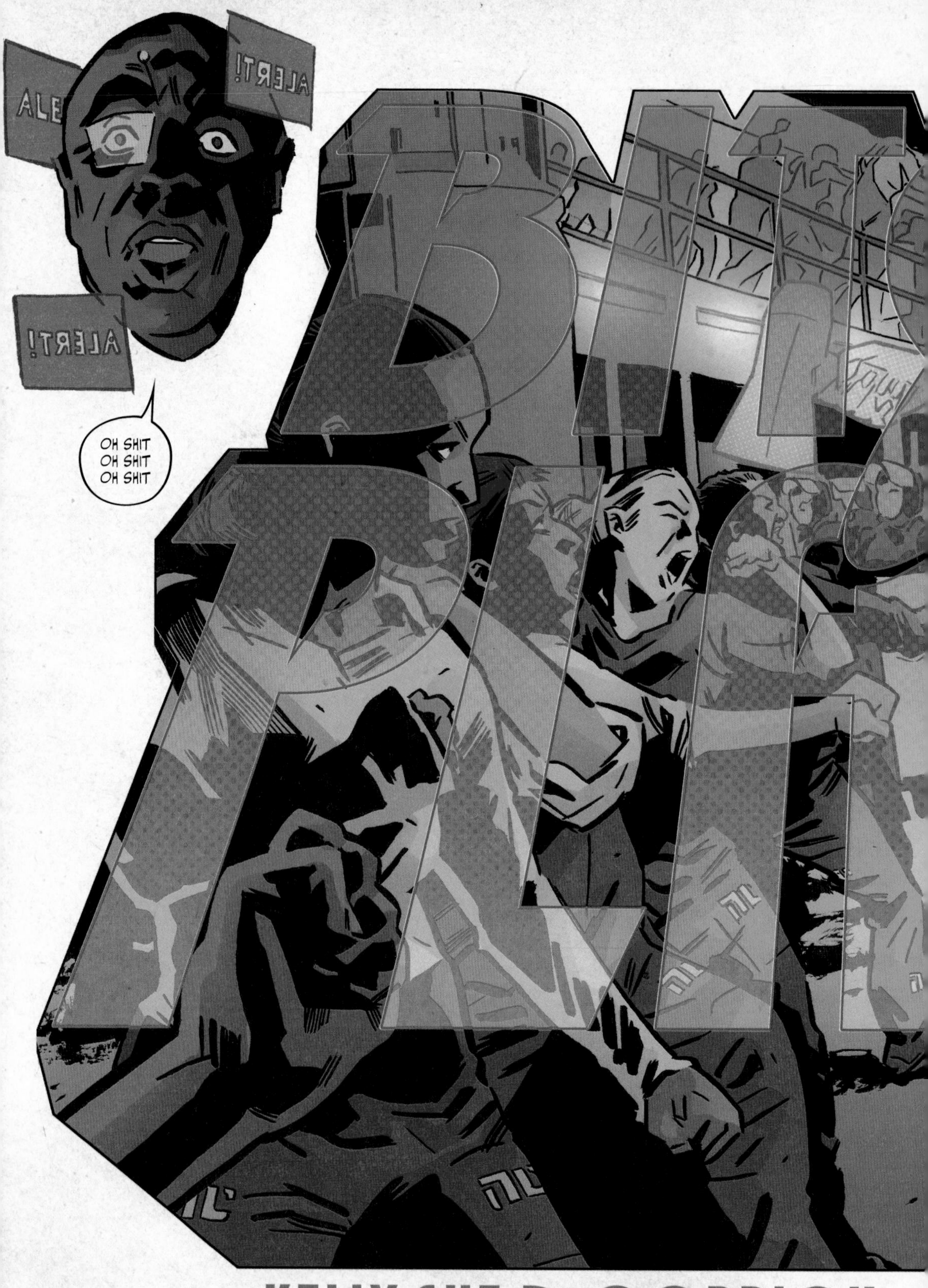
OH SHIT
OH SHIT
OH SHIT

KELLY SUE DECONNICK
SCRIPT

KELLY FITZPATRICK
COLORS

CLAYTON COWLES
LETTERS

RIAN HUGHES
COVER DESIGN & LOGO DESIGN

LAURENN McCUBBIN
BACKMATTER DESIGN

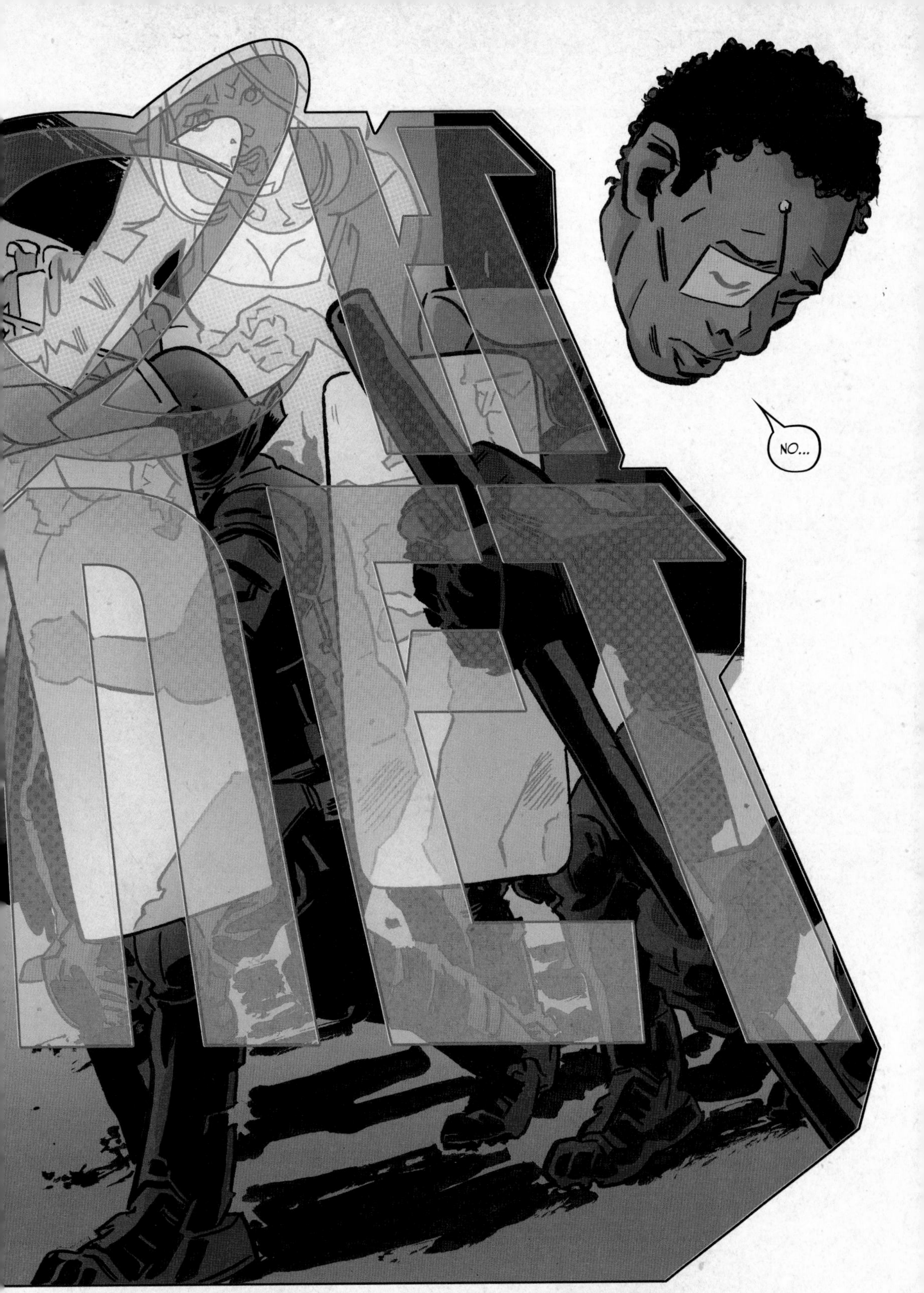
NO...

VALENTINE DE LANDRO
ART/COVERS

LAUREN SANKOVITCH
EDITOR

SPECIAL THANKS TO
ARIA EHREN, EMMA HOUXBOIS, MEY VALDIVIA RUDE & NICK SHADOW

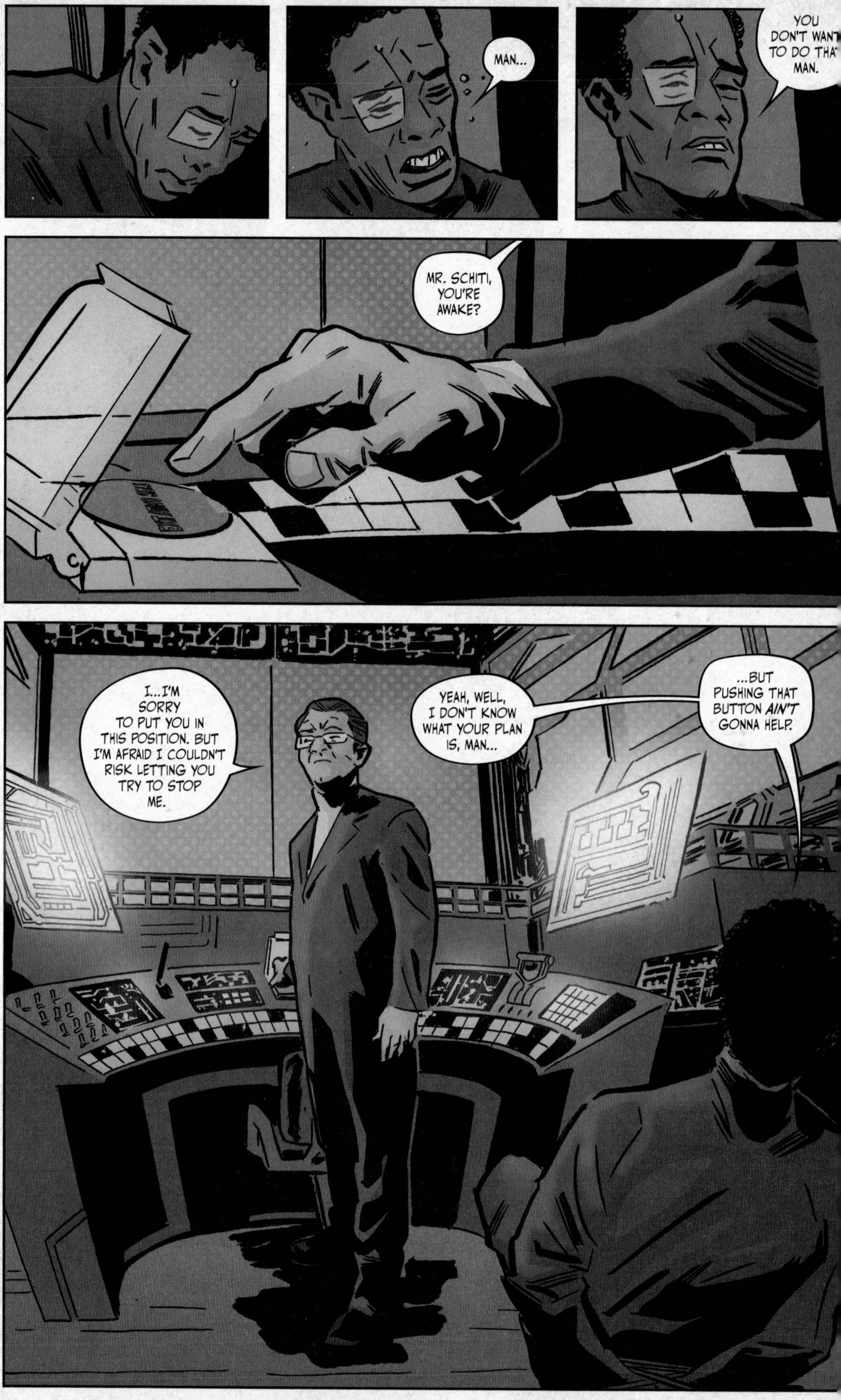
MAN...
YOU DON'T WANT TO DO THAT MAN.
MR. SCHITI, YOU'RE AWAKE?
I...I'M SORRY TO PUT YOU IN THIS POSITION. BUT I'M AFRAID I COULDN'T RISK LETTING YOU TRY TO STOP ME.
YEAH, WELL, I DON'T KNOW WHAT YOUR PLAN IS, MAN...
...BUT PUSHING THAT BUTTON *AIN'T* GONNA HELP.

I WANT TO...CHANGE THINGS. I WANT TO FREE THESE WOMEN. TO FREE US ALL.

YOU CAN'T JUST OPEN THE DOORS AND LET EVERYBODY GO HOME. WHERE DO YOU THINK YOU ARE?

THE ATMOSPHERE IS BREATHABLE. SENSORS SAY OXYGEN CONTENT IS HIGH.

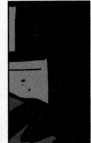

OXYGEN AIN'T THE PROBLEM. THIS PLANET GOT WAYS TO KILL YOU AIN'T NOTHING TO DO WITH OXYGEN.

MAYBE YOU'RE READY TO DIE FOR YOUR CAUSE OR WHATEVER, BUT...

YOU READY TO TAKE ALL'A US WITH YOU?

EXT ATMO SEAL

CLK

SOLID CHOICE, MAN.

WHAT NOW?

I DON'T KNOW.

HELLO.

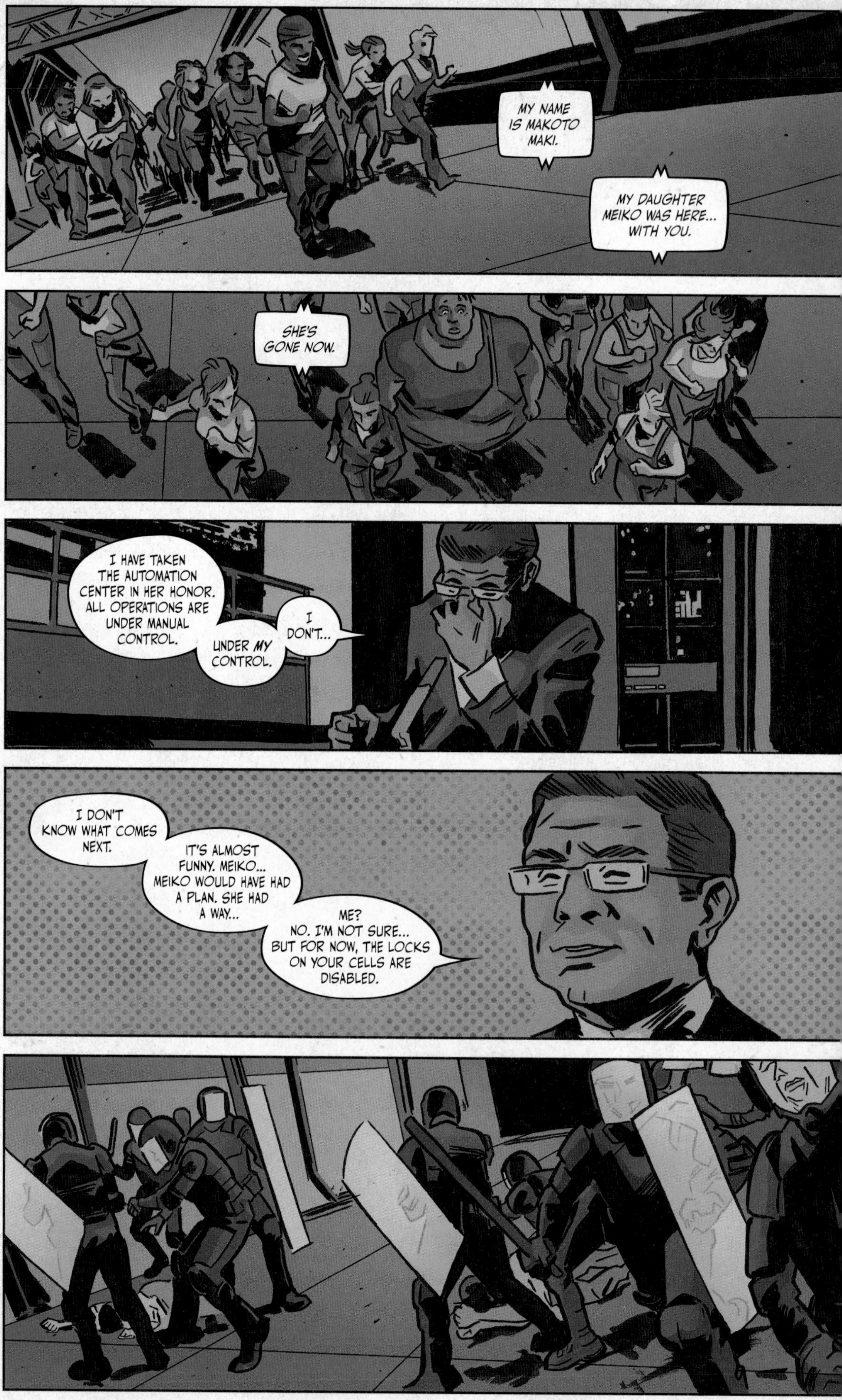
MY NAME IS MAKOTO MAKI.
MY DAUGHTER MEIKO WAS HERE... WITH YOU.
SHE'S GONE NOW.
I HAVE TAKEN THE AUTOMATION CENTER IN HER HONOR. ALL OPERATIONS ARE UNDER MANUAL CONTROL.
UNDER MY CONTROL.
I DON'T...
I DON'T KNOW WHAT COMES NEXT.
IT'S ALMOST FUNNY. MEIKO... MEIKO WOULD HAVE HAD A PLAN. SHE HAD A WAY...
ME? NO. I'M NOT SURE... BUT FOR NOW, THE LOCKS ON YOUR CELLS ARE DISABLED.

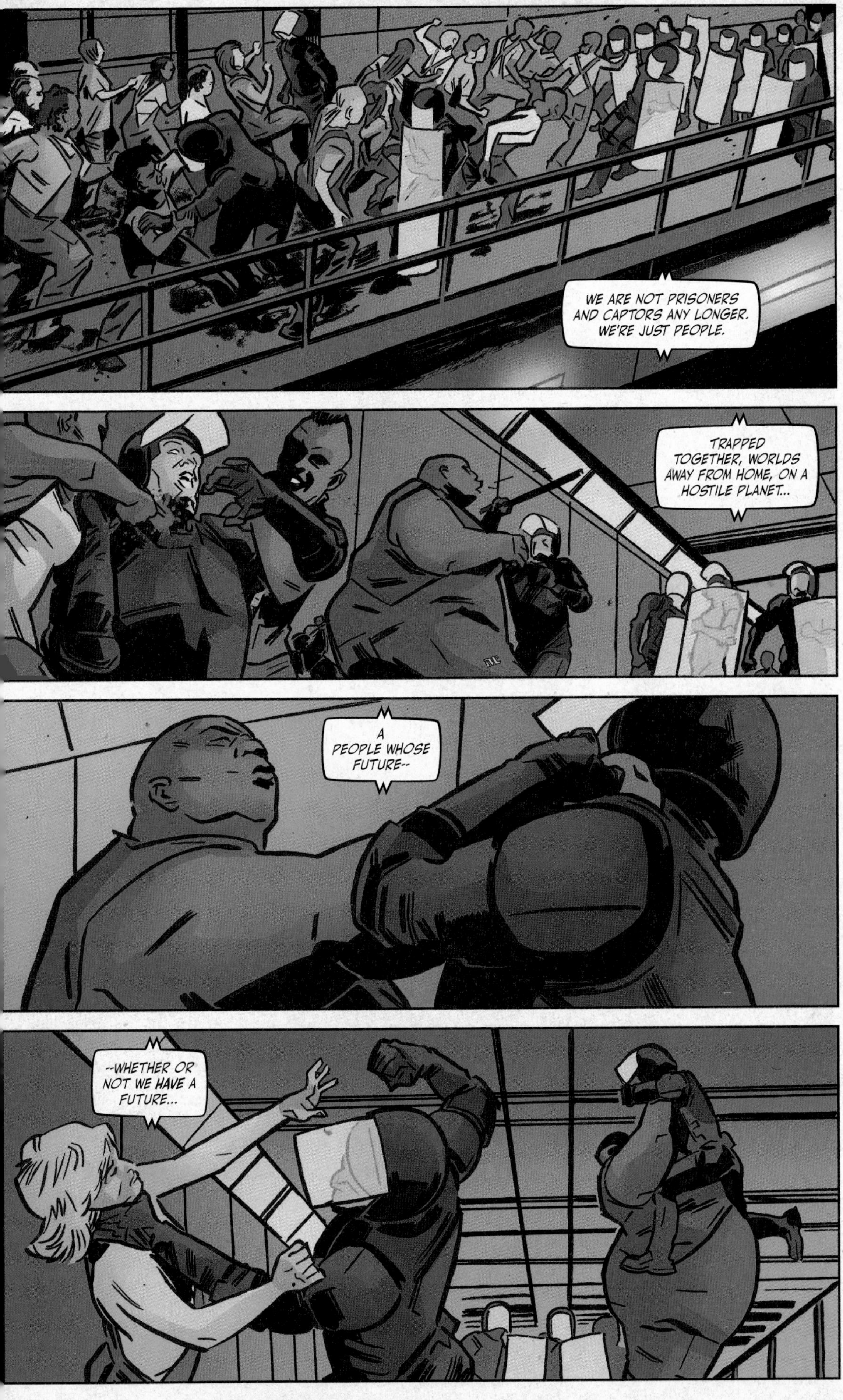
WE ARE NOT PRISONERS AND CAPTORS ANY LONGER. WE'RE JUST PEOPLE.
TRAPPED TOGETHER, WORLDS AWAY FROM HOME, ON A HOSTILE PLANET...
A PEOPLE WHOSE FUTURE--
--WHETHER OR NOT WE HAVE A FUTURE...

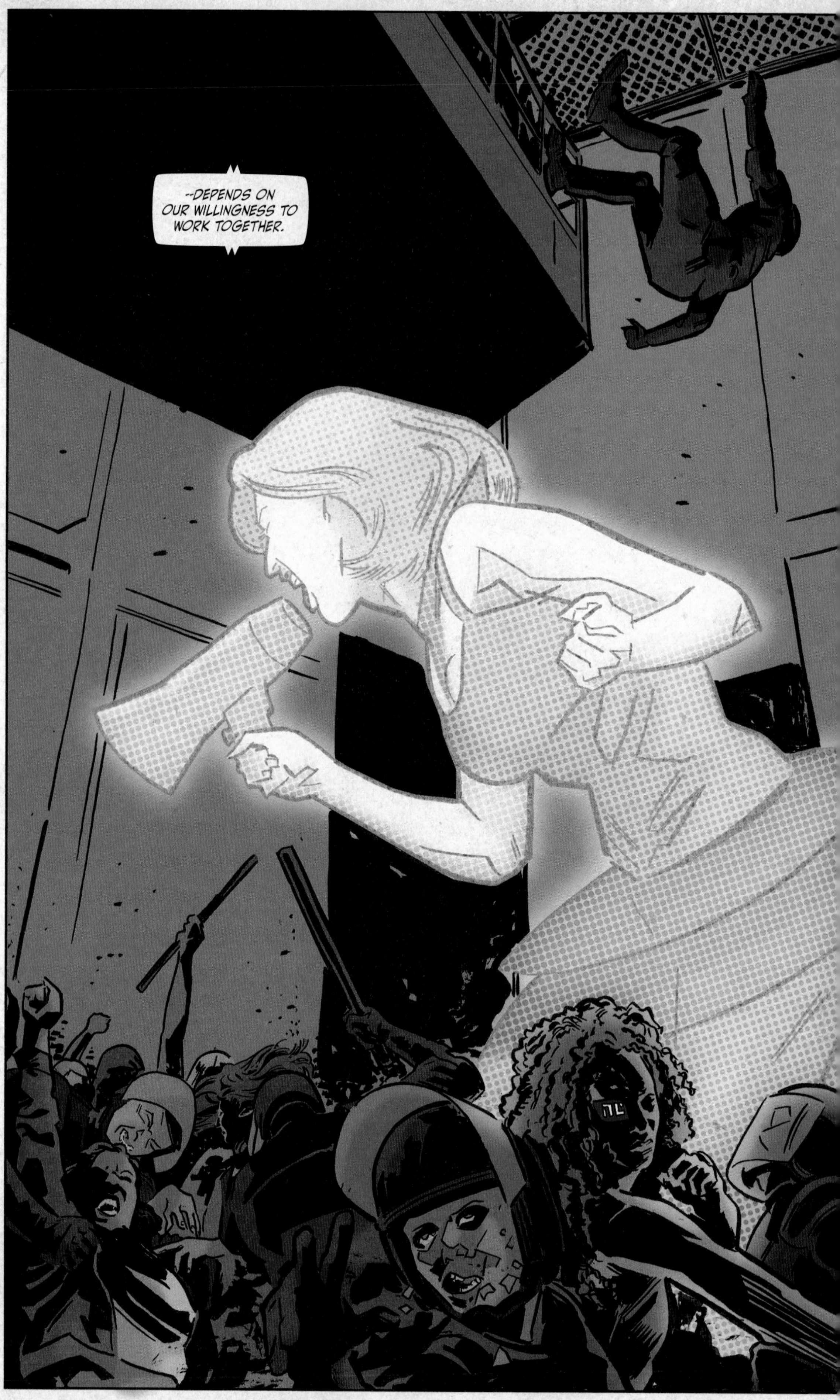
--DEPENDS ON OUR WILLINGNESS TO WORK TOGETHER.

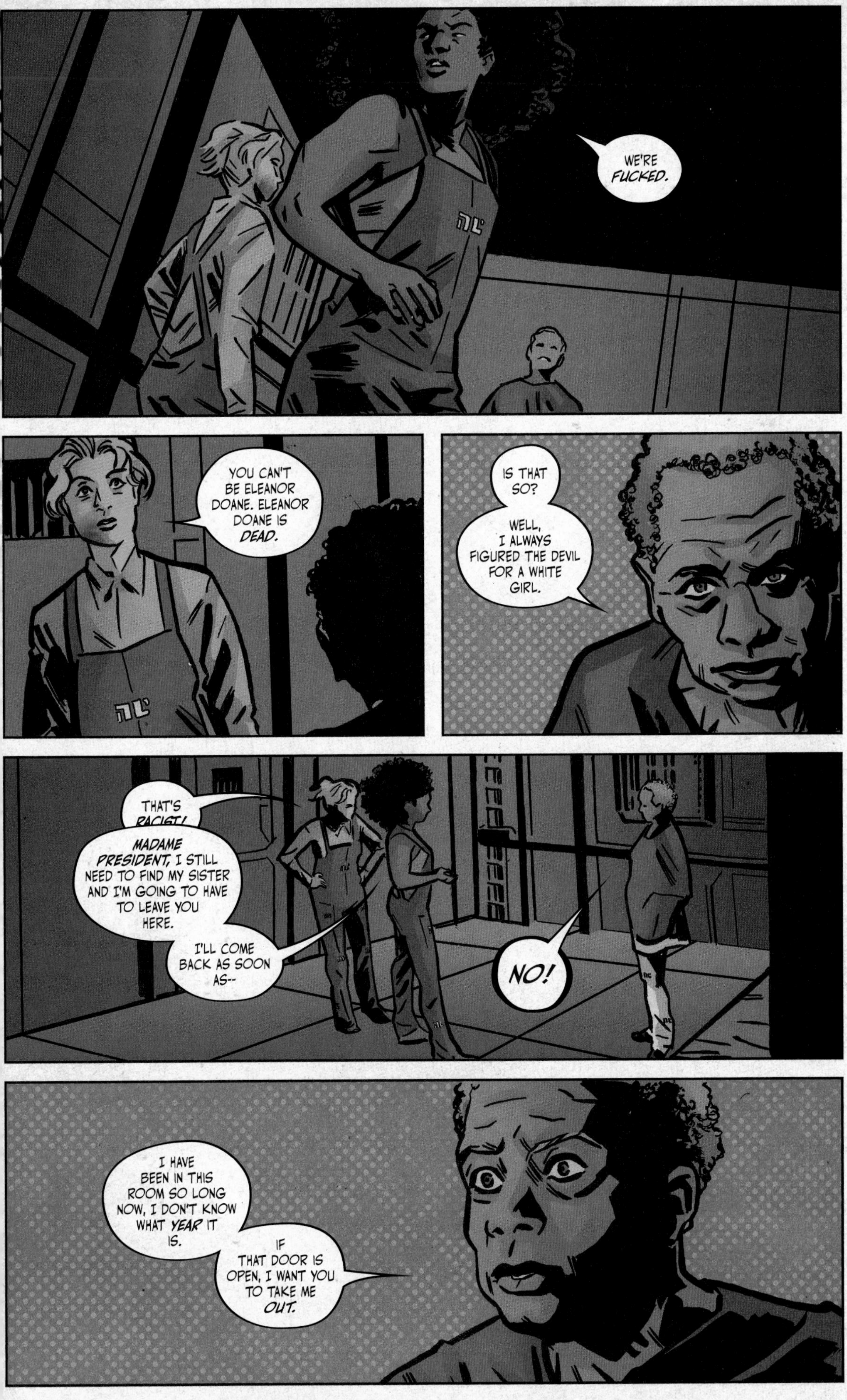
WE'RE FUCKED.
YOU CAN'T BE ELEANOR DOANE. ELEANOR DOANE IS DEAD.
IS THAT SO?
WELL, I ALWAYS FIGURED THE DEVIL FOR A WHITE GIRL.
THAT'S RACIST!
MADAME PRESIDENT, I STILL NEED TO FIND MY SISTER AND I'M GOING TO HAVE TO LEAVE YOU HERE.
I'LL COME BACK AS SOON AS--
NO!
I HAVE BEEN IN THIS ROOM SO LONG NOW, I DON'T KNOW WHAT YEAR IT IS.
IF THAT DOOR IS OPEN, I WANT YOU TO TAKE ME OUT.

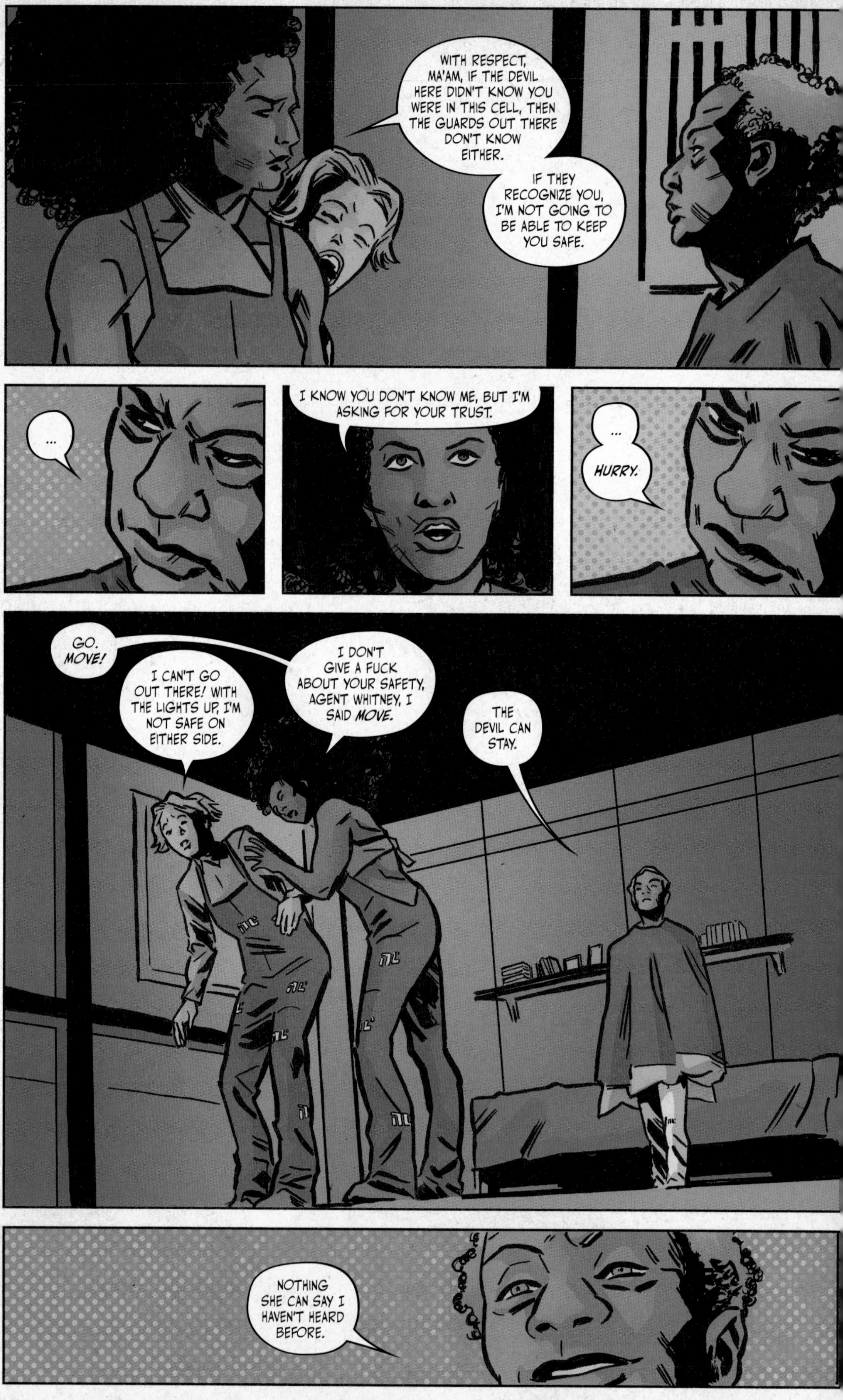
WITH RESPECT, MA'AM, IF THE DEVIL HERE DIDN'T KNOW YOU WERE IN THIS CELL, THEN THE GUARDS OUT THERE DON'T KNOW EITHER.
IF THEY RECOGNIZE YOU, I'M NOT GOING TO BE ABLE TO KEEP YOU SAFE.
...
I KNOW YOU DON'T KNOW ME, BUT I'M ASKING FOR YOUR TRUST.
...
HURRY.
GO. MOVE!
I CAN'T GO OUT THERE! WITH THE LIGHTS UP, I'M NOT SAFE ON EITHER SIDE.
I DON'T GIVE A FUCK ABOUT YOUR SAFETY, AGENT WHITNEY, I SAID MOVE.
THE DEVIL CAN STAY.
NOTHING SHE CAN SAY I HAVEN'T HEARD BEFORE.

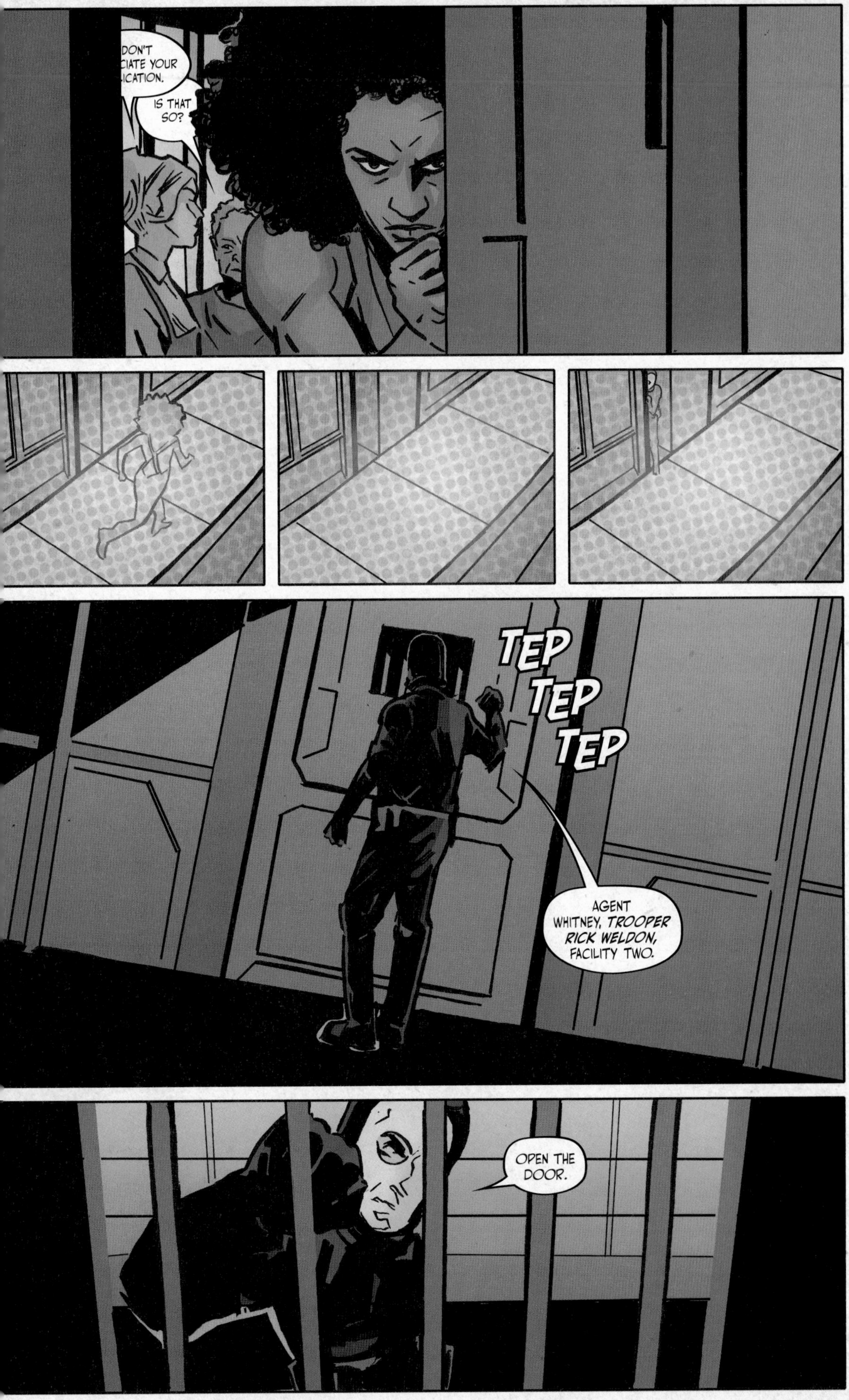

DON'T
CIATE YOUR
ICATION.
IS THAT SO?
TEP TEP TEP
AGENT WHITNEY, *TROOPER RICK WELDON,* FACILITY TWO.
OPEN THE DOOR.

FACILITY ONE.

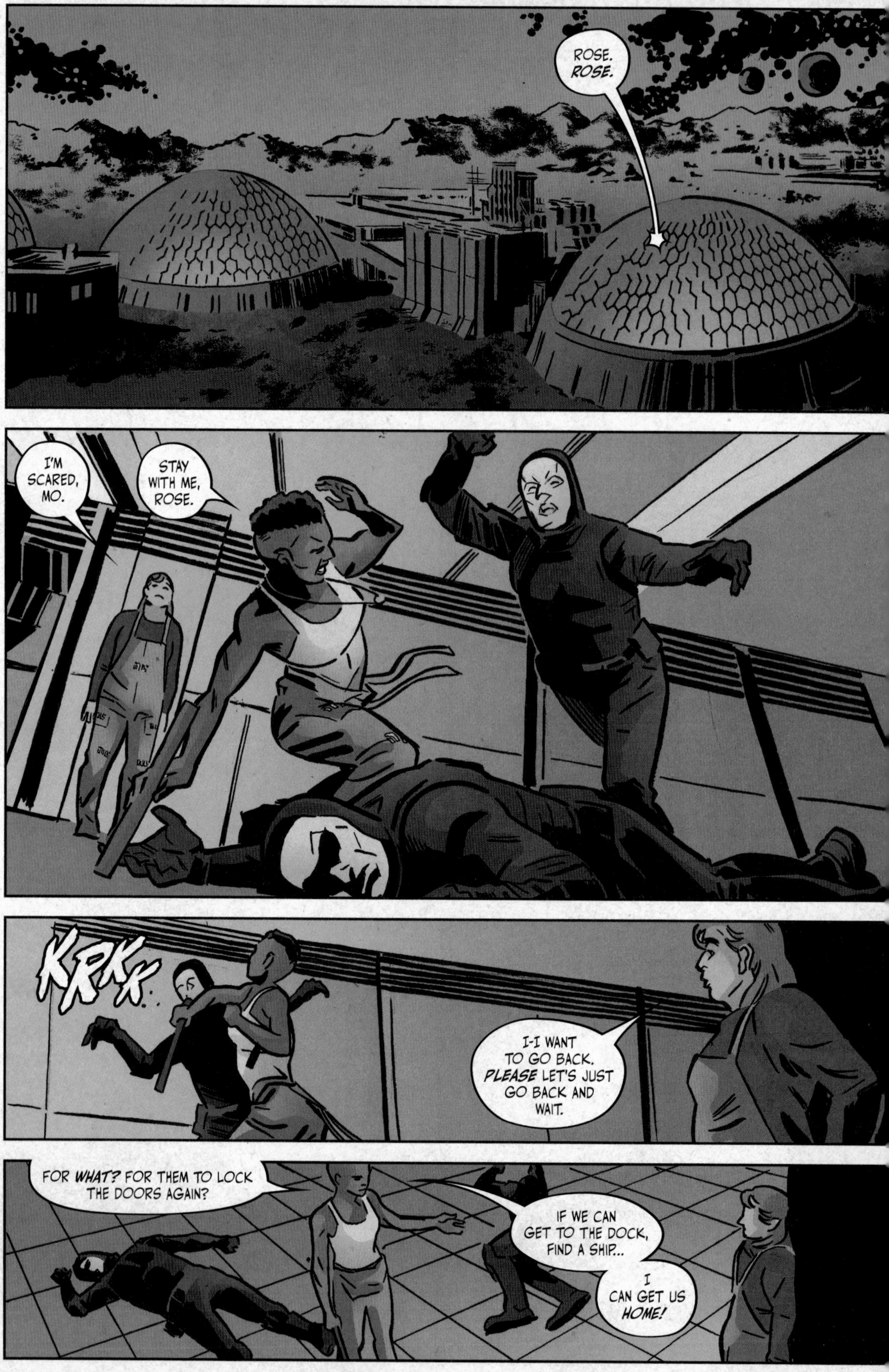
ROSE. *ROSE.*
I'M SCARED, MO.
STAY WITH ME, ROSE.
KRKK
I-I WANT TO GO BACK. *PLEASE* LET'S JUST GO BACK AND WAIT.
FOR *WHAT?* FOR THEM TO LOCK THE DOORS AGAIN?
IF WE CAN GET TO THE DOCK, FIND A SHIP...
I CAN GET US *HOME!*

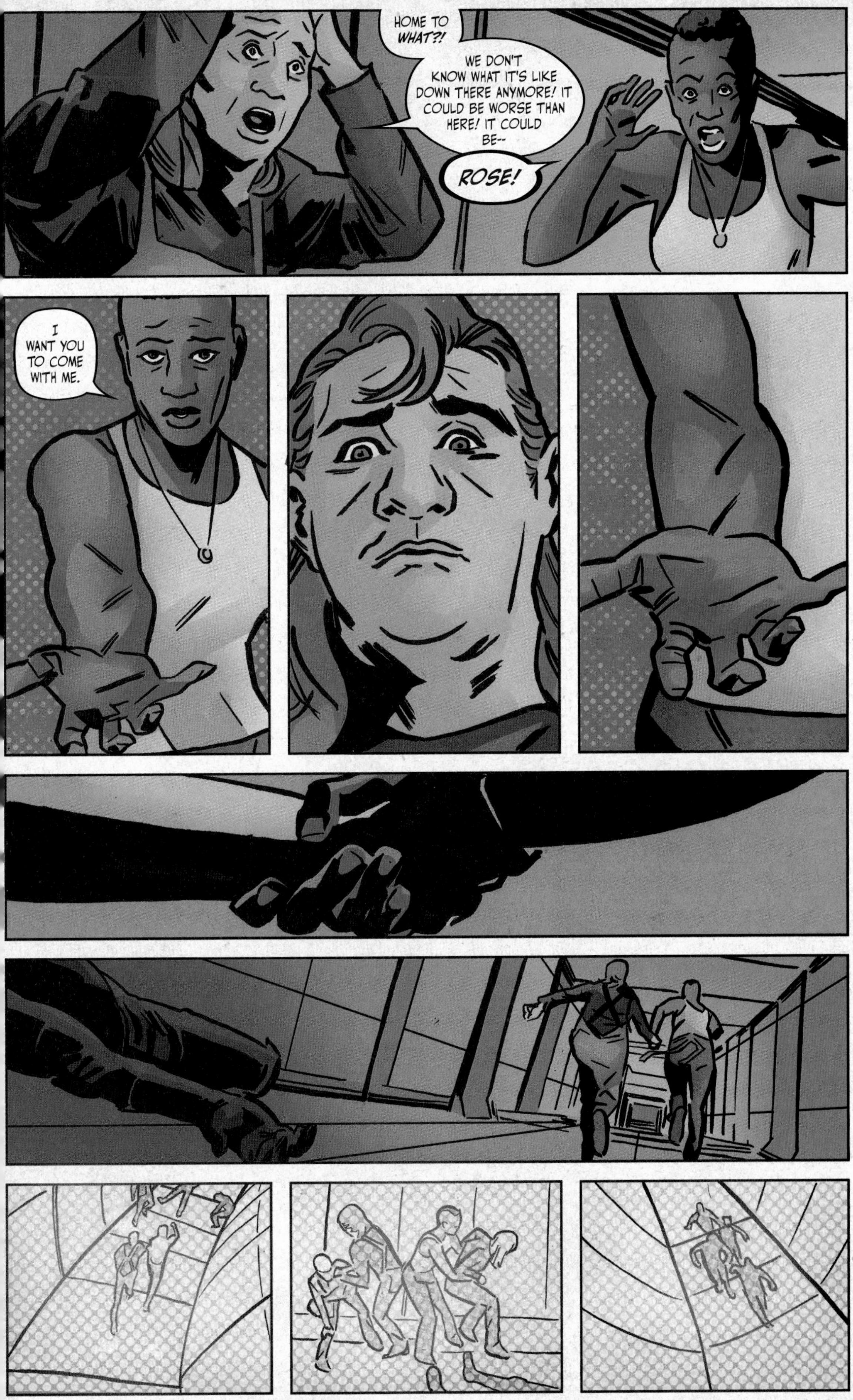
HOME TO WHAT?!
WE DON'T KNOW WHAT IT'S LIKE DOWN THERE ANYMORE! IT COULD BE WORSE THAN HERE! IT COULD BE--
ROSE!
I WANT YOU TO COME WITH ME.

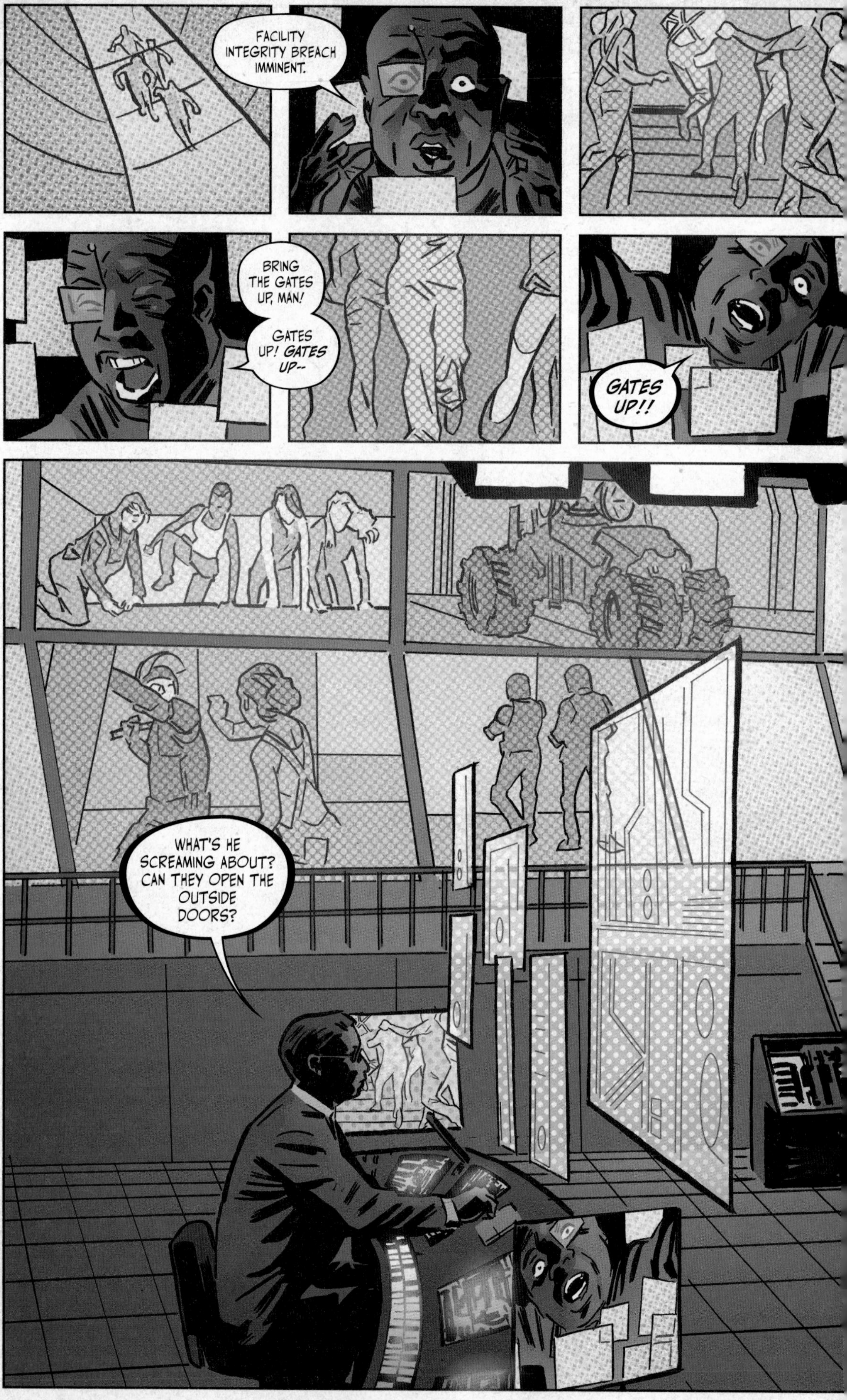
FACILITY INTEGRITY BREACH IMMINENT.
BRING THE GATES UP, MAN!
GATES UP! GATES UP--
GATES UP!!
WHAT'S HE SCREAMING ABOUT? CAN THEY OPEN THE OUTSIDE DOORS?

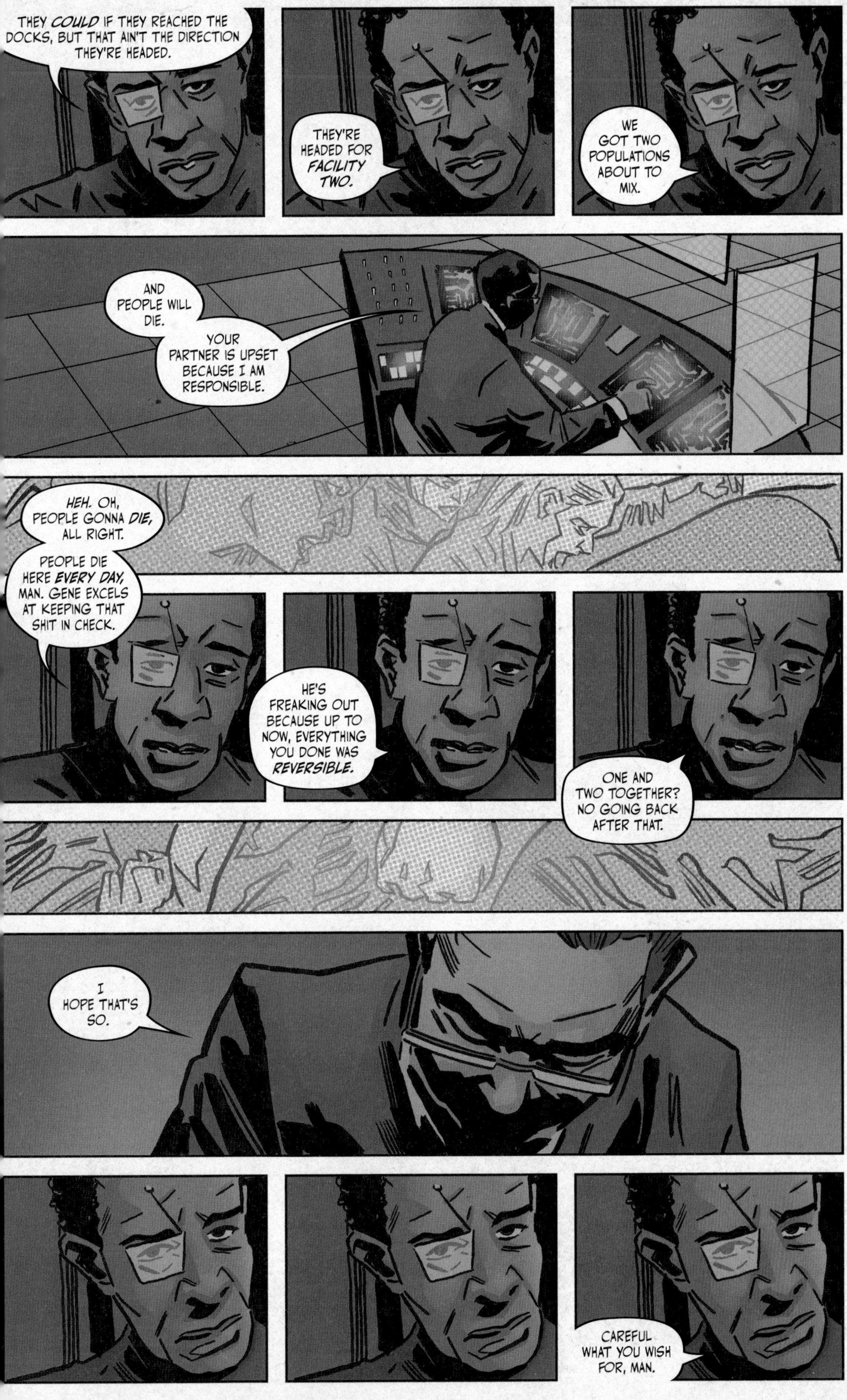
THEY *COULD* IF THEY REACHED THE DOCKS, BUT THAT AIN'T THE DIRECTION THEY'RE HEADED.
THEY'RE HEADED FOR *FACILITY TWO.*
WE GOT TWO POPULATIONS ABOUT TO MIX.
AND PEOPLE WILL DIE.
YOUR PARTNER IS UPSET BECAUSE I AM RESPONSIBLE.
HEH. OH, PEOPLE GONNA *DIE,* ALL RIGHT.
PEOPLE DIE HERE *EVERY DAY,* MAN. GENE EXCELS AT KEEPING THAT SHIT IN CHECK.
HE'S FREAKING OUT BECAUSE UP TO NOW, EVERYTHING YOU DONE WAS *REVERSIBLE.*
ONE AND TWO TOGETHER? NO GOING BACK AFTER THAT.
I HOPE THAT'S SO.
CAREFUL WHAT YOU WISH FOR, MAN.

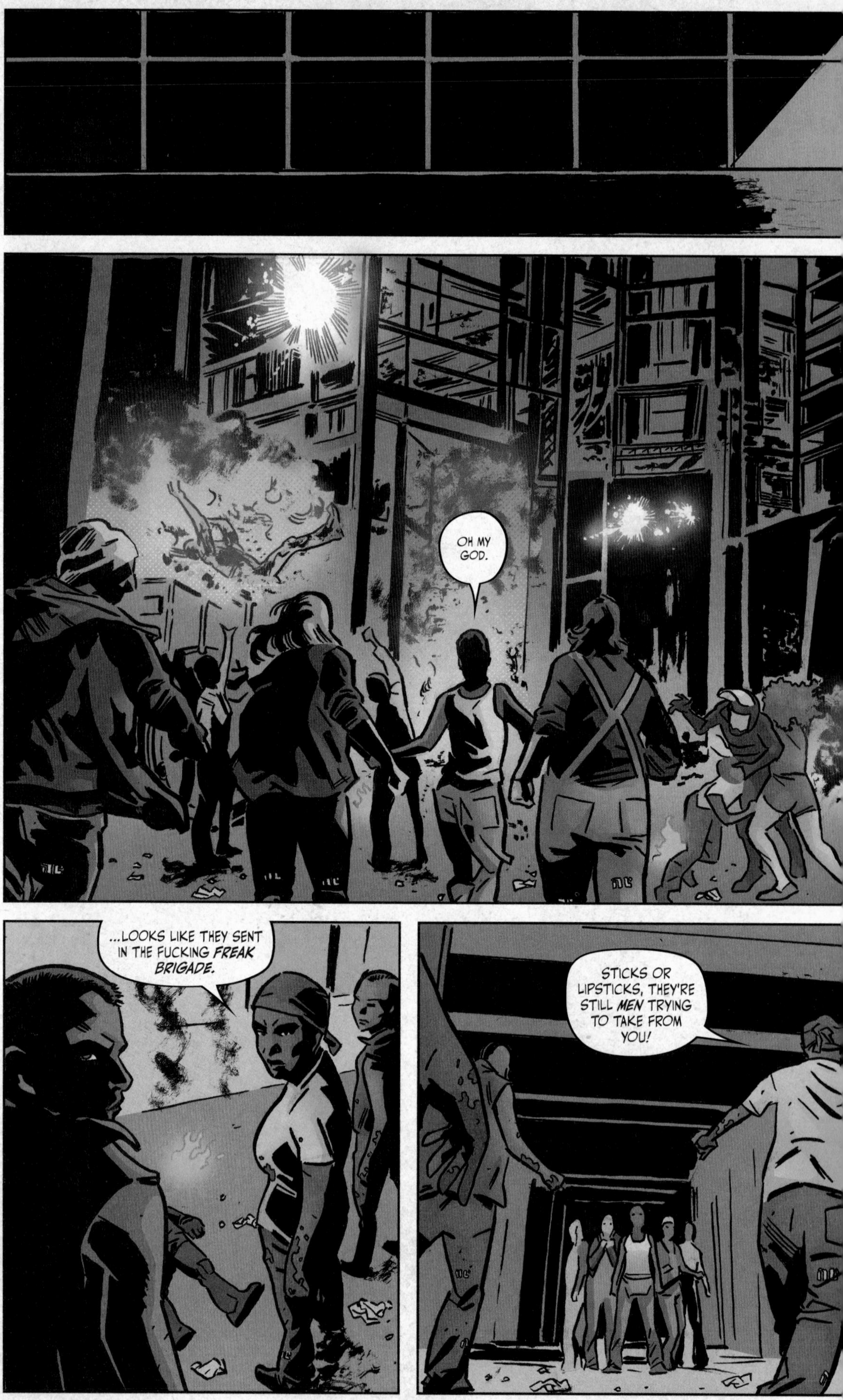
OH MY GOD.
...LOOKS LIKE THEY SENT IN THE FUCKING FREAK BRIGADE.
STICKS OR LIPSTICKS, THEY'RE STILL MEN TRYING TO TAKE FROM YOU!

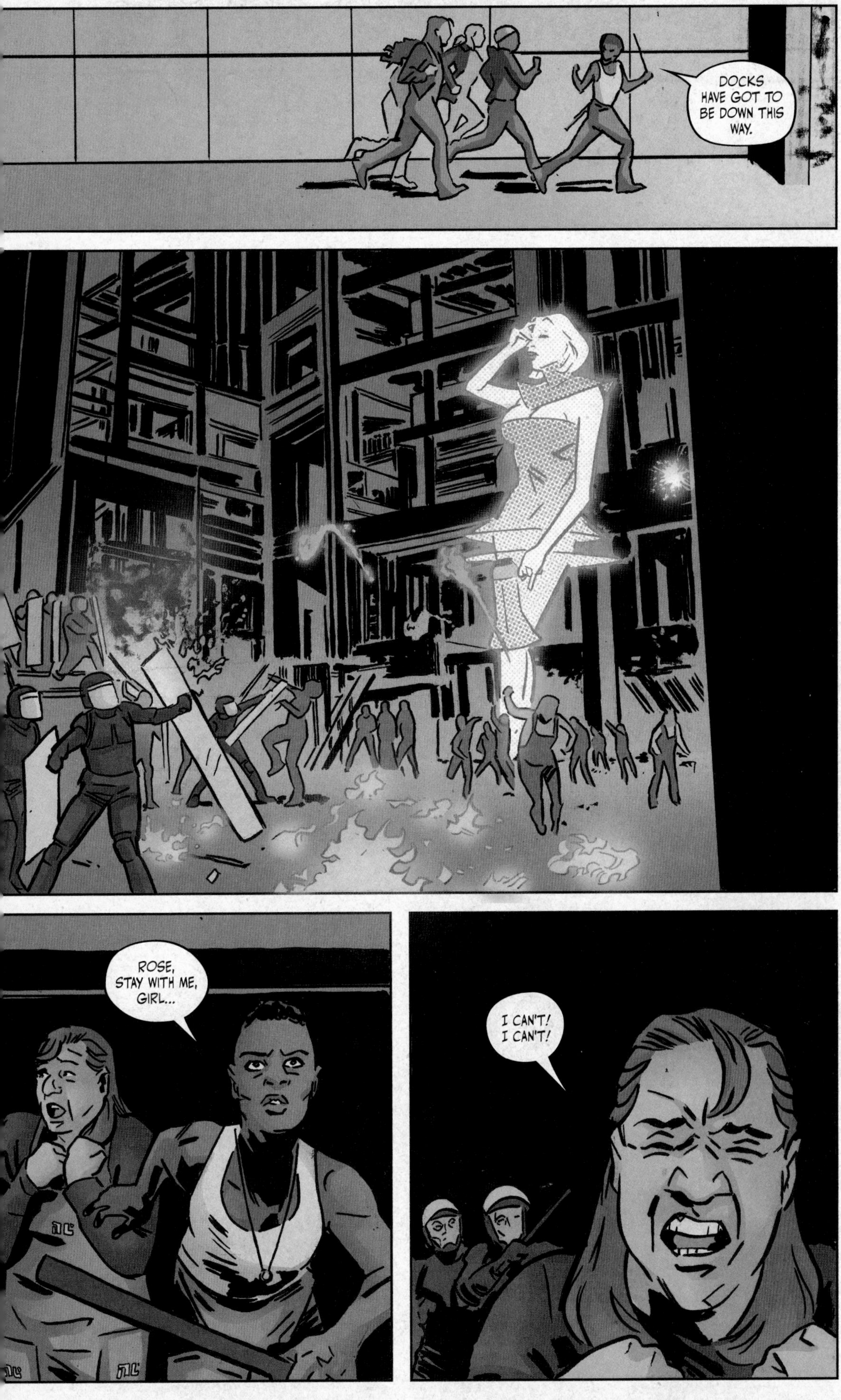
DOCKS HAVE GOT TO BE DOWN THIS WAY.
ROSE, STAY WITH ME, GIRL...
I CAN'T! I CAN'T!

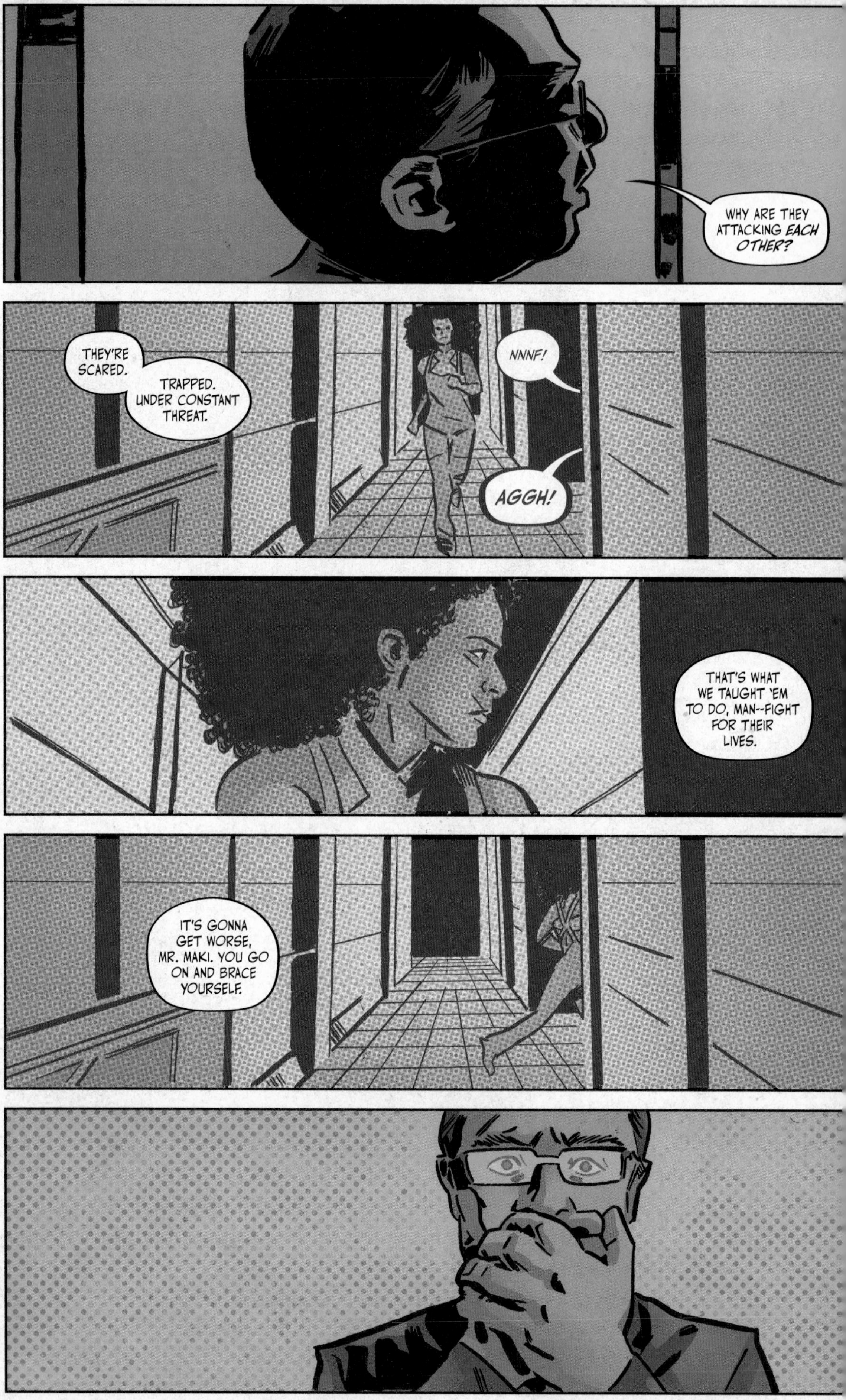
WHY ARE THEY ATTACKING EACH OTHER?
THEY'RE SCARED.
TRAPPED. UNDER CONSTANT THREAT.
NNNF!
AGGH!
THAT'S WHAT WE TAUGHT 'EM TO DO, MAN--FIGHT FOR THEIR LIVES.
IT'S GONNA GET WORSE, MR. MAKI. YOU GO ON AND BRACE YOURSELF.

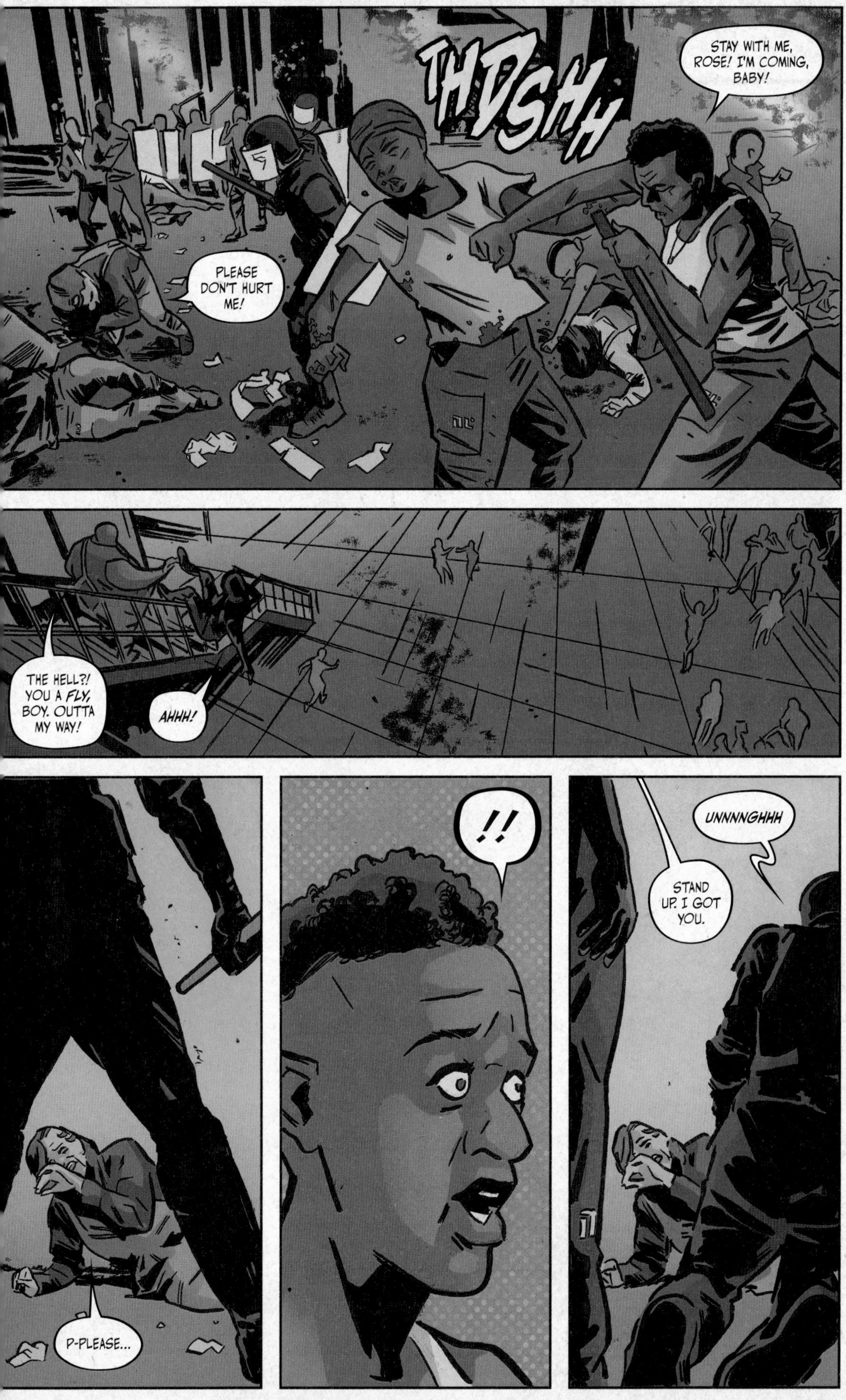
THDSHH
STAY WITH ME, ROSE! I'M COMING, BABY!
PLEASE DON'T HURT ME!
THE HELL?! YOU A FLY, BOY. OUTTA MY WAY!
AHHH!
P-PLEASE...
!!
UNNNNGHHH
STAND UP. I GOT YOU.

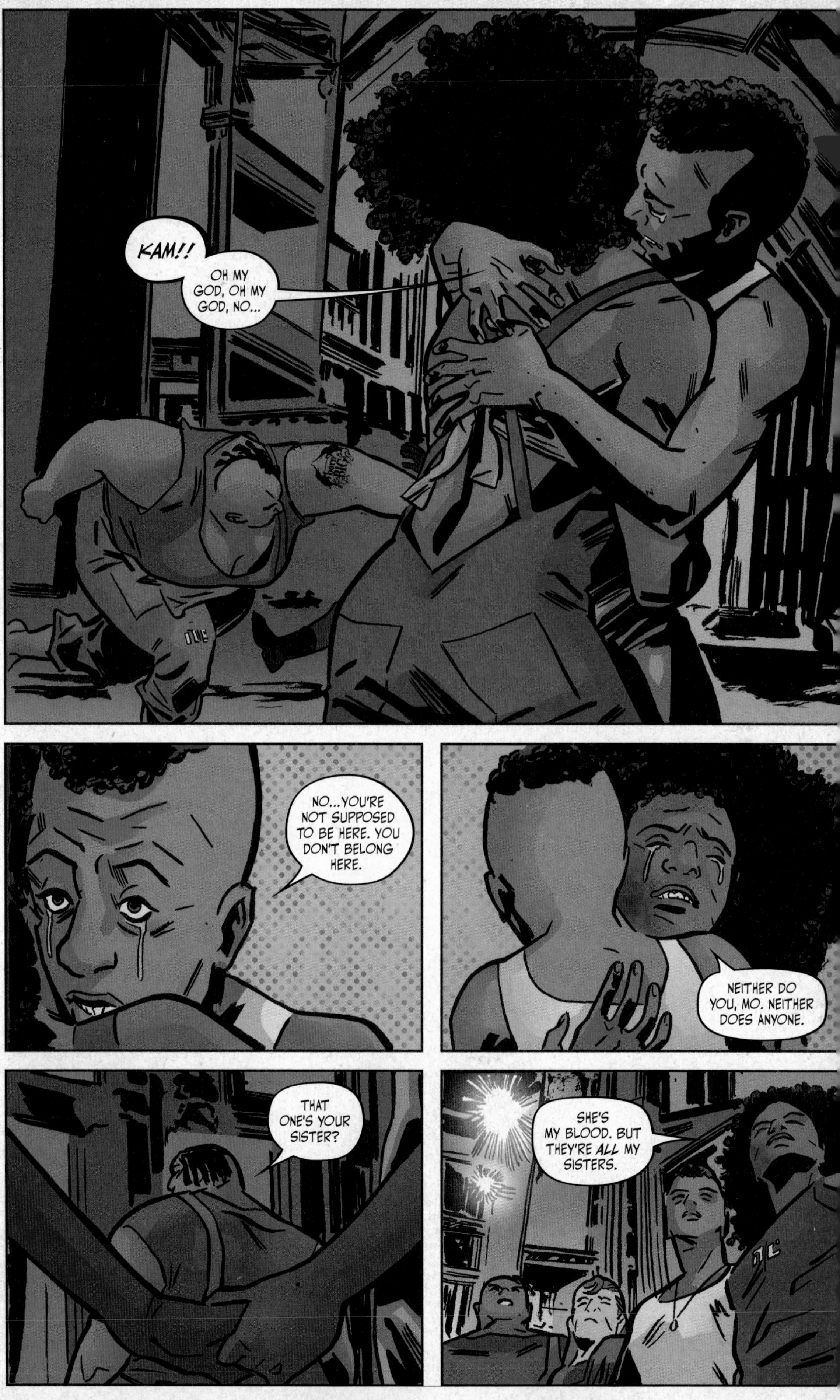
KAM!!
OH MY GOD, OH MY GOD, NO...
NO...YOU'RE NOT SUPPOSED TO BE HERE. YOU DON'T BELONG HERE.
NEITHER DO YOU, MO. NEITHER DOES ANYONE.
THAT ONE'S YOUR SISTER?
SHE'S MY BLOOD. BUT THEY'RE *ALL* MY SISTERS.

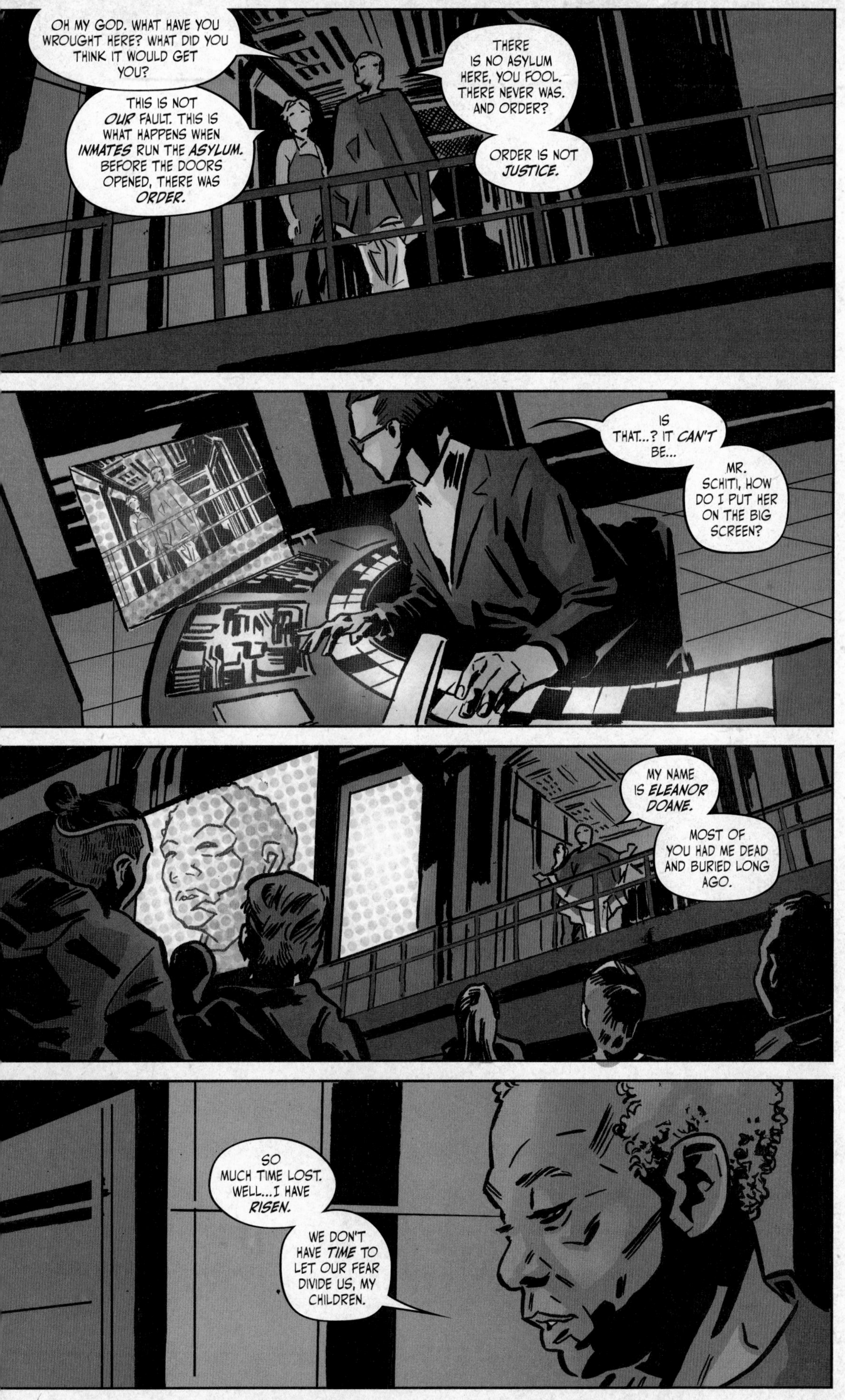
OH MY GOD. WHAT HAVE YOU WROUGHT HERE? WHAT DID YOU THINK IT WOULD GET YOU?
THIS IS NOT *OUR* FAULT. THIS IS WHAT HAPPENS WHEN *INMATES* RUN THE *ASYLUM.* BEFORE THE DOORS OPENED, THERE WAS *ORDER.*
THERE IS NO ASYLUM HERE, YOU FOOL. THERE NEVER WAS. AND ORDER?
ORDER IS NOT *JUSTICE.*
IS THAT...? IT *CAN'T* BE...
MR. SCHITI, HOW DO I PUT HER ON THE BIG SCREEN?
MY NAME IS *ELEANOR DOANE.*
MOST OF YOU HAD ME DEAD AND BURIED LONG AGO.
SO MUCH TIME LOST. WELL...I HAVE *RISEN.*
WE DON'T HAVE *TIME* TO LET OUR FEAR DIVIDE US, MY CHILDREN.

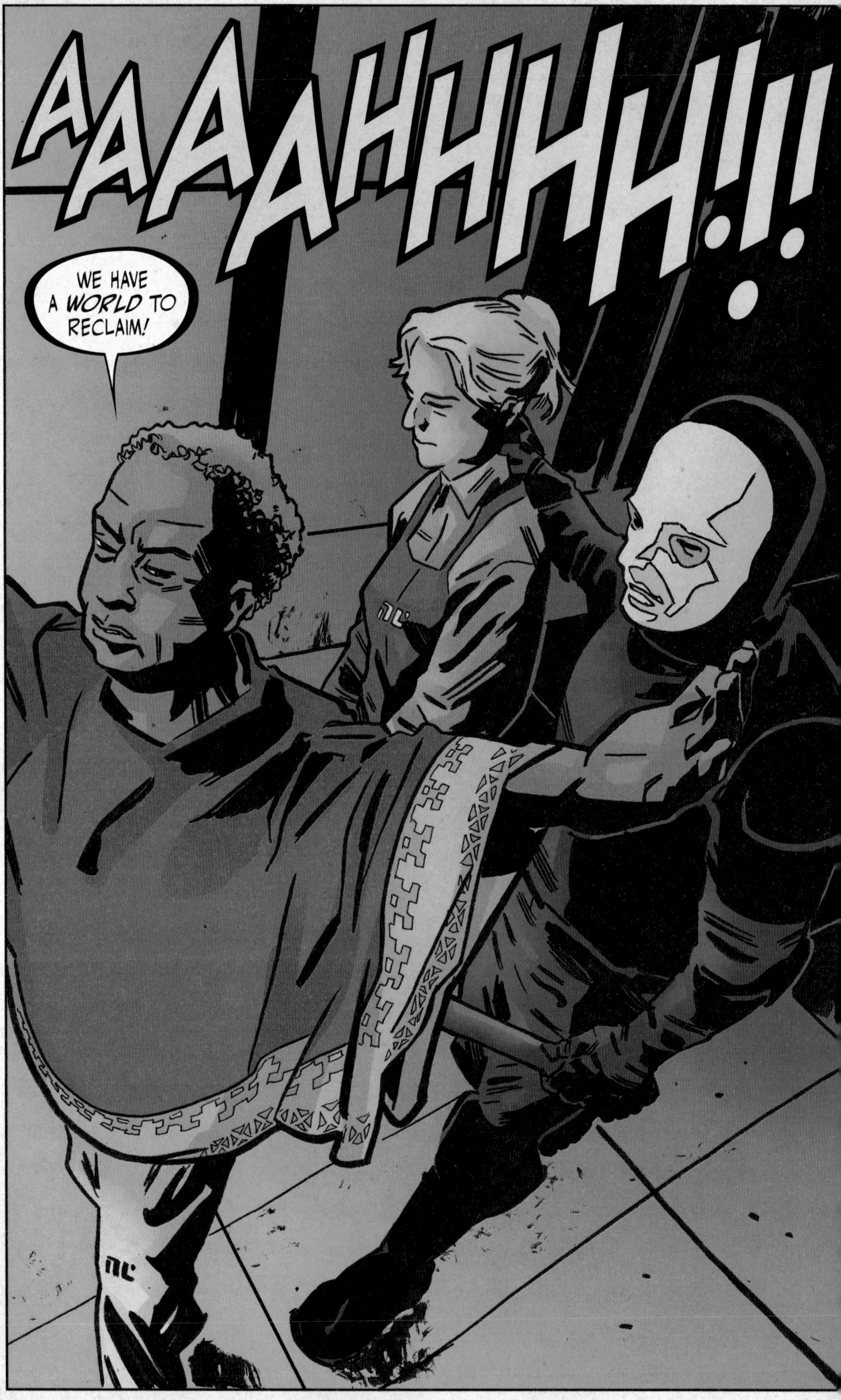
AAAHHHH!!!
WE HAVE A *WORLD* TO RECLAIM!

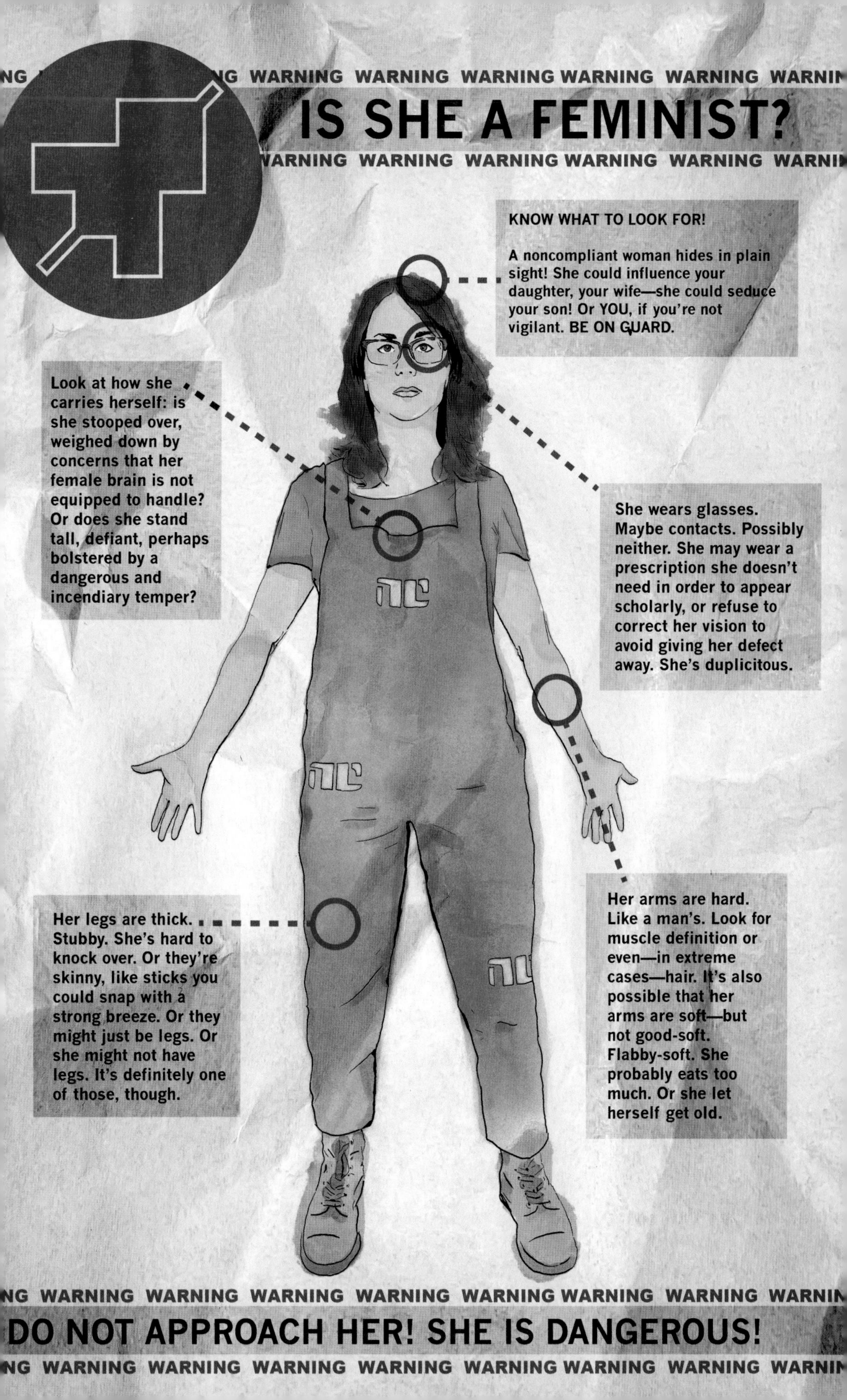
WARNING WARNING WARNING WARNING WARNING
IS SHE A FEMINIST?
WARNING WARNING WARNING WARNING WARNING
KNOW WHAT TO LOOK FOR!
A noncompliant woman hides in plain sight! She could influence your daughter, your wife—she could seduce your son! Or YOU, if you're not vigilant. BE ON GUARD.
Look at how she carries herself: is she stooped over, weighed down by concerns that her female brain is not equipped to handle? Or does she stand tall, defiant, perhaps bolstered by a dangerous and incendiary temper?
She wears glasses. Maybe contacts. Possibly neither. She may wear a prescription she doesn't need in order to appear scholarly, or refuse to correct her vision to avoid giving her defect away. She's duplicitous.
Her legs are thick. Stubby. She's hard to knock over. Or they're skinny, like sticks you could snap with a strong breeze. Or they might just be legs. Or she might not have legs. It's definitely one of those, though.
Her arms are hard. Like a man's. Look for muscle definition or even—in extreme cases—hair. It's also possible that her arms are soft—but not good-soft. Flabby-soft. She probably eats too much. Or she let herself get old.
WARNING WARNING WARNING WARNING WARNING WARNING WARNING
DO NOT APPROACH HER! SHE IS DANGEROUS!
WARNING WARNING WARNING WARNING WARNING WARNING WARNING

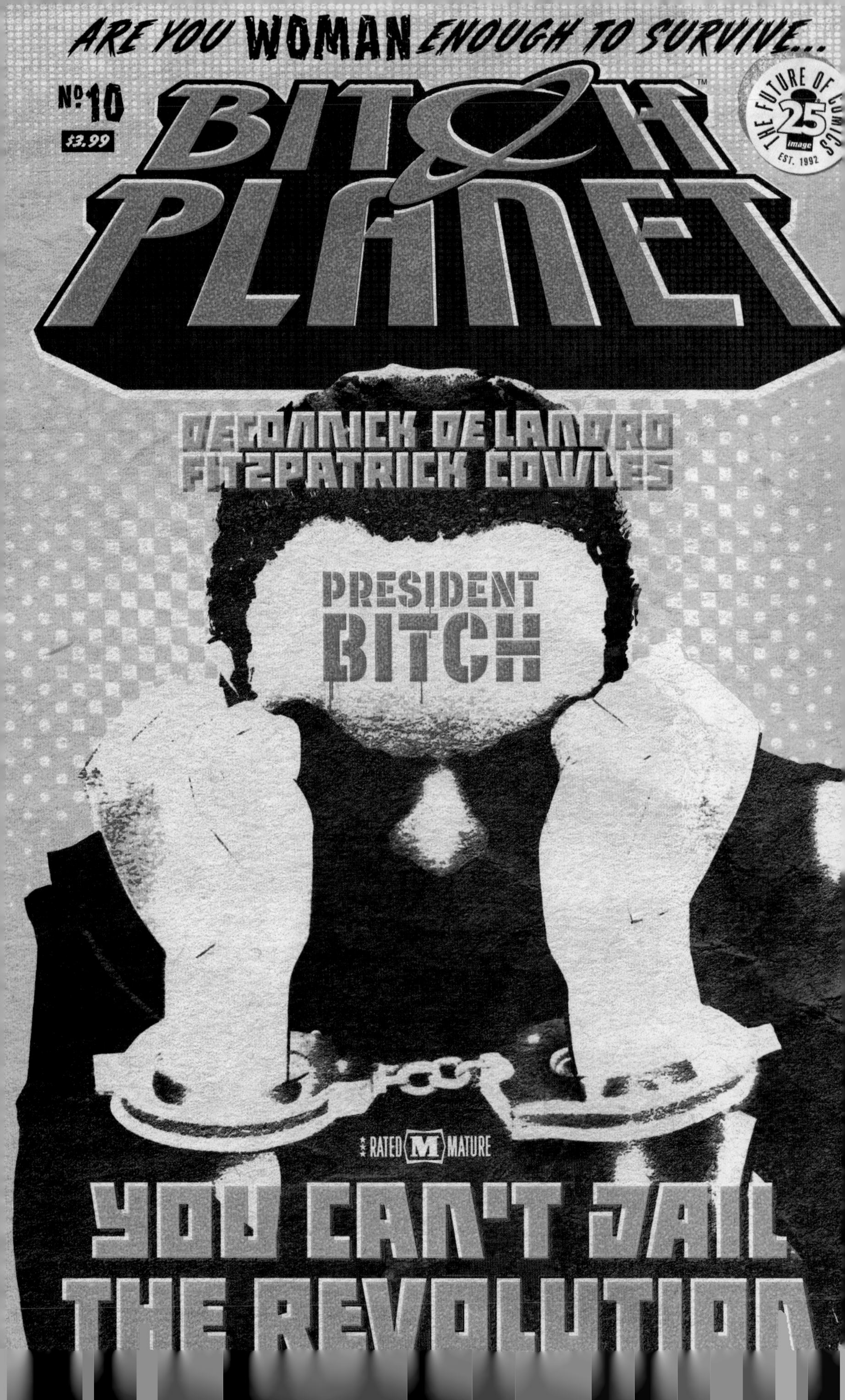
ARE YOU WOMAN ENOUGH TO SURVIVE...
№10
$3.99
BITCH PLANET
THE FUTURE OF COMICS 25 image EST. 1992
DECONNICK DE LANDRO
FITZPATRICK COWLES
PRESIDENT BITCH
RATED M MATURE
YOU CAN'T JAIL THE REVOLUTION

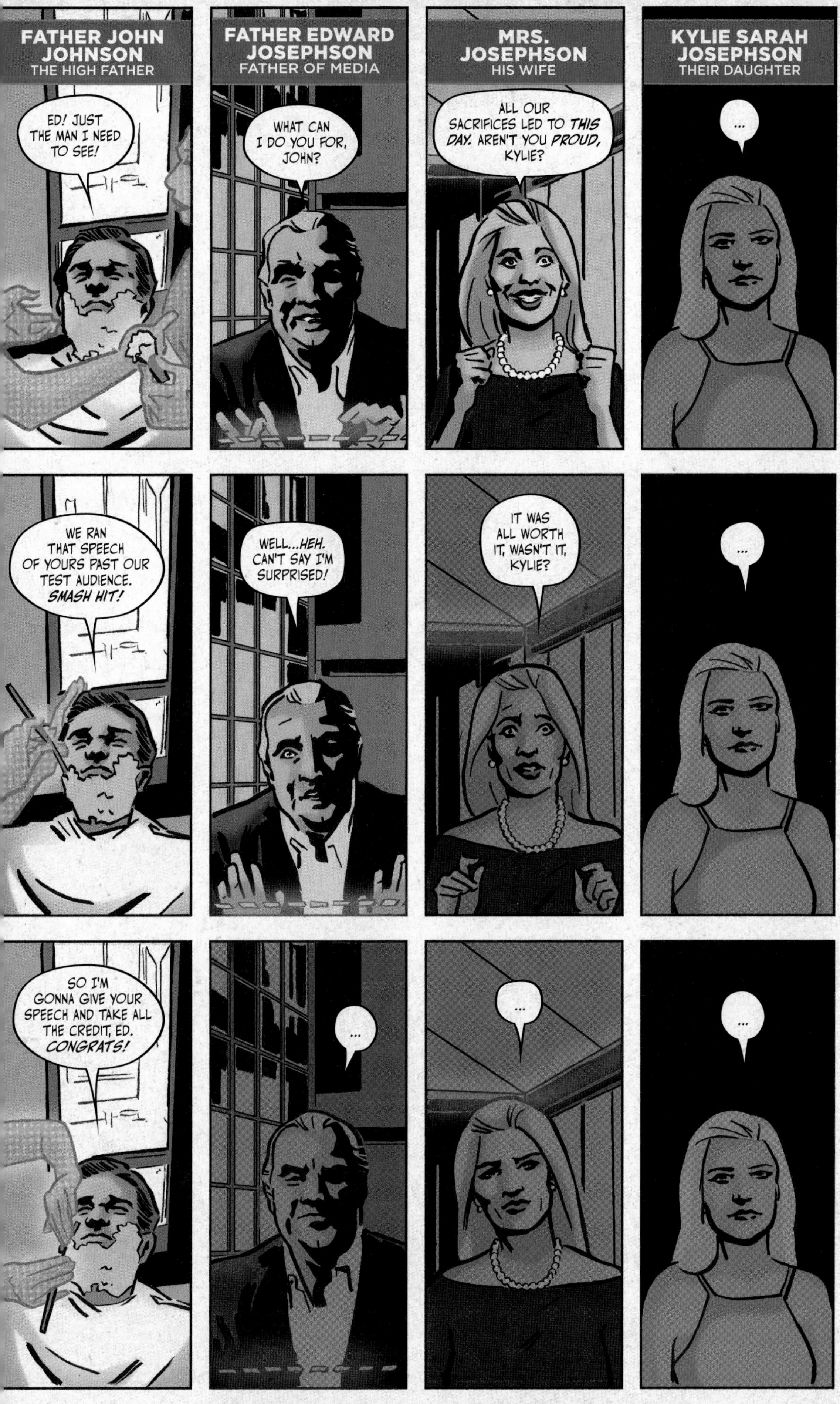
FATHER JOHN JOHNSON
THE HIGH FATHER
FATHER EDWARD JOSEPHSON
FATHER OF MEDIA
MRS. JOSEPHSON
HIS WIFE
KYLIE SARAH JOSEPHSON
THEIR DAUGHTER
ED! JUST THE MAN I NEED TO SEE!
WHAT CAN I DO YOU FOR, JOHN?
ALL OUR SACRIFICES LED TO THIS DAY. AREN'T YOU PROUD, KYLIE?
...
WE RAN THAT SPEECH OF YOURS PAST OUR TEST AUDIENCE. SMASH HIT!
WELL...HEH. CAN'T SAY I'M SURPRISED!
IT WAS ALL WORTH IT, WASN'T IT, KYLIE?
...
SO I'M GONNA GIVE YOUR SPEECH AND TAKE ALL THE CREDIT, ED. CONGRATS!
...
...
...

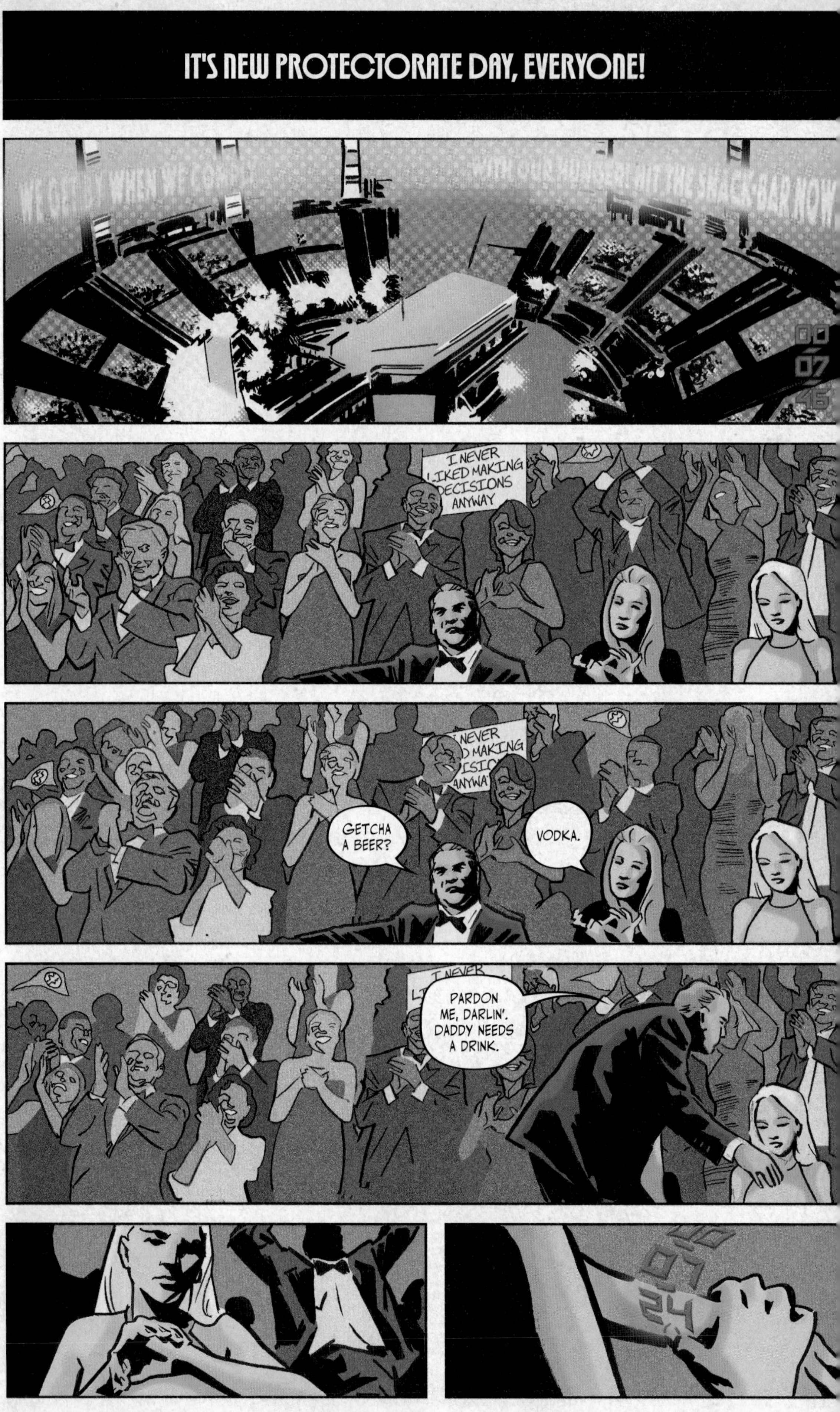
IT'S NEW PROTECTORATE DAY, EVERYONE!
I NEVER LIKED MAKING DECISIONS ANYWAY
GETCHA A BEER?
VODKA.
PARDON ME, DARLIN'. DADDY NEEDS A DRINK.

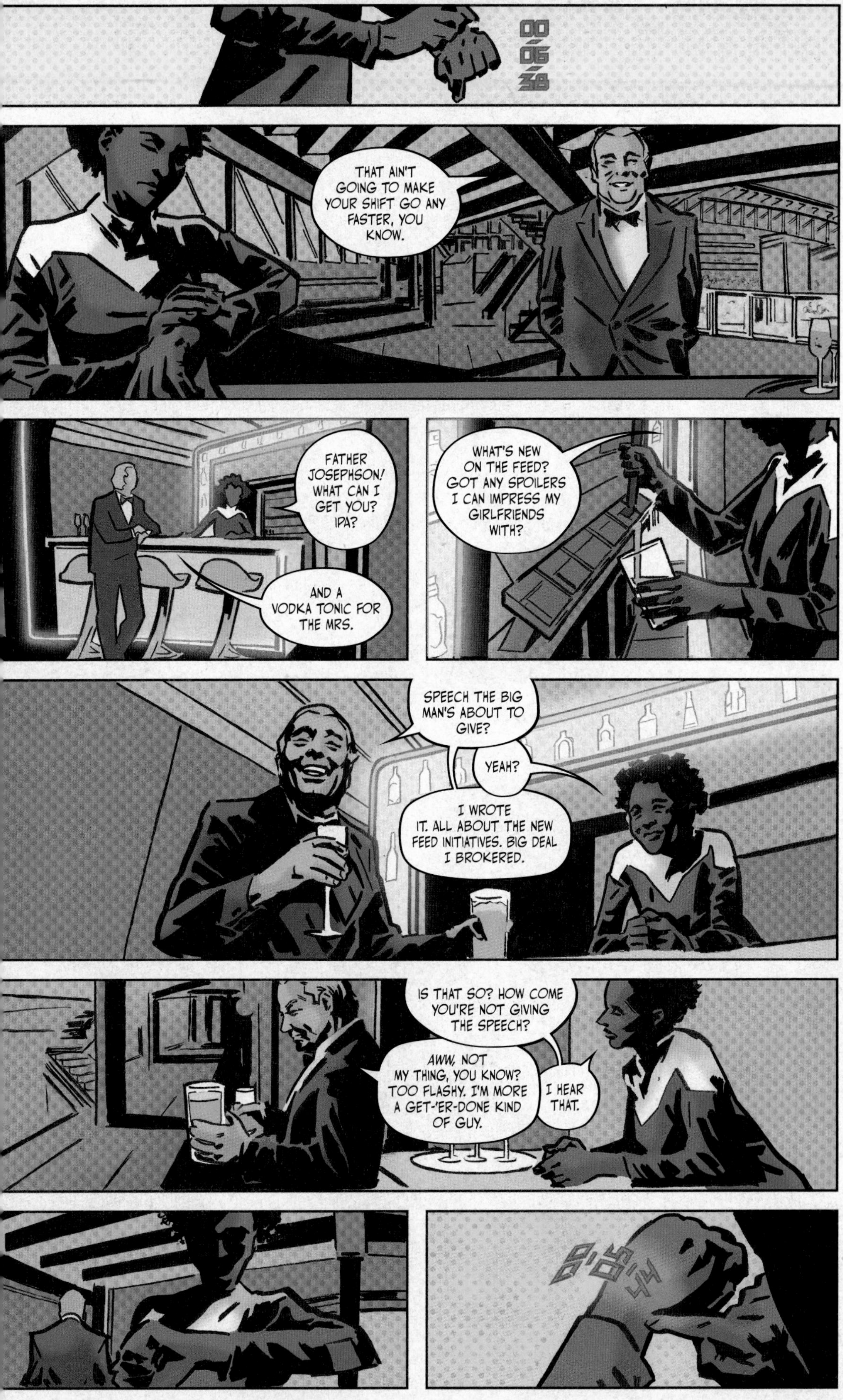
00
06
38
THAT AIN'T GOING TO MAKE YOUR SHIFT GO ANY FASTER, YOU KNOW.
FATHER JOSEPHSON! WHAT CAN I GET YOU? IPA?
AND A VODKA TONIC FOR THE MRS.
WHAT'S NEW ON THE FEED? GOT ANY SPOILERS I CAN IMPRESS MY GIRLFRIENDS WITH?
SPEECH THE BIG MAN'S ABOUT TO GIVE?
YEAH?
I WROTE IT. ALL ABOUT THE NEW FEED INITIATIVES. BIG DEAL I BROKERED.
IS THAT SO? HOW COME YOU'RE NOT GIVING THE SPEECH?
AWW, NOT MY THING, YOU KNOW? TOO FLASHY. I'M MORE A GET-'ER-DONE KIND OF GUY.
I HEAR THAT.

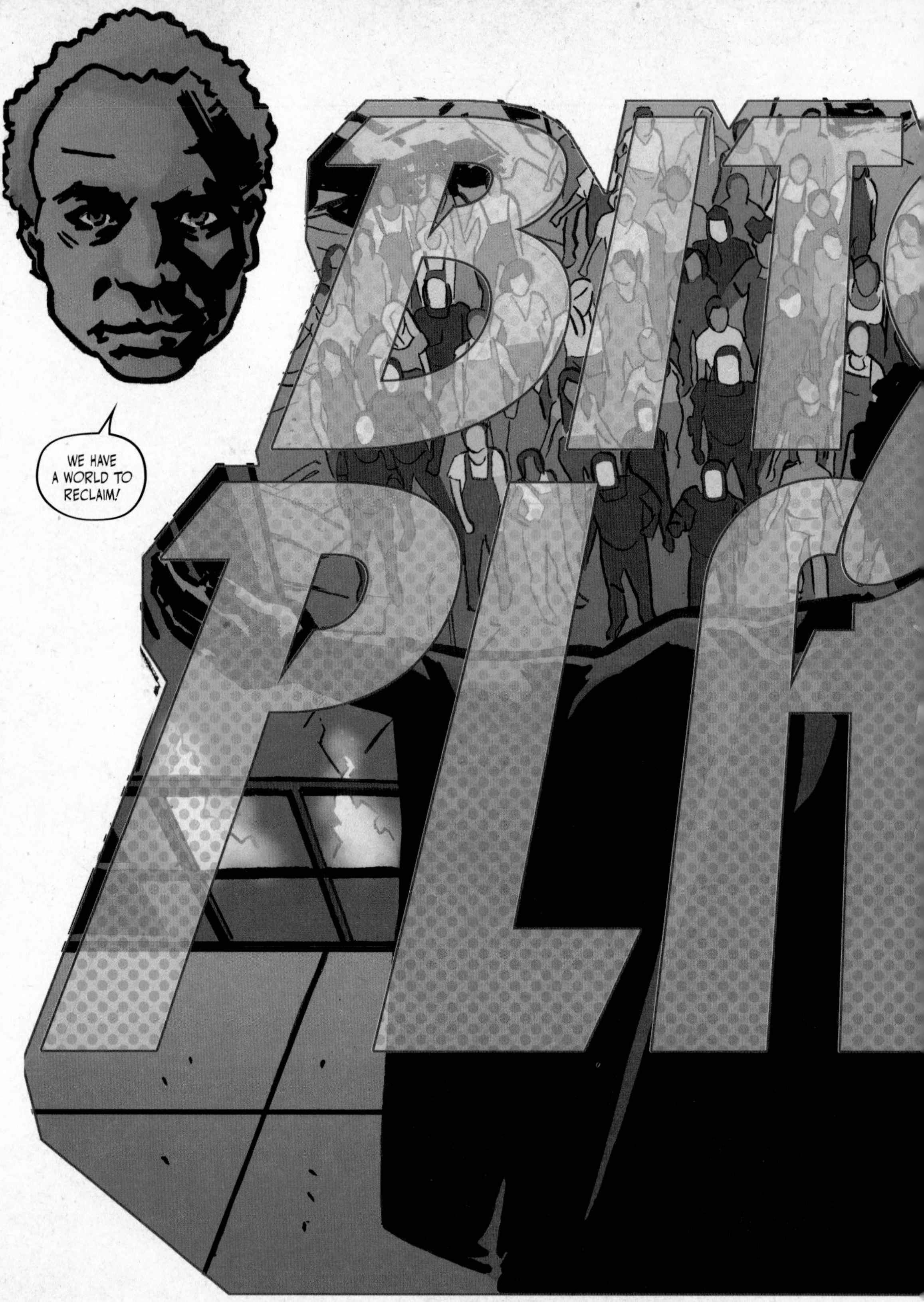
WE HAVE A WORLD TO RECLAIM!

KELLY SUE DECONNICK
SCRIPT

KELLY FITZPATRICK
COLORS

CLAYTON COWLES
LETTERS

RIAN HUGHES
COVER DESIGN & LOGO DESIGN

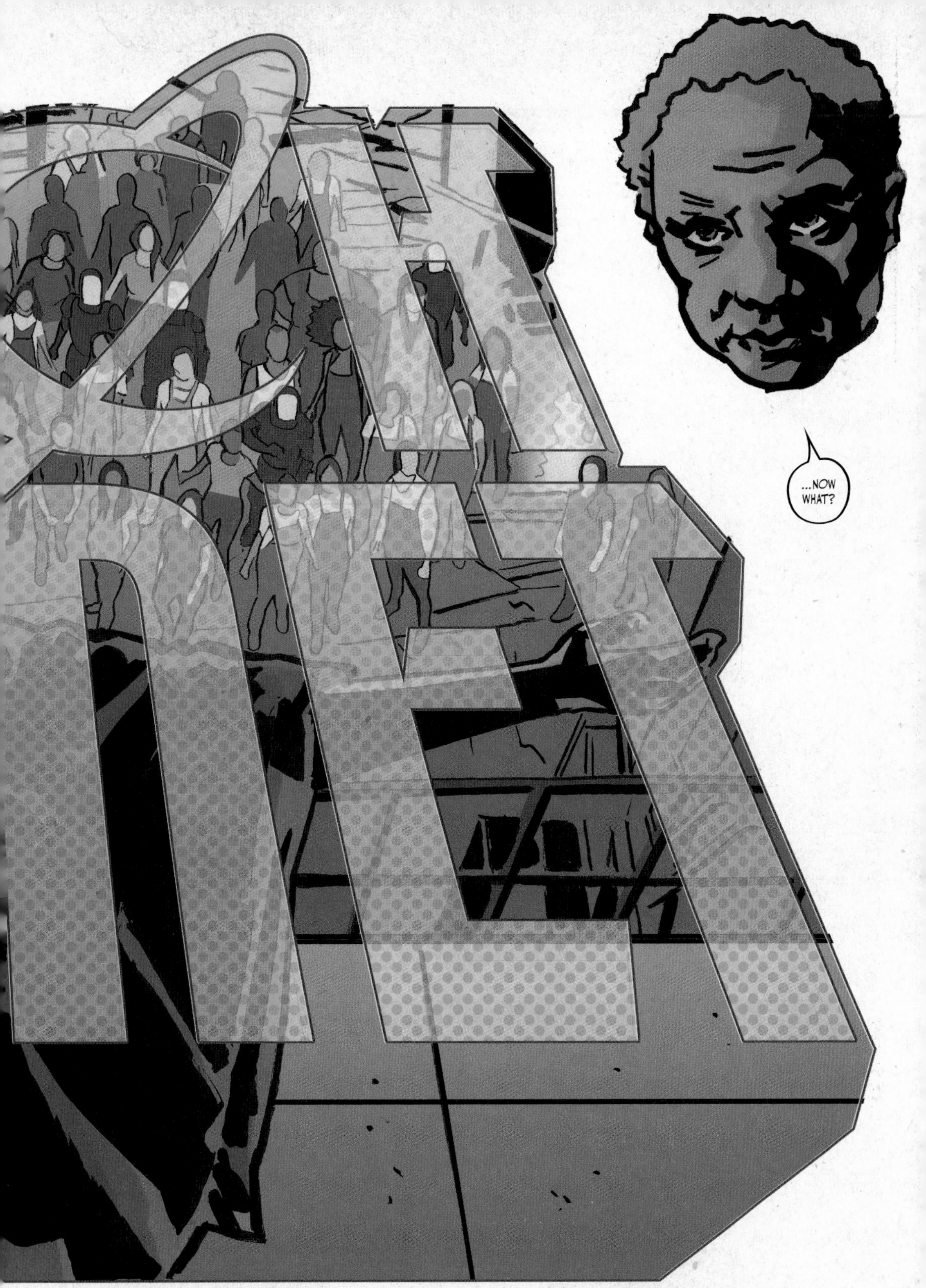
...NOW WHAT?

VALENTINE DE LANDRO

ART/COVERS

LAURENN McCUBBIN
BACKMATTER DESIGN

LAUREN SANKOVITCH
EDITOR

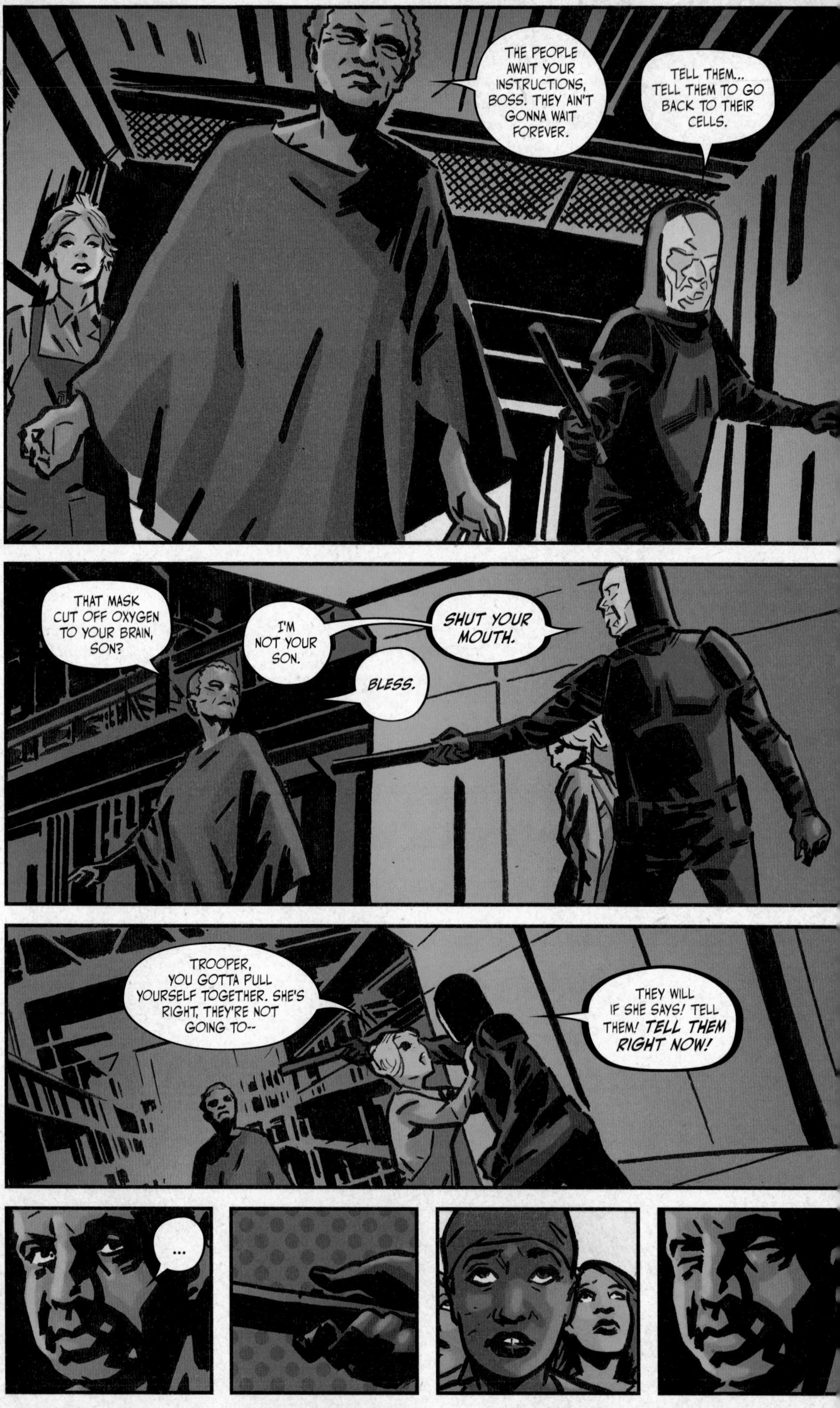
THE PEOPLE AWAIT YOUR INSTRUCTIONS, BOSS. THEY AIN'T GONNA WAIT FOREVER.
TELL THEM... TELL THEM TO GO BACK TO THEIR CELLS.
THAT MASK CUT OFF OXYGEN TO YOUR BRAIN, SON?
I'M NOT YOUR SON.
SHUT YOUR MOUTH.
BLESS.
TROOPER, YOU GOTTA PULL YOURSELF TOGETHER. SHE'S RIGHT, THEY'RE NOT GOING TO--
THEY WILL IF SHE SAYS! TELL THEM! TELL THEM RIGHT NOW!
...

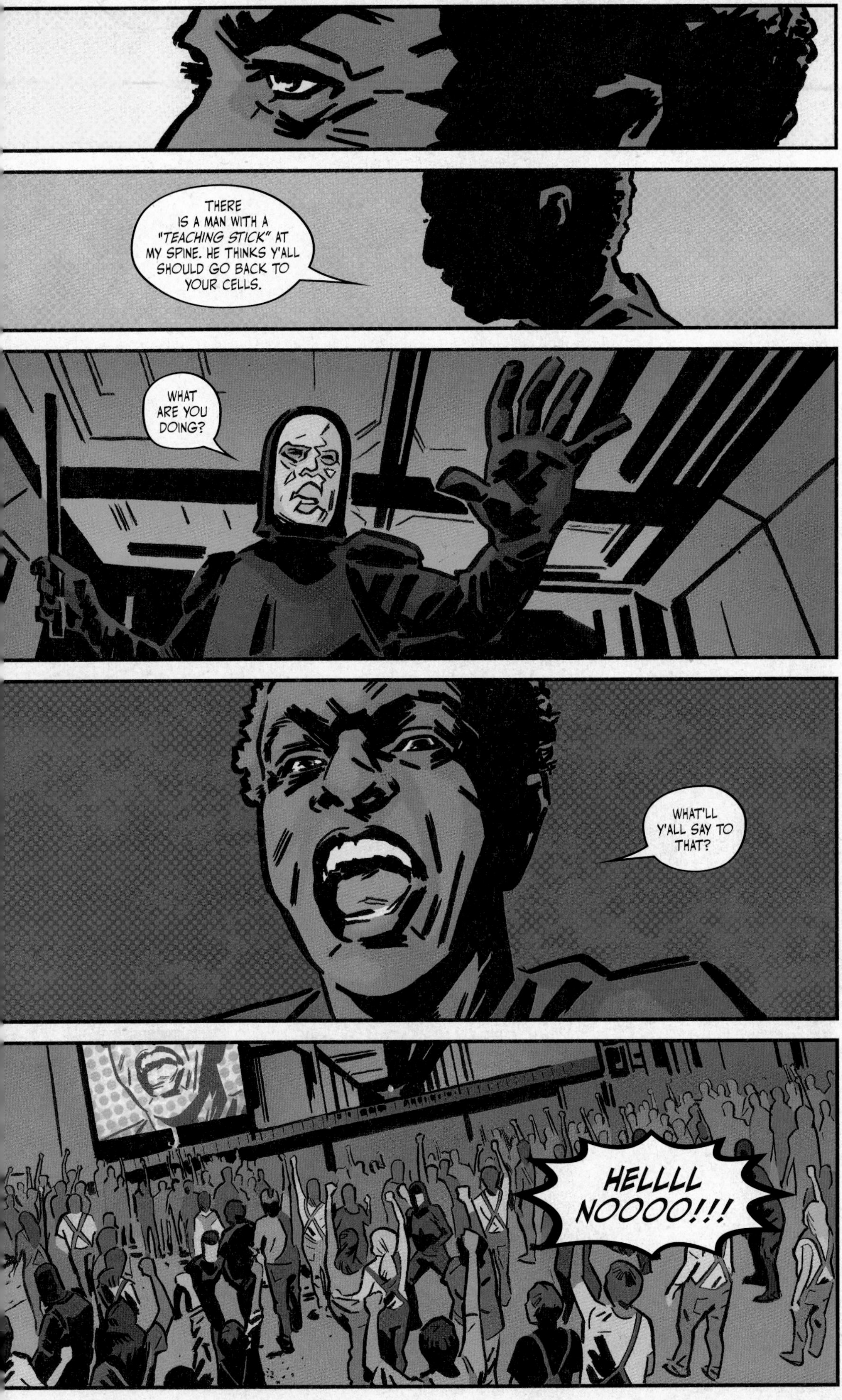
THERE IS A MAN WITH A "TEACHING STICK" AT MY SPINE. HE THINKS Y'ALL SHOULD GO BACK TO YOUR CELLS.
WHAT ARE YOU DOING?
WHAT'LL Y'ALL SAY TO THAT?
HELLLL NOOOO!!!

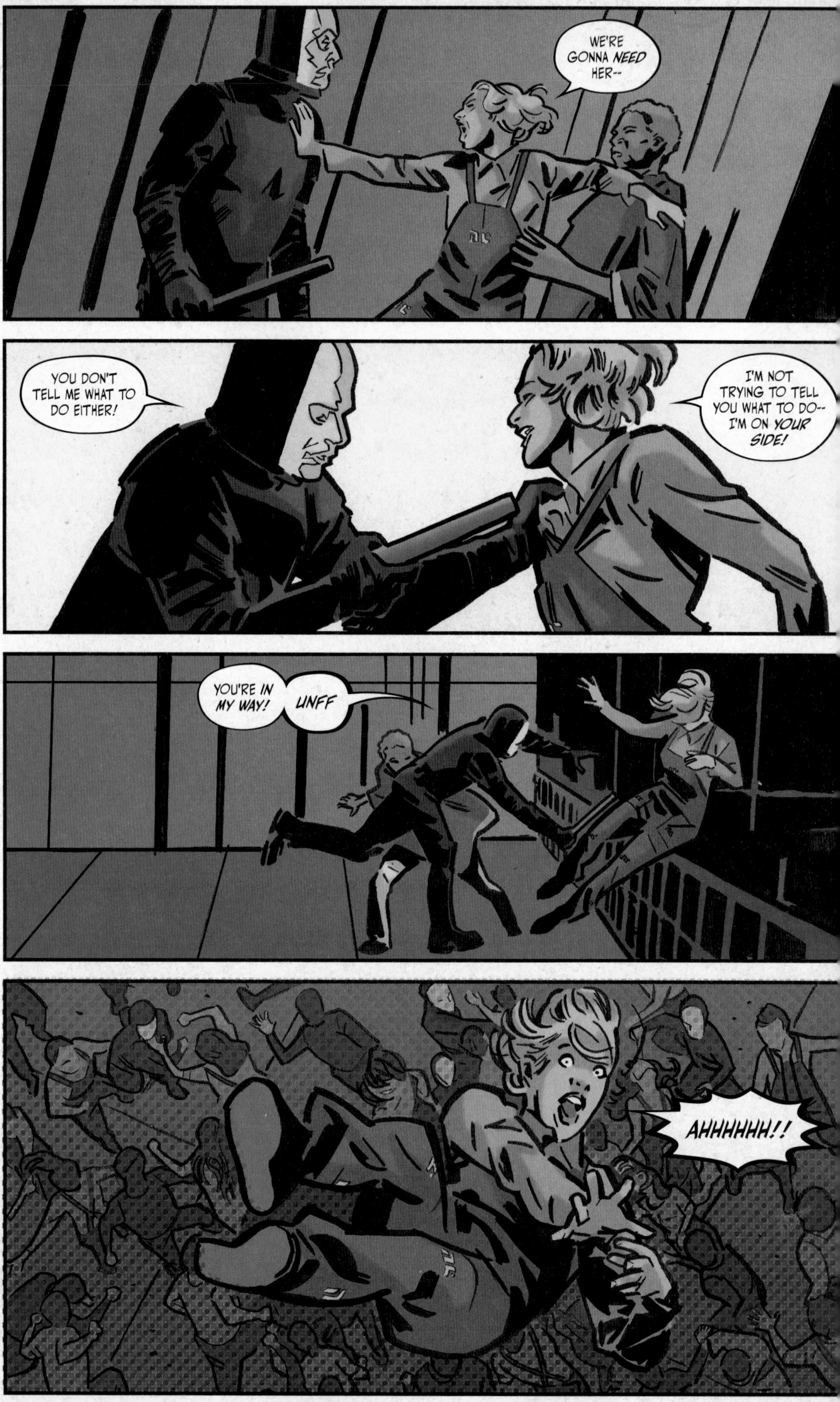
WE'RE GONNA NEED HER--
YOU DON'T TELL ME WHAT TO DO EITHER!
I'M NOT TRYING TO TELL YOU WHAT TO DO-- I'M ON YOUR SIDE!
YOU'RE IN MY WAY!
UNFF
AHHHHHH!!

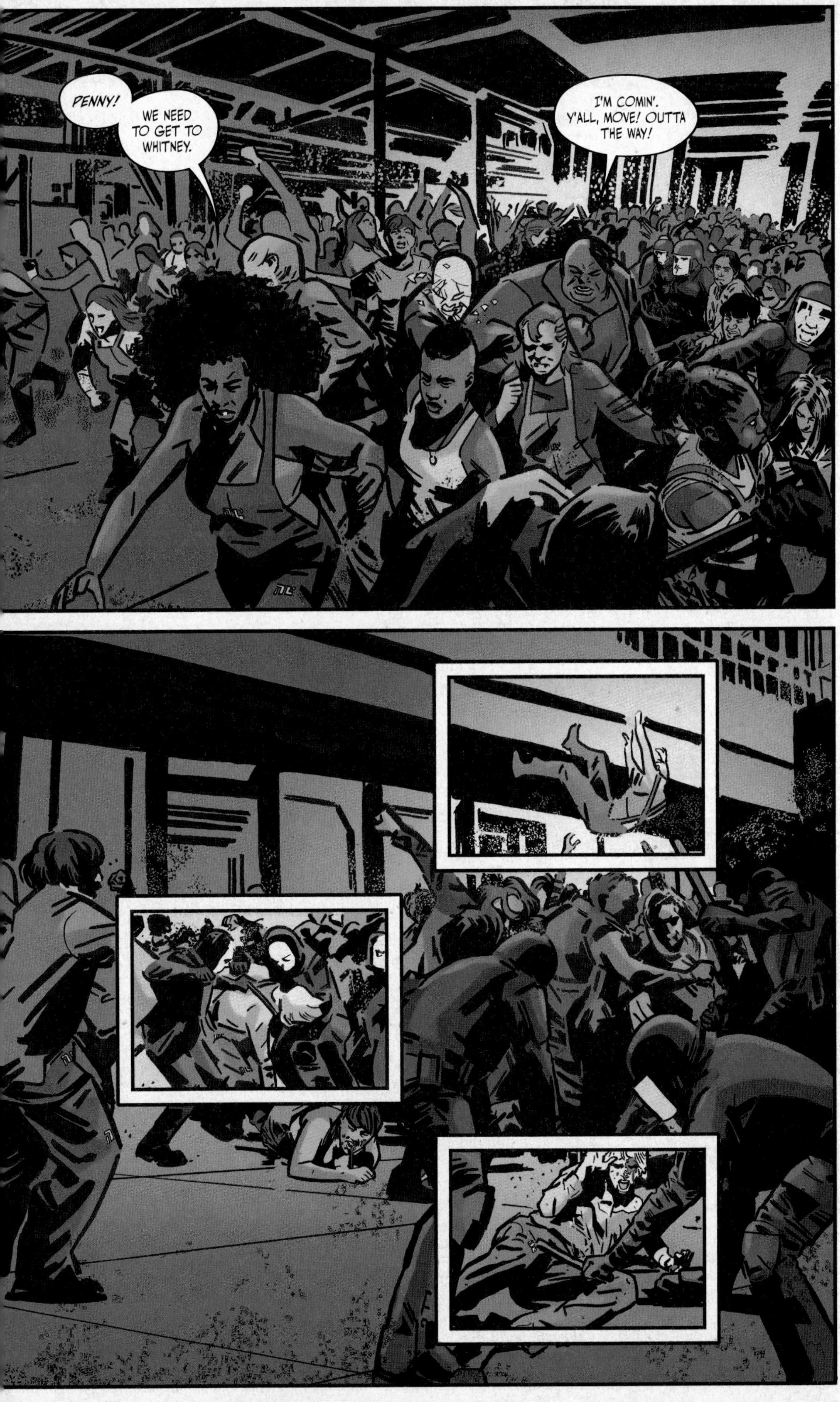
PENNY!
WE NEED TO GET TO WHITNEY.
I'M COMIN'. Y'ALL, MOVE! OUTTA THE WAY!

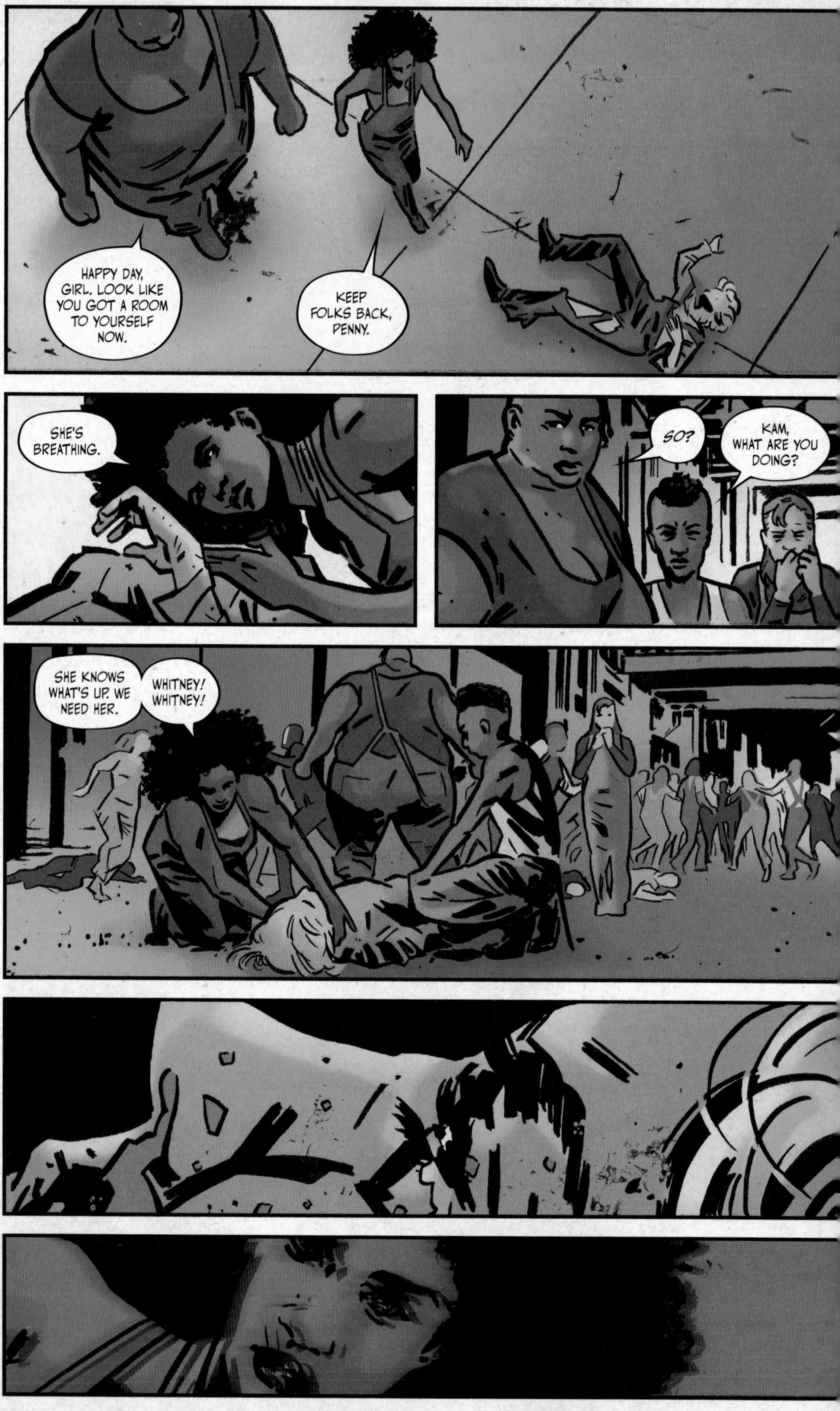
HAPPY DAY, GIRL. LOOK LIKE YOU GOT A ROOM TO YOURSELF NOW.
KEEP FOLKS BACK, PENNY.
SHE'S BREATHING.
SO?
KAM, WHAT ARE YOU DOING?
SHE KNOWS WHAT'S UP. WE NEED HER.
WHITNEY! WHITNEY!

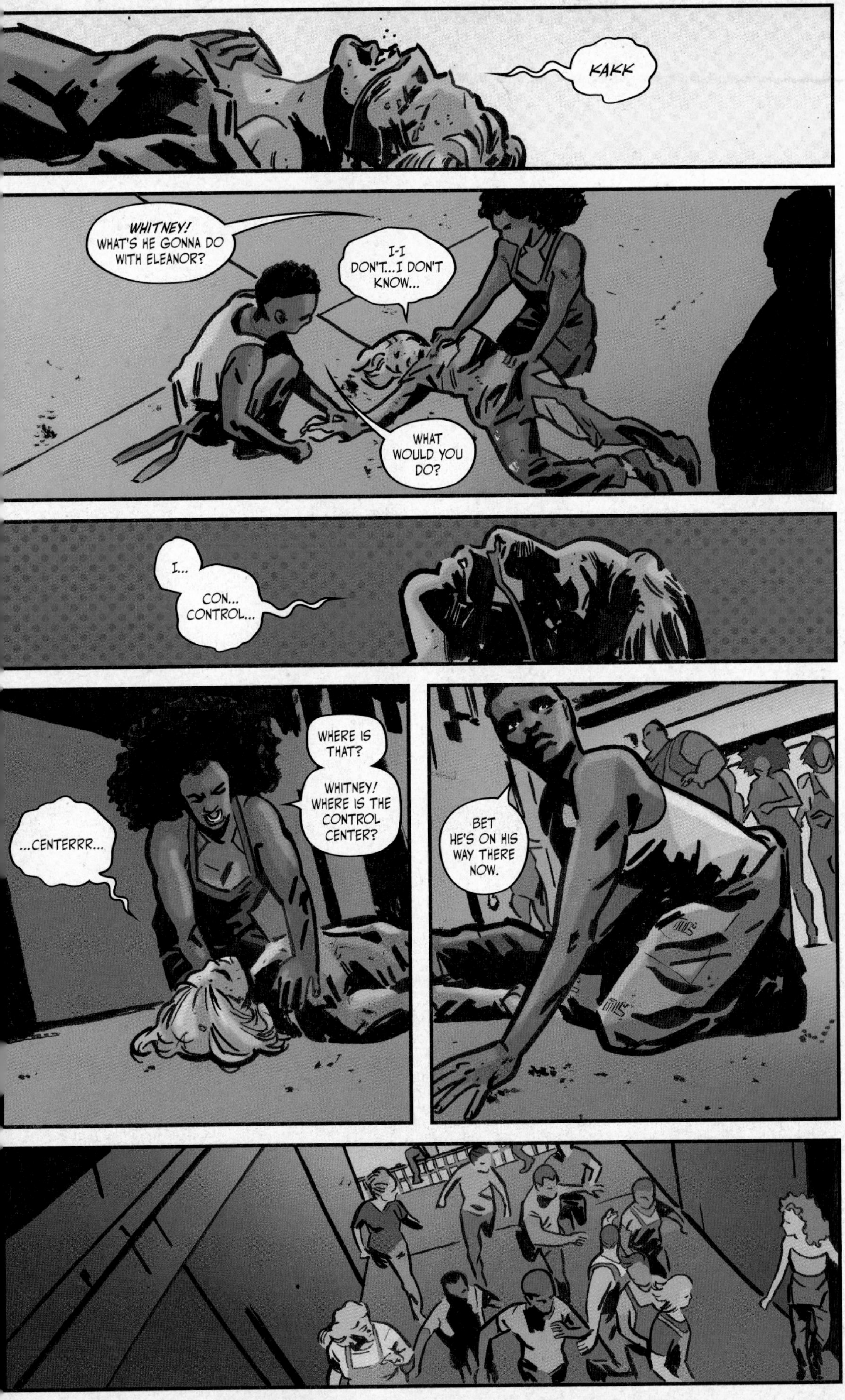
KAKK
WHITNEY! WHAT'S HE GONNA DO WITH ELEANOR?
I-I DON'T...I DON'T KNOW...
WHAT WOULD YOU DO?
I...
CON... CONTROL...
...CENTERRR...
WHERE IS THAT?
WHITNEY! WHERE IS THE CONTROL CENTER?
BET HE'S ON HIS WAY THERE NOW.

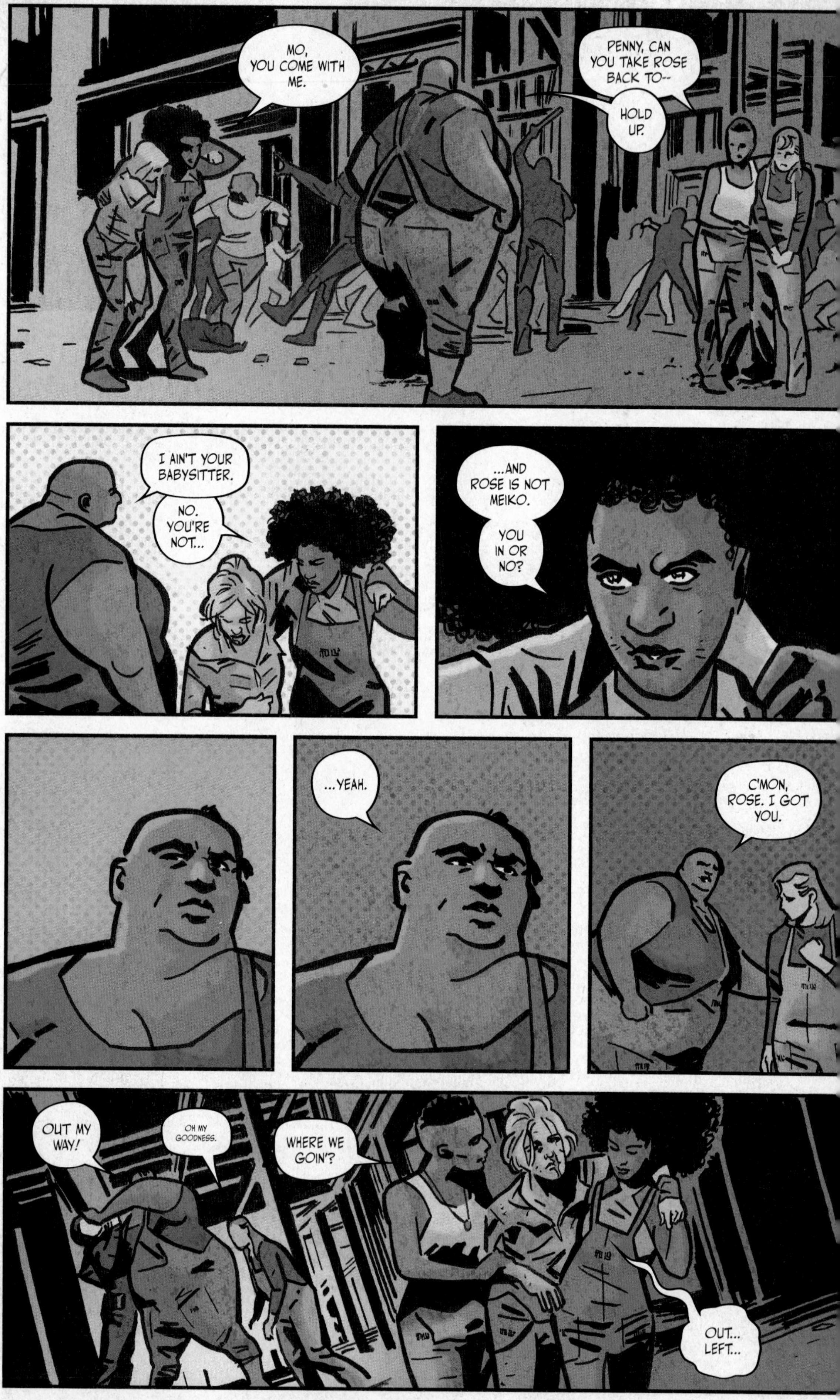
MO, YOU COME WITH ME.
PENNY, CAN YOU TAKE ROSE BACK TO--
HOLD UP.
I AIN'T YOUR BABYSITTER.
NO. YOU'RE NOT...
...AND ROSE IS NOT MEIKO.
YOU IN OR NO?
...YEAH.
C'MON, ROSE. I GOT YOU.
OUT MY WAY!
OH MY GOODNESS.
WHERE WE GOIN'?
OUT... LEFT...

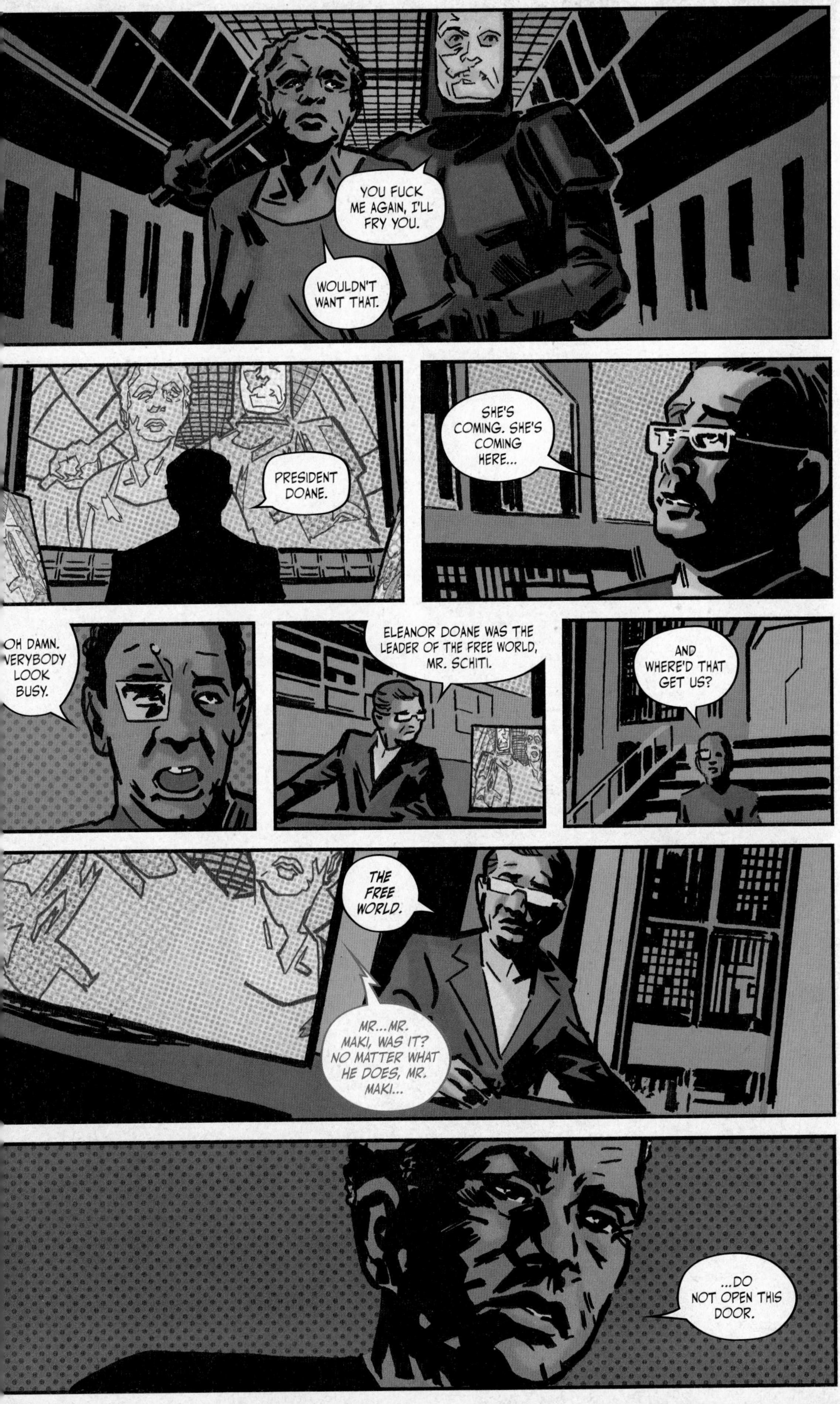
YOU FUCK ME AGAIN, I'LL FRY YOU.
WOULDN'T WANT THAT.
PRESIDENT DOANE.
SHE'S COMING. SHE'S COMING HERE...
OH DAMN. EVERYBODY LOOK BUSY.
ELEANOR DOANE WAS THE LEADER OF THE FREE WORLD, MR. SCHITI.
AND WHERE'D THAT GET US?
THE FREE WORLD.
MR... MR. MAKI, WAS IT? NO MATTER WHAT HE DOES, MR. MAKI...
...DO NOT OPEN THIS DOOR.

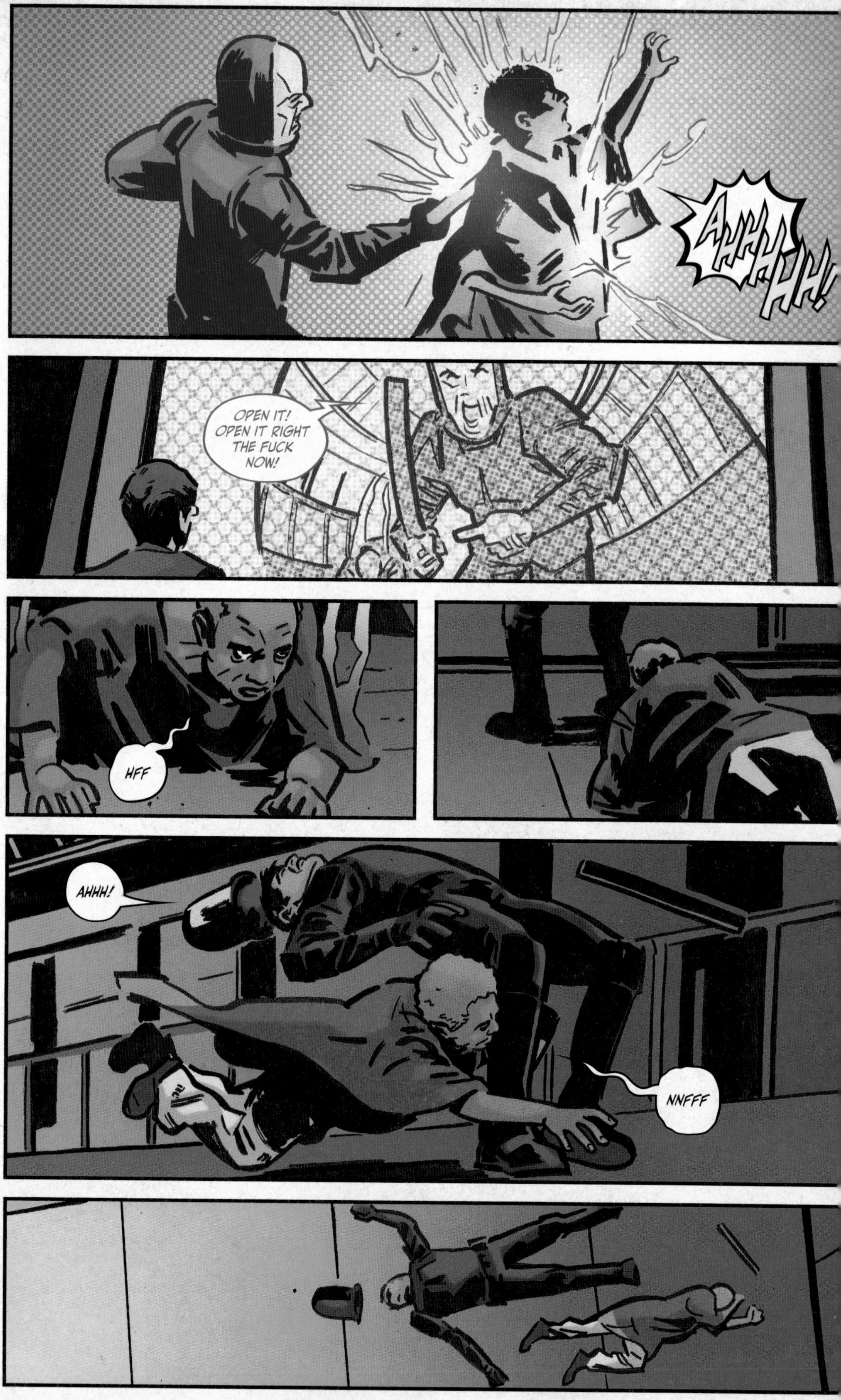
AHHHHH!
OPEN IT! OPEN IT RIGHT THE FUCK NOW!
HFF
AHHH!
NNFFF

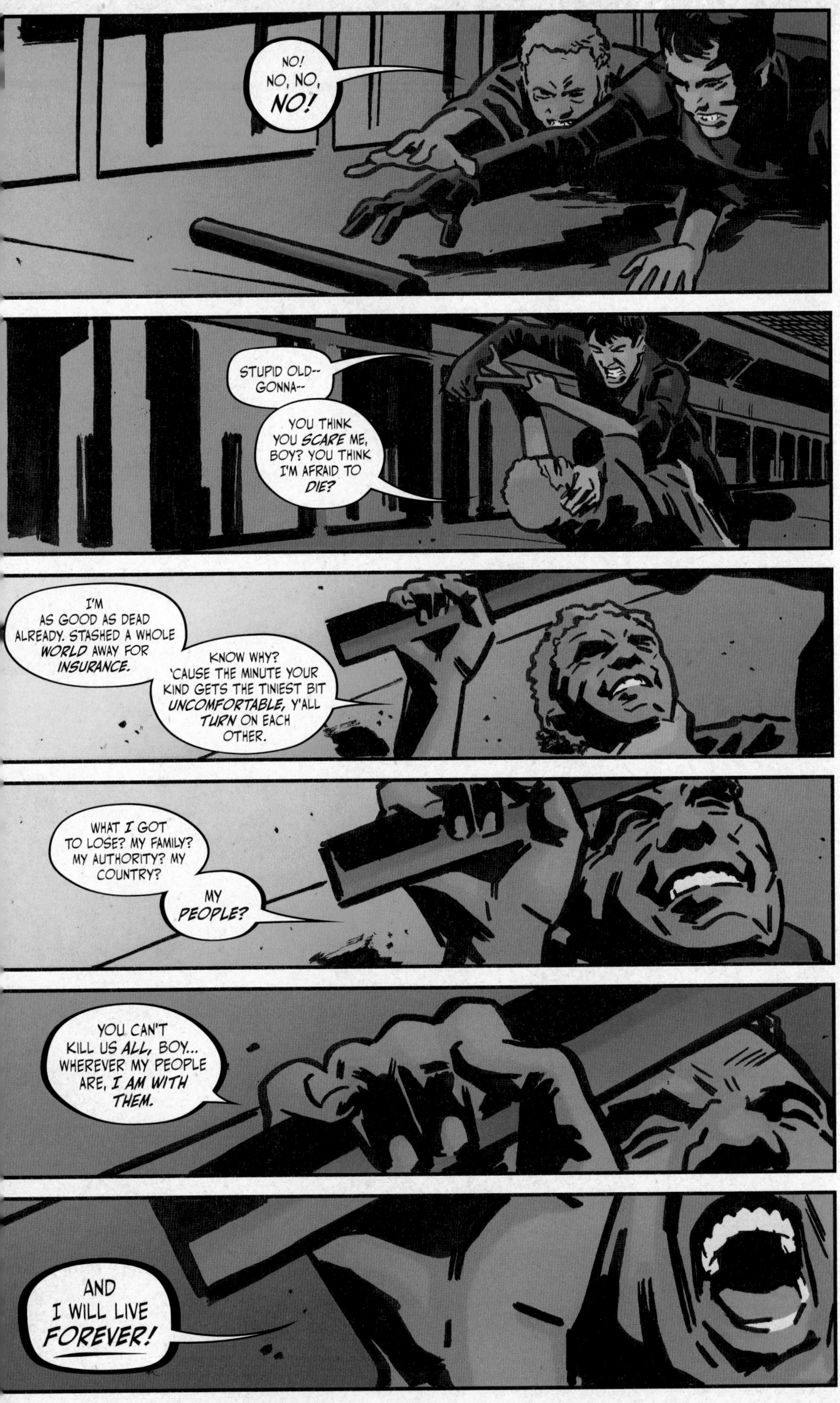
NO! NO, NO, NO!
STUPID OLD-- GONNA--
YOU THINK YOU SCARE ME, BOY? YOU THINK I'M AFRAID TO DIE?
I'M AS GOOD AS DEAD ALREADY. STASHED A WHOLE WORLD AWAY FOR INSURANCE.
KNOW WHY? 'CAUSE THE MINUTE YOUR KIND GETS THE TINIEST BIT UNCOMFORTABLE, Y'ALL TURN ON EACH OTHER.
WHAT I GOT TO LOSE? MY FAMILY? MY AUTHORITY? MY COUNTRY?
MY PEOPLE?
YOU CAN'T KILL US ALL, BOY... WHEREVER MY PEOPLE ARE, I AM WITH THEM.
AND I WILL LIVE FOREVER!

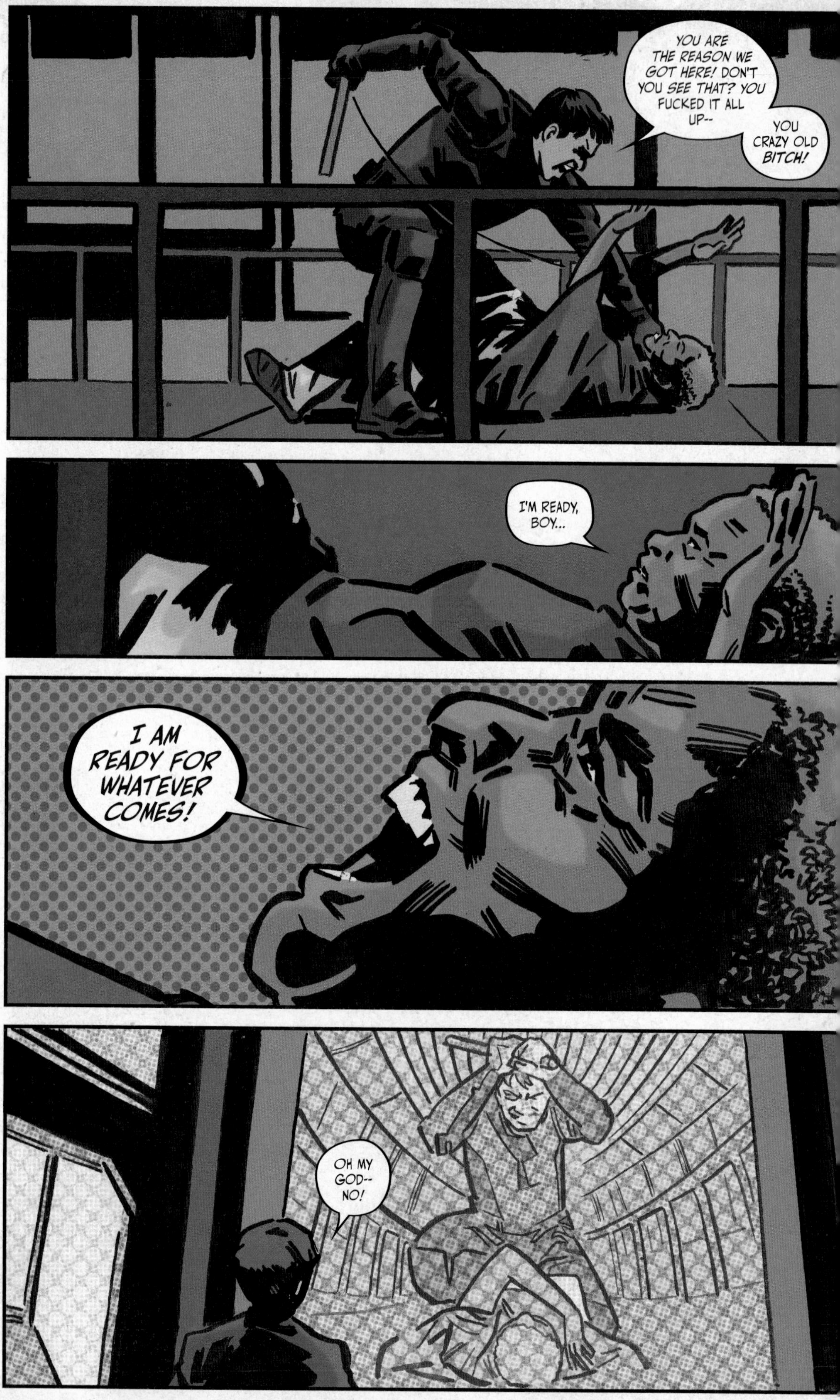
YOU ARE THE REASON WE GOT HERE! DON'T YOU SEE THAT? YOU FUCKED IT ALL UP--
YOU CRAZY OLD BITCH!
I'M READY, BOY...
I AM READY FOR WHATEVER COMES!
OH MY GOD-- NO!

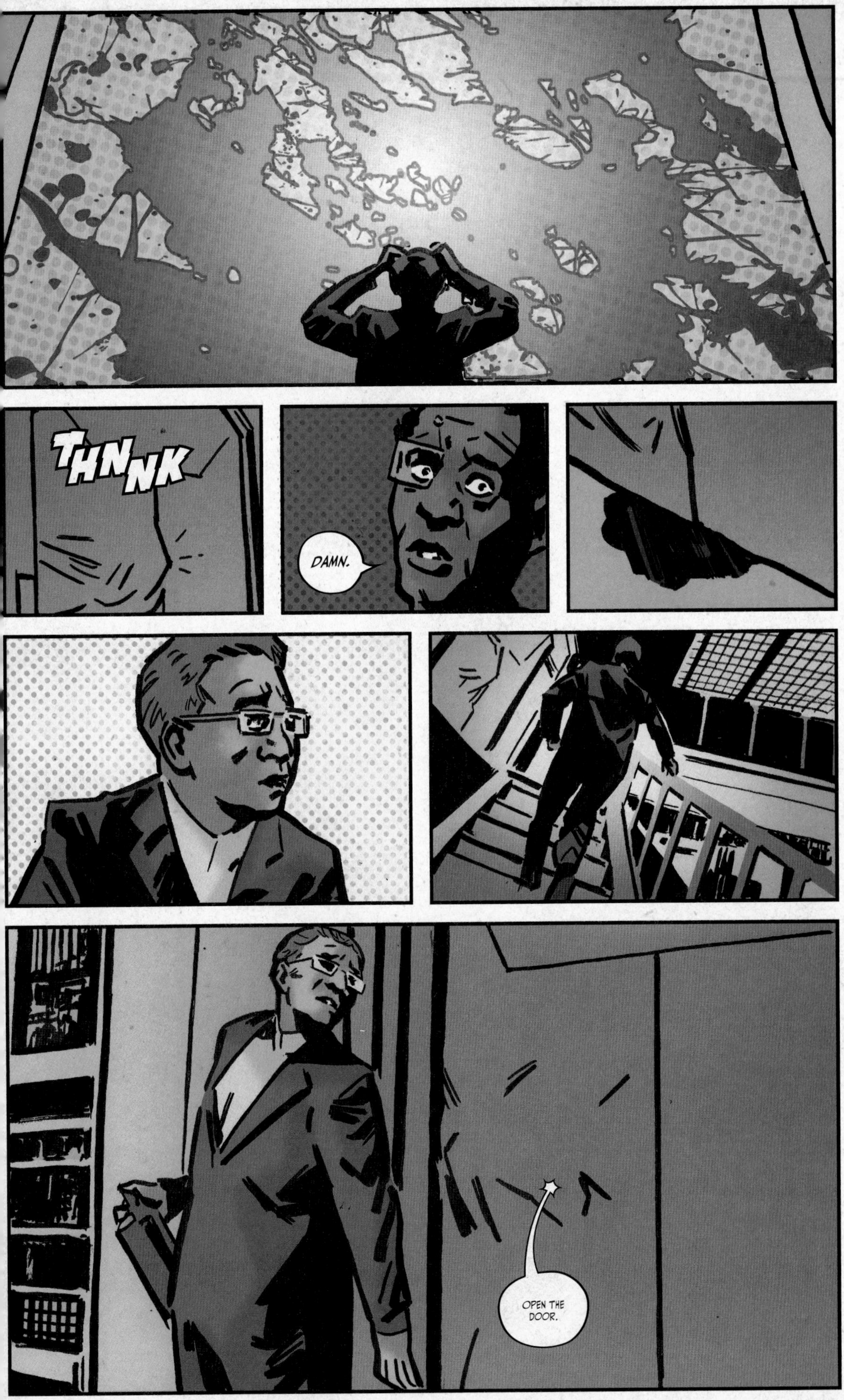
THNNK
DAMN.
OPEN THE DOOR.

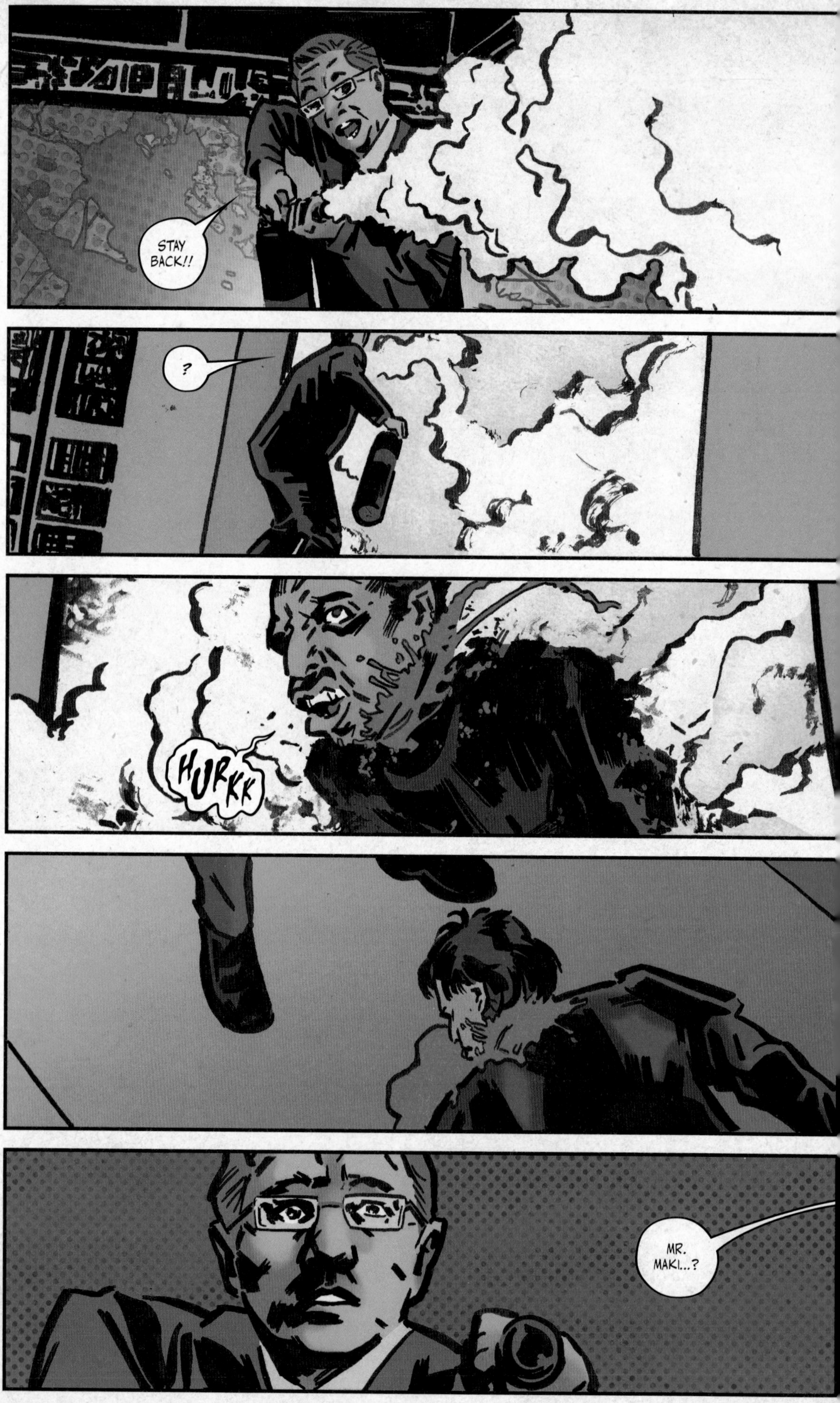
STAY BACK!!
?
HURKK
MR. MAKI...?

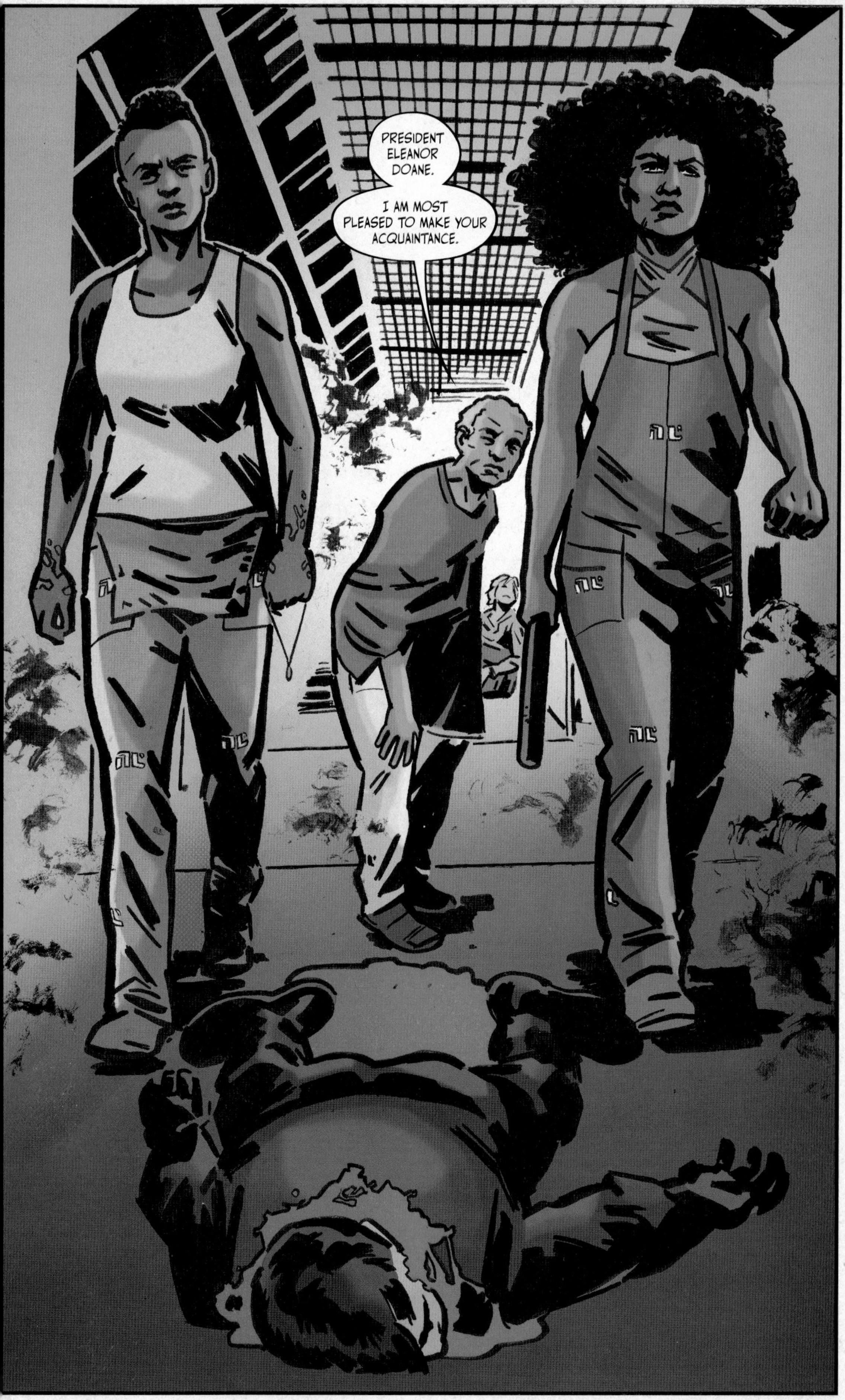
PRESIDENT ELEANOR DOANE.
I AM MOST PLEASED TO MAKE YOUR ACQUAINTANCE.

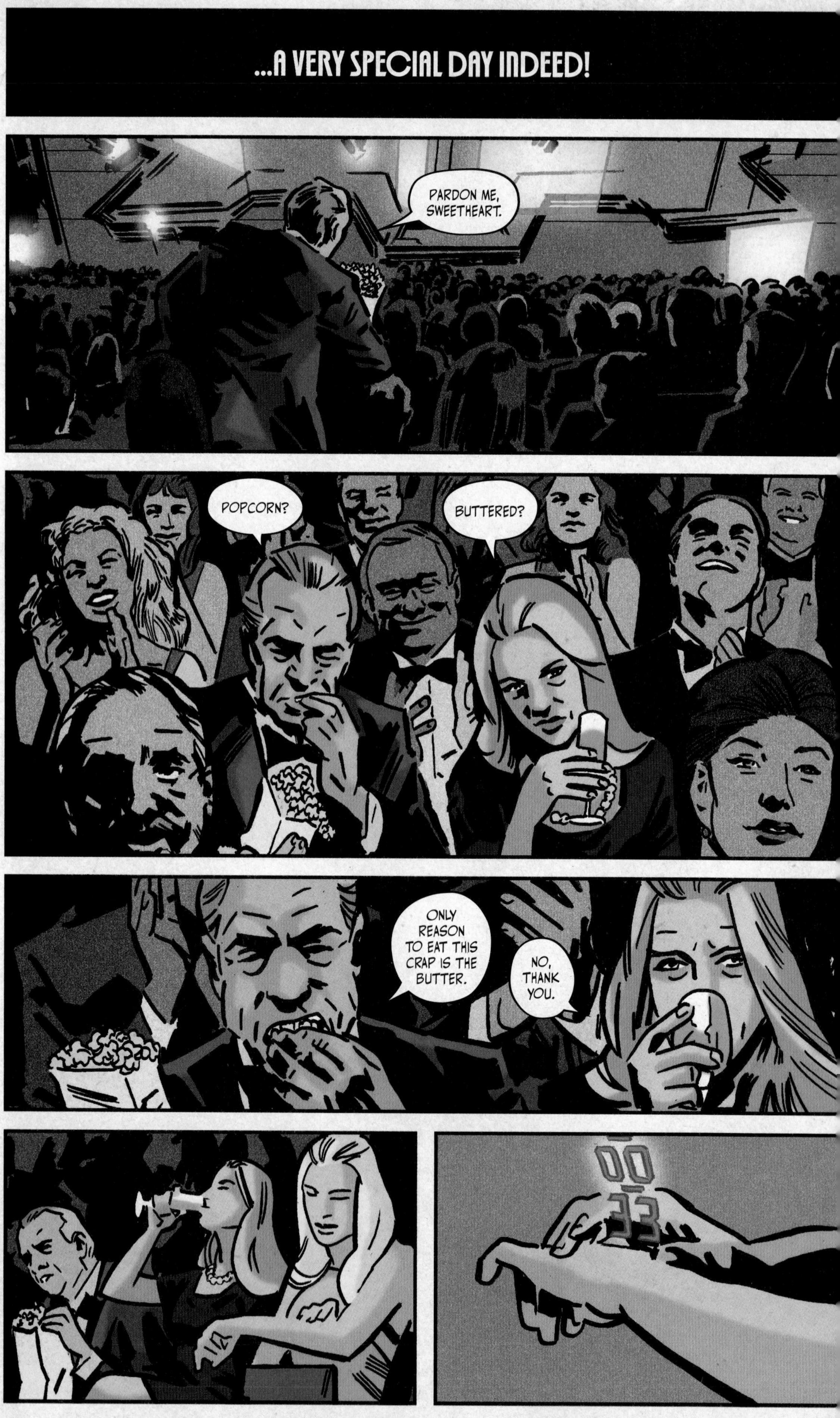
...A VERY SPECIAL DAY INDEED!
PARDON ME, SWEETHEART.
POPCORN?
BUTTERED?
ONLY REASON TO EAT THIS CRAP IS THE BUTTER.
NO, THANK YOU.

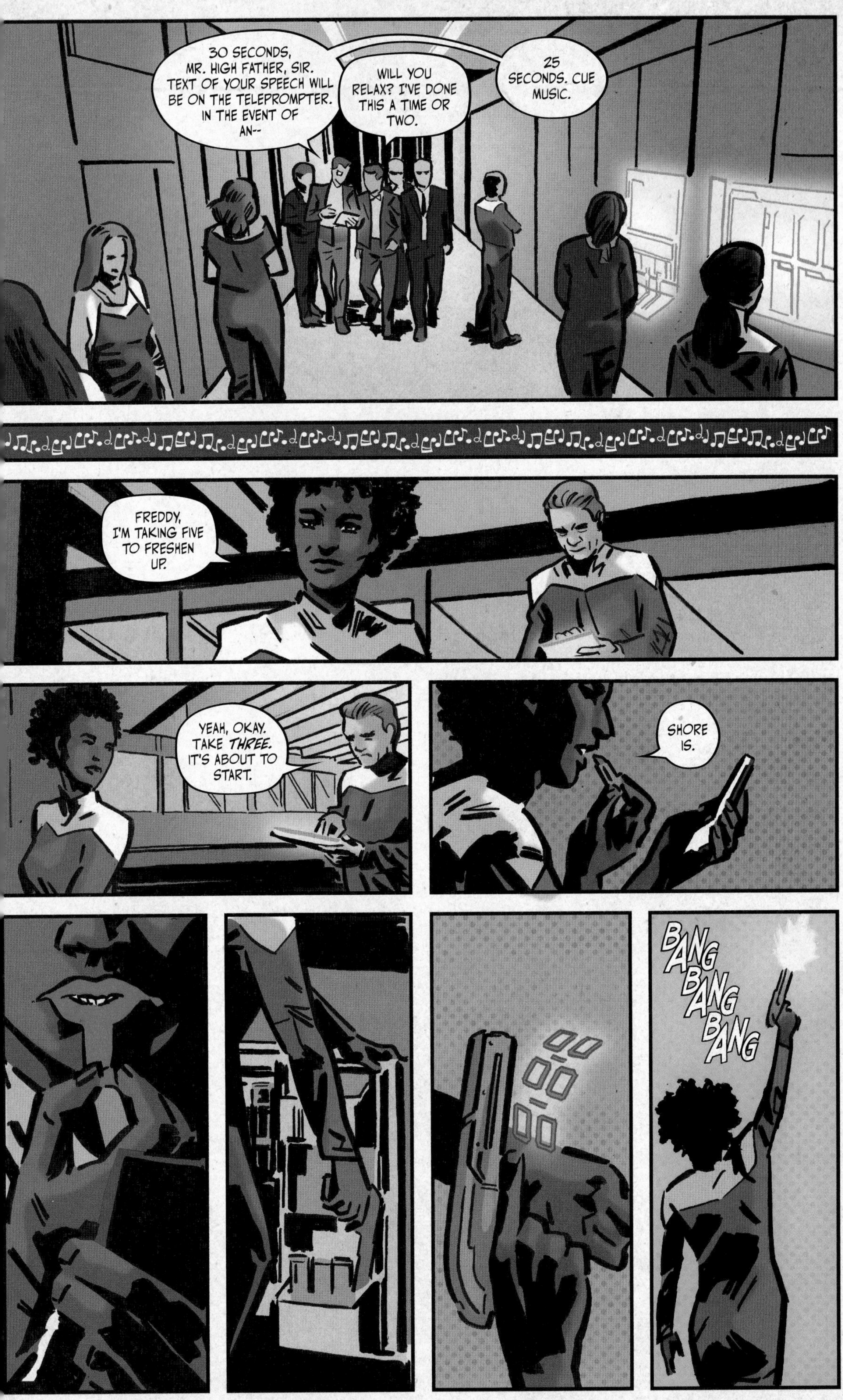
30 SECONDS, MR. HIGH FATHER, SIR. TEXT OF YOUR SPEECH WILL BE ON THE TELEPROMPTER. IN THE EVENT OF AN--
WILL YOU RELAX? I'VE DONE THIS A TIME OR TWO.
25 SECONDS. CUE MUSIC.
FREDDY, I'M TAKING FIVE TO FRESHEN UP.
YEAH, OKAY. TAKE THREE. IT'S ABOUT TO START.
SHORE IS.
BANG BANG BANG

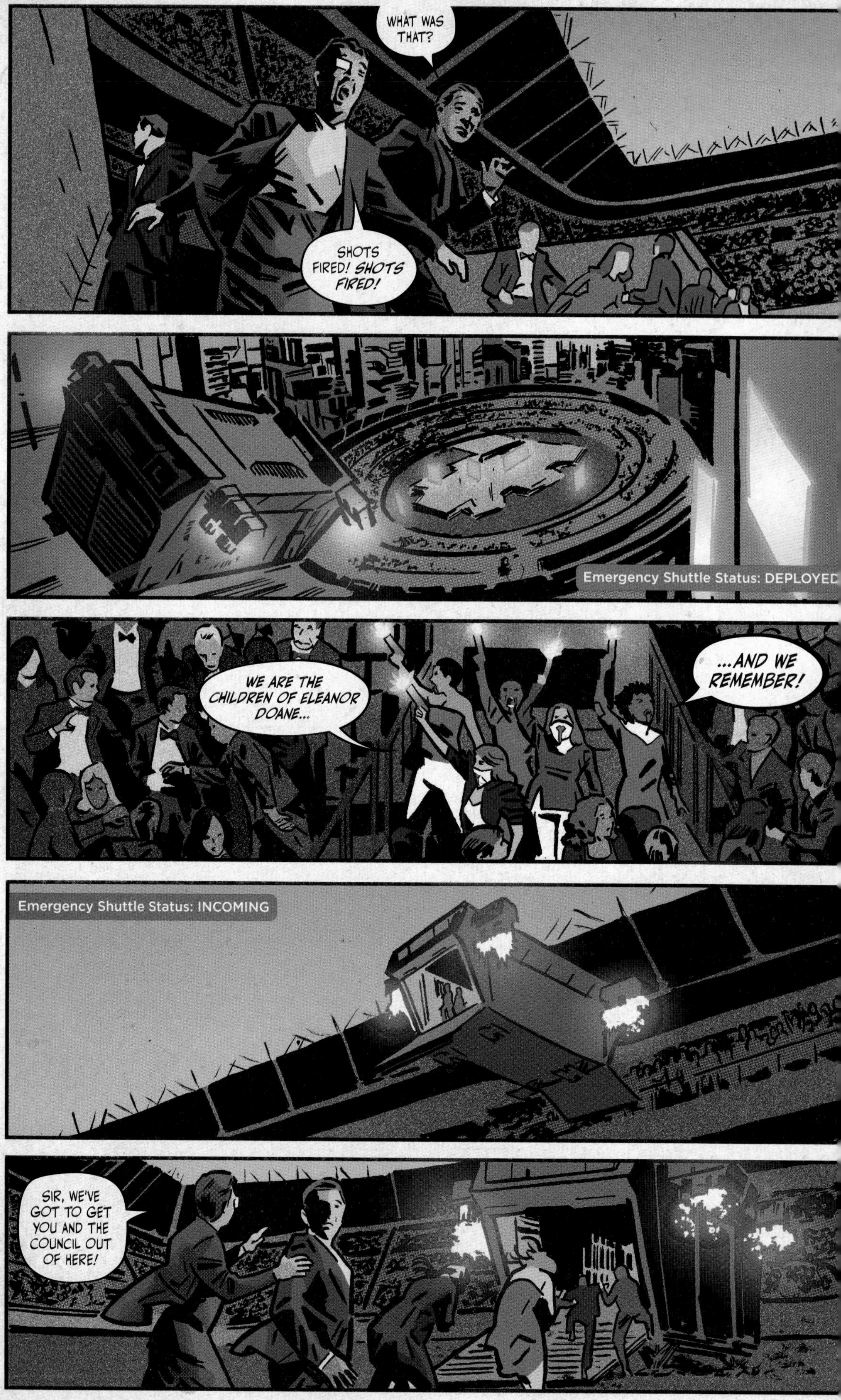

WHAT WAS THAT?
SHOTS FIRED! SHOTS FIRED!
Emergency Shuttle Status: DEPLOYED
WE ARE THE CHILDREN OF ELEANOR DOANE...
...AND WE REMEMBER!
Emergency Shuttle Status: INCOMING
SIR, WE'VE GOT TO GET YOU AND THE COUNCIL OUT OF HERE!

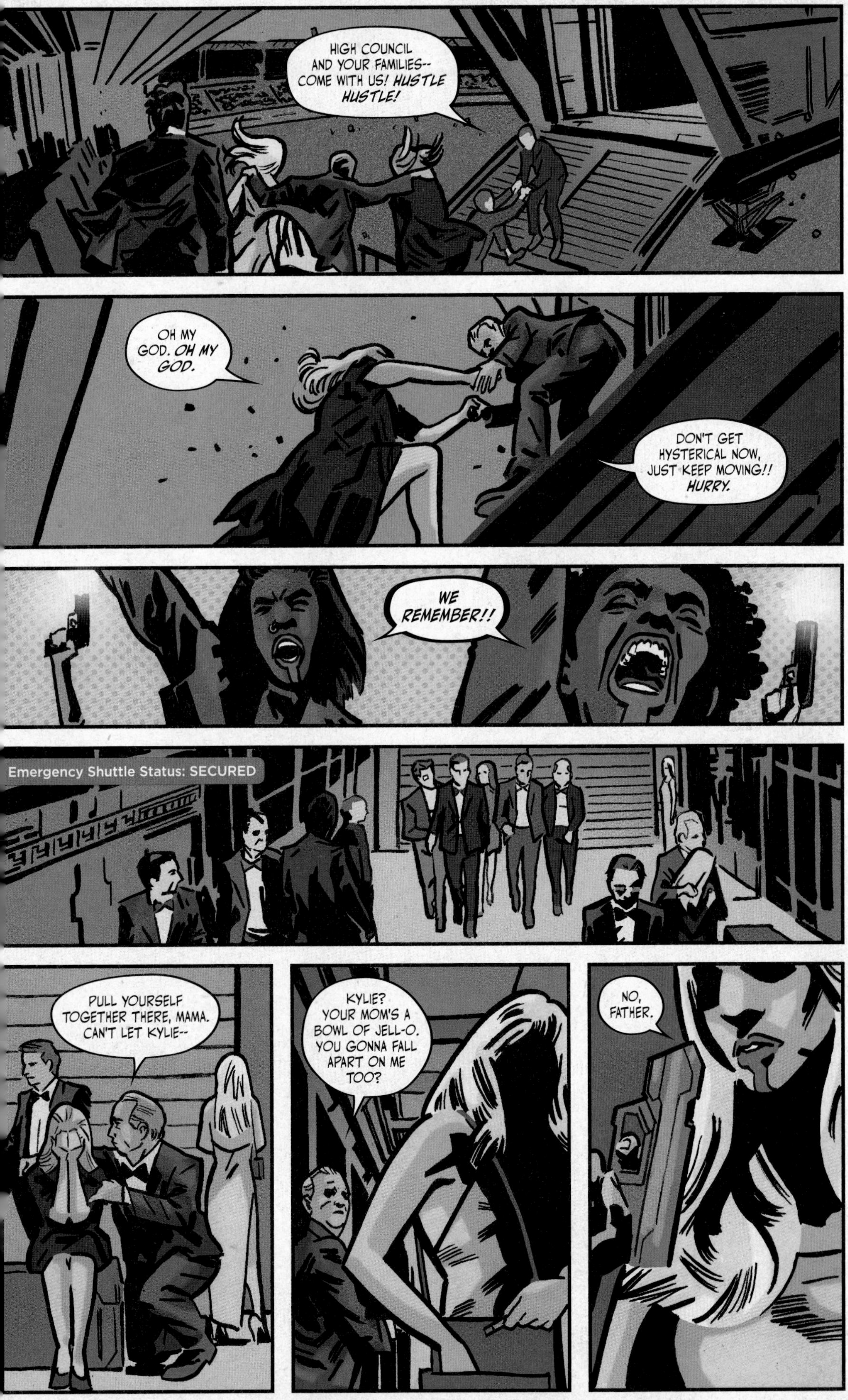
HIGH COUNCIL AND YOUR FAMILIES-- COME WITH US! HUSTLE HUSTLE!
OH MY GOD. OH MY GOD.
DON'T GET HYSTERICAL NOW, JUST KEEP MOVING!! HURRY.
WE REMEMBER!!
Emergency Shuttle Status: SECURED
PULL YOURSELF TOGETHER THERE, MAMA. CAN'T LET KYLIE--
KYLIE? YOUR MOM'S A BOWL OF JELL-O. YOU GONNA FALL APART ON ME TOO?
NO, FATHER.

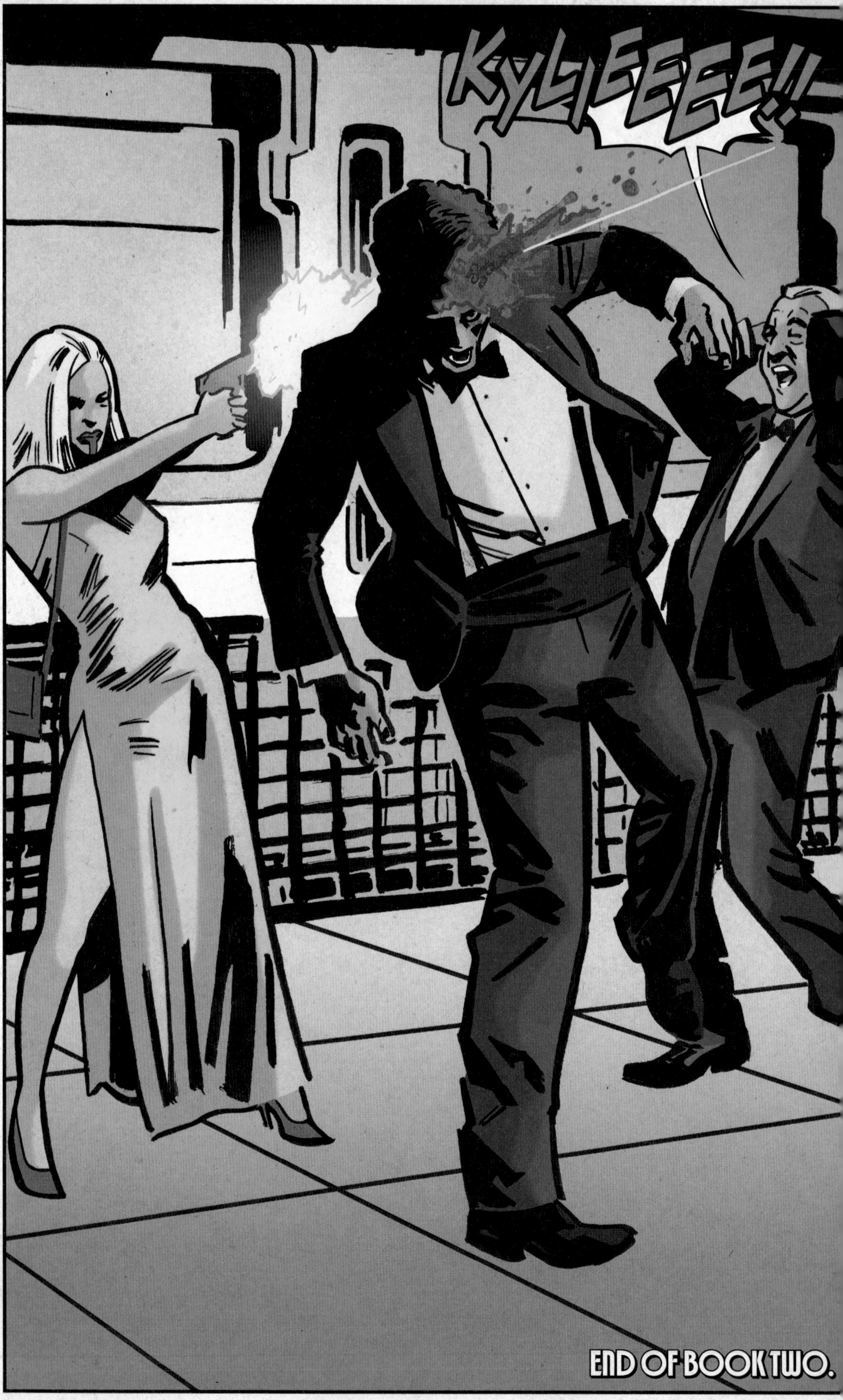
KYLIEEEE!!
END OF BOOK TWO.

Compliant Woman's Weekly

Keeping you in line since 2017!

Always Stressed?
Gaining an Unsightly Middle?

YOUR BRAIN IS MAKING YOU FAT!

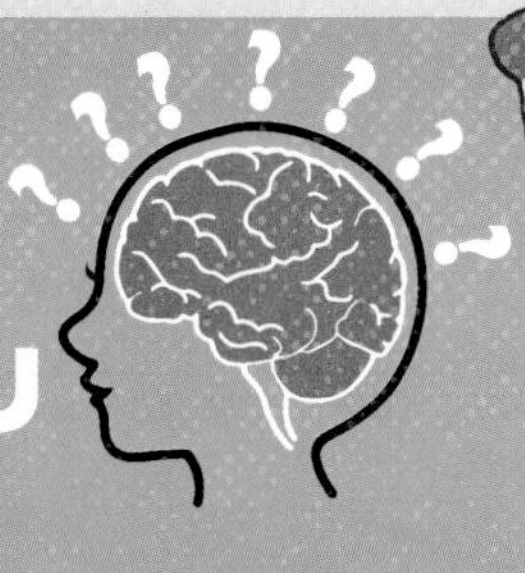

It thinks you should EAT when you are HUNGRY — Silly Brain!
Can your brain tell which of these articles are REAL? Email your guess to blahblahblah@bitchpla.net to find out!

page 20

HAILEY & KAILEY

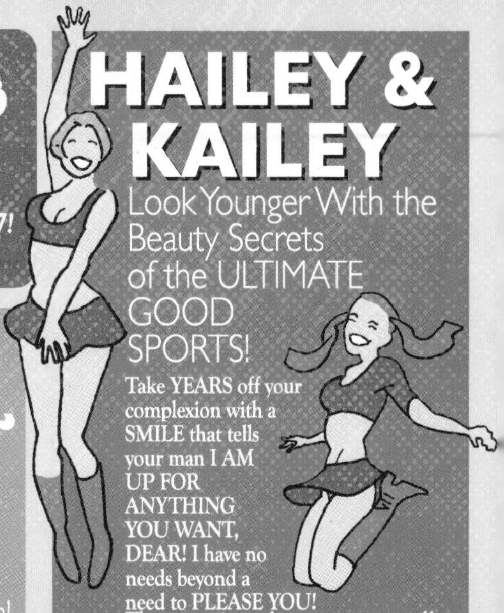

Look Younger With the Beauty Secrets of the ULTIMATE GOOD SPORTS!

Take YEARS off your complexion with a SMILE that tells your man I AM UP FOR ANYTHING YOU WANT, DEAR! I have no needs beyond a need to PLEASE YOU! These practices take so many years off your life you'll look like a fetus. A SEXY, SEXY DTF FETUS!

HOLO-MODELS TELL ALL!

page 45

Celebrate Your Friendships!

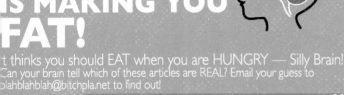

The women in your life are the center of your world. But be careful! Besties can be the Worsties, demanding time and attention you owe to your family first. This simple quiz tells you if it's time to tell your "B-F-F" "B-Y-E."

page 35

---

3 WAYS TO FIND *MORE* TIME!

Organize Your Mess!

It can be hard to keep an organized home — and let's face it ladies, men are no help around the house! Instead of working against him, work WITH him. Does he always leave his socks by the bed? Start keeping a small laundry basket right there — problem solved!

Be More Efficient!

Plan Ahead and Plan to Plan! Did you know the average woman has a half an hour of free time a week? If you're like me, you're asking—Where's mine?! Find it by keeping a "mom" calendar of everyone's activities. Don't forget to carve out 30 minutes for you — you're worth it!

Nobody Likes A Whiner!

We all face disappointments, but taking yours to the internet or even the hair salon is a bad look. Keep a journal of your fuss and counter every complaint with two items of gratitude. You'll feel better in no time!

How's Your Husband's Disposition?

Is he irritable, moody, hard to please?

You feel discouraged, hurt—but it is probably all your own fault! Disposition depends largely on digestion–you don't cook him well-balanced meals. Fats, vitamins, carbohydrates, proteins, minerals—all of them are needed to keep the human machine in good running order. Valuable facts on nutrition are available in

The New BUTTERICK COOK BOOK

page 19

Breakthrough research:
Bird Droppings
PREVENT WRINKLES!

Powerful anti-aging treatments are one step closer now that scientists have isolated the enzyme responsible for youthful skin in the most UNLIKELY of places! The secret to combating decreased bio-energy and harmful free radicals is as close as the nearest statue.

page 31

Surprising *FAT-BURNING* Foods!

Called NEGATIVE CALORIE FOODS, these 15 "superfoods" may not contain any actual "nutrients" but they do burn more calories in their digestion than they bring in, so go ahead and for once in your life EAT YOUR FILL!

page 17

On the issue 7 opening scene (shown right):

KELLY SUE: I was at a birthday swim party with my daughter, making small talk with other parents, and one dad and I got onto roleplaying games. Turned out he ran a dystopian game of some sort (I'm sorry I don't remember the details—it may have been one of his own design). I told him about BP and we chatted elements we thought were modern horrors. I brought up corporate personhood and he told me, in his game, the rights afforded by the second amendment were extended to corporate "persons."

I don't know why that had never occurred to me before—it's apparently a fairly common concern on the topic—but it hadn't, and I remember getting chills.

Every issue—except the spotlight issues—begins with an opening twelve-panel grid, divided into six and six, most often with six panels of high status and six panels of low status (sometimes public and private—the nature of the binary isn't set in stone). Here, I wanted to force myself to consider how the horror of Trayvon Martin and Tamir Rice could become even more casual in a situation where a corporation was afforded the protections of something like "stand your ground."

BITCH PLANET SKETCHBOOK
Conversations with Kelly Sue and Valentine

On the issue 8 introduction of the Facility One prisoners (Images after page turn):

KELLY SUE: We can't really talk about this scene without talking about Emma, Mey and Aria—the trans women who acted as consultants for us. The book is so much better for their work.

VALENTINE: We've been so lucky to have generous people to consult with. I'm glad that they were willing to help us with the introduction to these characters.

KELLY SUE: Initially, I thought we should reprint the panel description for the first panel in full here and talk about what changed after our consultants had a look, but—ha ha—the panel description is 1008 words. That...that is insane. My panel descriptions (aside from first issues, which are always wordier because of worldbuilding) usually average around thirty words.

VALENTINE: This was the most considerate panel description I've ever read.

KELLY SUE: The most CONSIDERED I've ever written to be sure, but still, a lot to saddle you with. I'm going to pull out a couple

And this is what we got.

I "love" the body language of the security guard in particular; how walled off he is from the humanity of the children.

VALENTINE: It's all in a day's work for him. He'd rather just put in his time and punch the clock. Instead there's this nuisance. If he spends one second longer on it, that threatens his mandatory break time.

The striking thing about this scene for me is how much it reminds me of my own after-school walk from home. I used to get off the school bus with my younger cousin and sister. We'd walk and cut through the parking lot of a commercial property. But we weren't allowed to.

We'd get hollered at by the superintendent sometimes if he saw us. There were some liability issues for the building, I'm sure. We were kids essentially walking into live traffic. But we had a five-minute walk and our cartoons started at three. This shortcut was necessary.

I feel like it's always something so innocuous that precedes these horrible events. Trying to save a few minutes on our trek from school. Out buying a bag of Skittles.

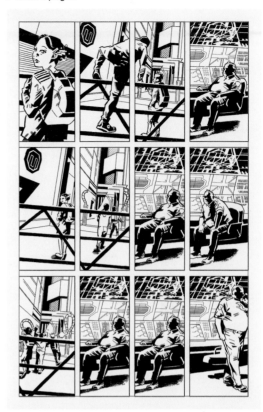

of excerpts instead of reprinting in full.

[See p2]. Here's a note to Kelly Fitzpatrick, our colorist, on why the trans women and cis women should have differently colored overalls:

> This gives us a simple visual shorthand for who is trans going forward so we don't need to have any awkward exposition or a display of anatomy that doesn't mean anything anyway; and once the facilities are mingled, seeing the various expressions of gender across the trans and cis women should drive home the fact that gender is a spectrum, as we'll see folks in both colors of overalls presenting all over that spectrum.

VALENTINE: You had a really great idea here. It visually unifies and separates the inmates at the same time. Seeing it with Fitz's colors brought this to a different level.

KELLY SUE: On presentation of anatomy:

> Many of these women, if not most, will have penises. This is a fact that we want to show without fetishizing—no close-ups, no centering of the penis in this frame. Let

that shit dangle where it goes, but we don't want to treat it as any more interesting than we would if we were showing a room full of men with penises, follow? Normalize our presentation. Subtext is: "Some of these women have dicks. Get over it."

(We've never shied away from nudity in our book before and we're not going to start now—but we're not looking to titillate the reader or pass judgment on these bodies in any way.)

VALENTINE: I personally felt a lot of pressure trying to work the layouts and compose the first page of the scene. After we gauged reactions to the introduction of trans characters in comics—and other media—I realized that this is something that we could do both ineffectively and inappropriately.

KELLY SUE: [See p3]. Again, not for us to decide if we've been successful or not, but I love what you did and think your thoughtfulness shows. Some notes on presentation:

> Fathers wouldn't help them transition— they would withhold their meds, deny them

2 Issue 8 page 4

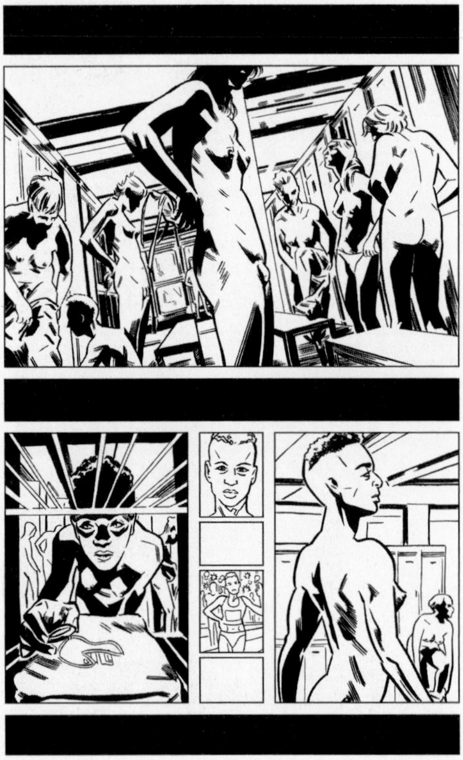

3 Issue 8 page 5

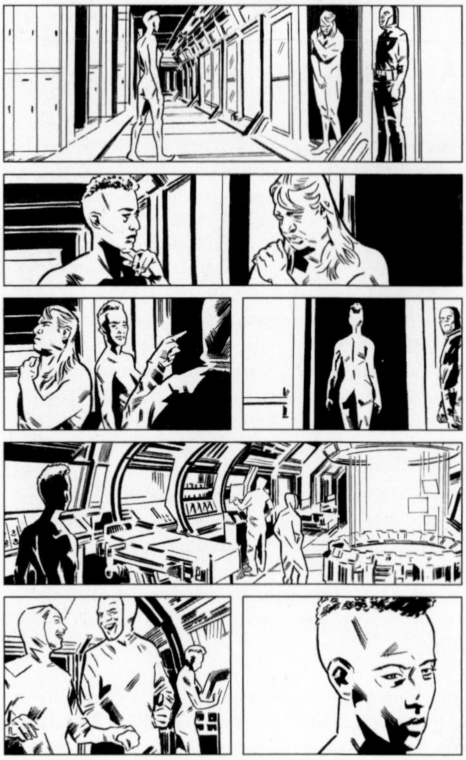

any surgical requests—but I don't think they'd care enough to enforce their notions of masculine presentation. My suspicion is that the women here with short hair would either be the gender fluid (some non-binary/gender fluid characters would be housed in Facility Two as well, dependent upon gender assignment at birth) new, or a few may simple prefer a shorter hairstyle. (This is a sweeping generalization, but my research suggests more trans women prefer to grow their hair out or wear a shoulder-length to long wig because it is still so socially coded as 'feminine' to have long hair. My son Henry Leo was repeatedly misgendered on our cruise, for example, because he has long-ISH hair and delicate features and people read that as "girl.")

I think it was Aria who nudged me away from that generalization about how trans women may choose to present, reminding me that as a straight, cis woman I might be projecting a bit. "Queers gonna queer," she said sweetly.

VALENTINE: Henry Leo's hair is RAD.

KELLY SUE: The fact is not in dispute! For real. But the rest we can rethink.

VALENTINE: [See p4]. Yep, long hair and fair facial composition is still an illustrator's shorthand to represent women. It's how I was taught. Rose has this weird mullet going one. So not short or long. Mo I've always pictured with short hair. Maybe to show a contrast with Kam.

KELLY SUE: On Morowa's anatomy:

My first impulse was to have Morowa be post-op. Kam had money. She would have been able to send her sister away for gender reassignment surgery if she chose. If we went that way, Morowa would be one of very few. In part because the surgery would be expensive and difficult to obtain (and not every woman WANTS the surgery), and in part because post-surgical trans women would have an easier time hiding from authorities. Kam and her sister were well-known professional athletes, and so Morowa couldn't stay hidden.

BUT, I was concerned about having a very traditionally feminine-looking woman be our central trans character—concerned that the unintentional message would be that her body was somehow more acceptable. If we simple refuse to decide

4 *Issue 8 page 6*

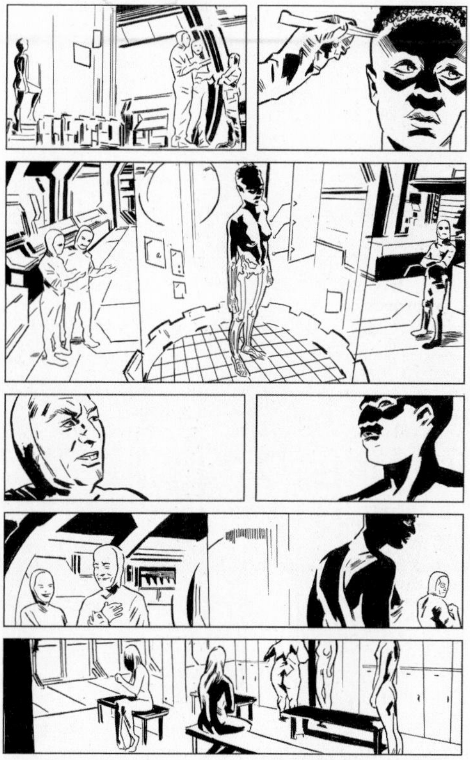

5 *Issue 8 page 7*

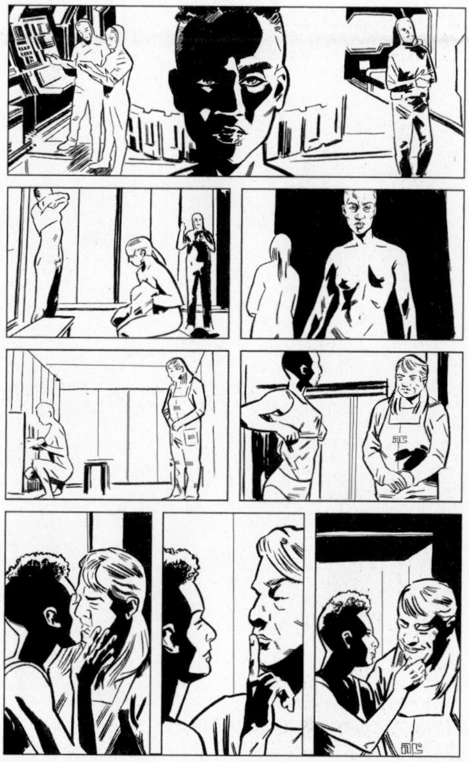

anything about Morowa, we avoid sending that message and because of the variety of bodies and presentations we're still presenting, we're not putting a different standard on trans women than on cis women. We're simply not making a decision about Morowa's anatomy because it's irrelevant and not our business anyway.

VALENTINE: I liked this challenge. A reverse-*reverse* modesty conceal. I think we pulled this off...?

KELLY SUE: I hope? I guess we'll find out. Mo's necklace, as I recall, was one of those things, like Penny's curl, that you added without really knowing why, yeah?

VALENTINE: Yeah, I had an idea for some kind of jewelry that Mo could keep concealed if necessary.

KELLY SUE: I love this part of the collaborative process. Sondheim talks about writing lyrics as being analogous to puzzle-solving, or tickling the same part of his brain anyway. I feel that way about comics collaborations. You write the music, I write the lyrics. You lay down a line that forms the image of the necklace and my job is the solve the puzzle of how it fits.

VALENTINE: Oh, I was relieved when you said you liked solving these things. Pulls my fat out of the fire. I was sure you'd think I was just messing with you. "Hey Kel, here's something I drew. Figure it out, okay?"

KELLY SUE: Nah, I love it. That's collaboration, you know?

Let's talk about Rose. [See p5].

VALENTINE: Ah, Rose. She's a beauty. One of my favorite additions to our cast. That means we have to kill her off, of course.

KELLY SUE: YOU'RE A MONSTER.

VALENTINE: Not untrue.

I think that Rose is coming off gentler in design than I wanted at first. I think it's because of how we've introduced her. Hopefully there's still some runway left to go with her, so we can show her a bit tougher.

You know. Before we kill her off.

KELLY SUE: ...Welp.

ELEANORIANS

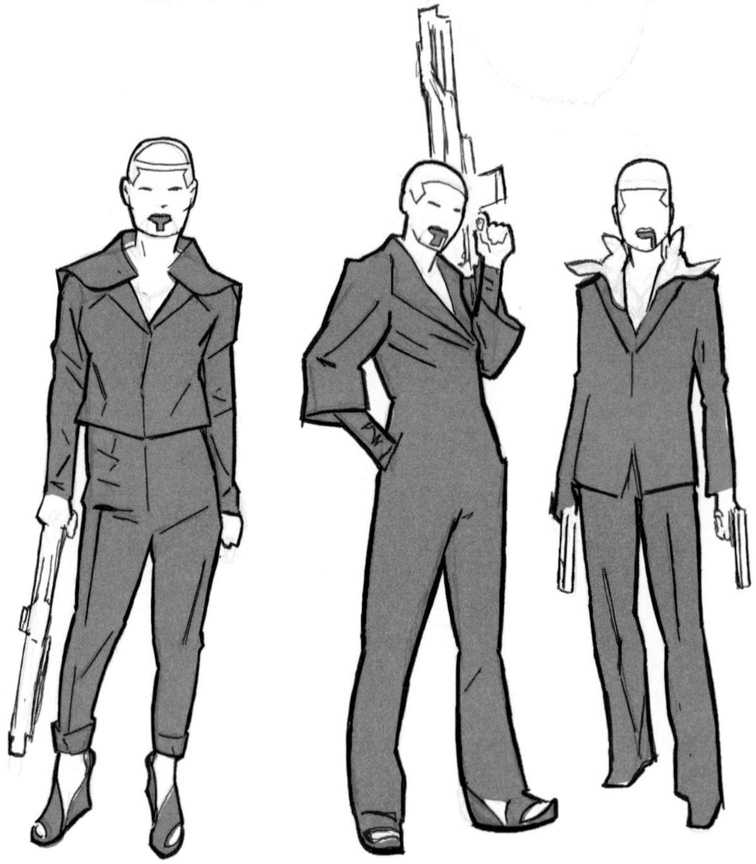

BP MEGATON TEAM

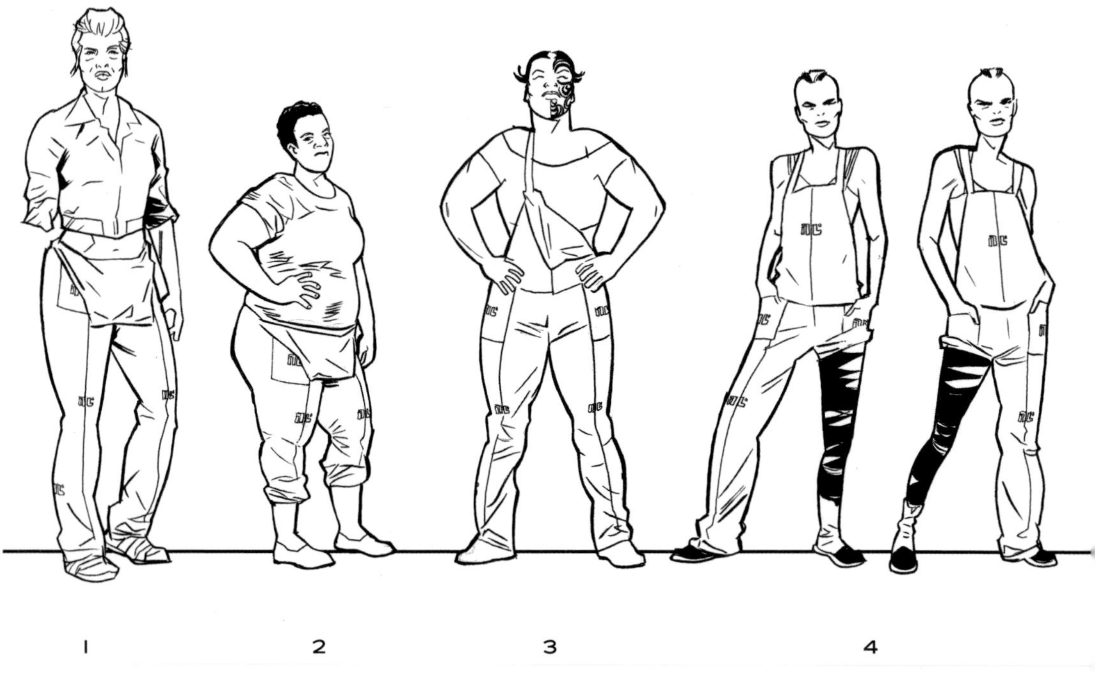
1
2
3
4

VALENTINE'S NOTES:
Thinking of using all of these in some form, unless you think it's better they have a more unified look. I think they should have the same color (Red? Too close to ACO dungarees?)

Nothing more powerful than a woman in a suit.
—Dani V.

Head gear is silver/chrome. (Lights?)

1 **KATRINA "KAT" JAIMES-FREYRE**
WELTERWEIGHT
W: 145 lbs. H: 6ft 2in

2 **DANIELLE ZUBIATE**
CRUISERWEIGHT
W: 180 lbs. H: 5ft 5in

3 **ALIKA "THE HOUSE" KAHALE**
SUPER MIDDLEWEIGHT
W: 164 lbs. H: 5ft 10in

4 **APRIL LIU & MAY LIU**
FEATHERWEIGHT
W: 125 lbs. H: 5ft 7in (EACH)

5 **MARILYN GUNNING**
LIGHT MIDDLEWEIGHT
W: 156 lbs. H: 5ft 2in

6 **NUT SUHAIR**
HEAVYWEIGHT
W: 233 lbs. H: 6ft

BITCH PLANET VOLUME TWO

DISCUSSION GUIDE

By Professor Ben Saunders,
University of Oregon

Professor Ben Saunders is the author
of two books, *Desiring Donne* (Harvard
University Press, 2006) and *Do The
Gods Wear Capes?: Spirituality, Fantasy,
and Superheroes* (Continuum, 2011) and
co-editor of two critical anthologies,
*Rock Over The Edge: Transformations in
Popular Music Culture* (Duke University
Press, 2002) with Roger Beebe and
Denise Fulbrook and *Comic Book
Apocalypse: The Graphic Worlds of Jack
Kirby* (IDW, 2015) with Charles Hatfield.
He has also published numerous essays
on topics ranging from the plays of
Shakespeare to the drumming of Keith
Moon, and curated several exhibitions of
comic art. He founded and currently directs
the Undergraduate Minor in Comics
Studies at the University of Oregon (the
first Minor of its kind in the country).

● This volume of *Bitch Planet* is filled with women (CIS and trans) who have been denied the most basic freedoms and who nevertheless refuse to be "compliant." Their stories can be very moving and compelling. Which struck you as most powerful, and why?

● Not all the male characters in *Bitch Planet* are happy living in an anti-feminist society. Makoto Maki is the most obvious example of a man who rejects the culture of male dominance. He not only attempts to subvert the system through technological sabotage, but also struggles to raise two daughters to be safe and strong, despite the fact that they live in a world that oppresses women. How would you describe his parenting style?

● How else is the role of father imagined in a culture that insists women must always be subservient and men dominant? Is it possible for a man to be a "good" father in such a world? What other ideas about fathers and fathering do you see at work in the text?

● Not all the female characters in *Bitch Planet* reject the anti-feminist culture in which they live. Operative Whitney Nestpas clearly thinks the system can work in her favor. Even when she is reduced to the status of those she once helped to oppress, Whitney still does not see herself as one of them. (She shows no guilt over Meiko's death, for example, and when she discovers Kam's map of the complex she calls for the guards.) What kinds of fears, desires or beliefs might prompt someone from an oppressed group to collude with a system that sustains that oppression?

● How might factors such as race, education, wealth or other forms of privilege factor into Whitney's decision to collaborate with a male-dominated hierarchy?

● Whitney happily works within a prejudiced prison system that incarcerates women of color at a much higher rate than white women; nevertheless, she accuses another character (Eleanor Doane) of racism. What do you think about this moment? Can you think of any real-life examples of a privileged white person attacking a person of color for being racist?

● *Bitch Planet* is sometimes described as a satire. Satire is a genre that often employs exaggeration, distortion, and cruel humor in order to make a social or political point. What aspects of *Bitch Planet* strike you as satirical? For example, can you point to a specific moment where an act of exaggeration or caricature (either visual or at the level of plot) is clearly intended as a commentary upon contemporary western society?

● This volume of *Bitch Planet* introduces us to the trans women of Facility One. DeConnick and De Landro's decision to include transgender people in their dystopian fantasy suggests (among other things) that the project of feminist liberation overlaps significantly with the project of transgender liberation. In this context, it is interesting to consider the following quotations. The first comes from feminist critic Jacqueline Rose, responding to the accusation that transgender women cannot be as critical of patriarchy as cis women because they generally were not raised as women:

> [I]t is because of the journey they have made, and because so many of them have suffered such pain in prising open the question 'Who is a real woman?' that transgender women should be listened to.

The second quotation comes from trans author Susan Stryker. Stryker is responding to the accusation that trans women are not "real" women:

> The Nature you bedevil me with is a lie. Do not trust it to protect you from what I represent, for it is a fabrication that cloaks the groundlessness of the privilege you seek to maintain for yourself at my expense. You are as constructed as me; the same anarchic Womb has birthed us both.

How do you understand Rose and Stryker's claims here? Is *Bitch Planet* making similar claims? If so, in which scenes?

DEDICATIONS

TO THE FIGHTERS.
— VALENTINE

FOR HILLARY RODHAM CLINTON AND EVERY NASTY
WOMAN WHO HAS EVER COMMITTED THE CARDINAL
SIN OF LIVING IN PUBLIC.
FOR TALLULAH LOUISE FRITCHMAN: YOU TELL THE
WORLD YOU'RE HERE, BABY GIRL.
— KELLY SUE

DEDICATED TO MY FAMILY WHO ENCOURAGES MY
RADICAL NOTIONS.
— KELLY

TO MY SISTER.
— CLAYTON

KELLY SUE DECONNICK - @KELLYSUE
VALENTINE DE LANDRO - @VAL_DELANDRO
TAKI SOMA - @TAKISOMA
KELLY FITZPATRICK - @WASTEDWINGS
CLAYTON COWLES - @CLAYTONCOWLES
RIAN HUGHES - @RIANHUGHES
LAURENN MCCUBBIN - @LAURENNMCC
LAUREN SANKOVITCH - @PANCAKELADY

#BITCHPLANET

TUMBLR: WWW.BITCHPLA.NET

MILKFED CRIMINAL MASTERMINDS: WWW.MILKFED.US

KELLY SUE DECONNICK got her start in the comic industry adapting Japanese and Korean comics into English. Five years and more than ten thousand pages of adaptation later, she transitioned to American comics with 30 DAYS OF NIGHT: EBEN AND STELLA, for Steve Niles and IDW. Work for Image, Boom, Oni, Humanoids, Dark Horse, DC, Vertigo and Marvel soon followed. Today, DeConnick is best known for surprise hits like Carol Danvers' rebranding as Captain Marvel and the Eisner-nominated mythological western, PRETTY DEADLY, the latter was co-created with artist Emma Rios. DeConnick's most recent venture, the Eisner-nominated sci-fi kidney-punch called BITCH PLANET, co-created with Valentine De Landro, launched to rave reviews in December 2014 and has received multiple awards. DeConnick lives in Portland, Oregon with her husband, Matt Fraction, and their two children. Under their company Milkfed Criminal Masterminds, Inc., DeConnick and Fraction are currently developing television for NBC/Universal.

VALENTINE DE LANDRO is a Canadian comic book artist, illustrator, and designer. His credits include titles from Marvel, DC Comics, IDW, Valiant, and Dark Horse. He's known for MARVEL KNIGHTS: 4 and X-FACTOR. He is the co-creator of BITCH PLANET with Kelly Sue DeConnick. De Landro lives east of Toronto, Ontario with his wife Maya and their two children.

IMAGE COMICS, INC.

ROBERT KIRKMAN—CHIEF OPERATING OFFICER
ERIK LARSEN—CHIEF FINANCIAL OFFICER
TODD MCFARLANE—PRESIDENT
MARC SILVESTRI—CHIEF EXECUTIVE OFFICER
JIM VALENTINO—VICE-PRESIDENT
ERIC STEPHENSON—PUBLISHER
COREY MURPHY—DIRECTOR OF SALES
JEFF BOISON—DIRECTOR OF PUBLISHING PLANNING & BOOK TRADE SALES
CHRIS ROSS—DIRECTOR OF DIGITAL SALES
JEFF STANG—DIRECTOR OF SPECIALTY SALES
KAT SALAZAR—DIRECTOR OF PR & MARKETING
BRANWYN BIGGLESTONE—CONTROLLER
SUE KORPELA—ACCOUNTS MANAGER
DREW GILL—ART DIRECTOR
BRETT WARNOCK—PRODUCTION MANAGER
MEREDITH WALLACE—PRINT MANAGER
TRICIA RAMOS—TRAFFIC MANAGER
BRIAH SKELLY—PUBLICIST
ALY HOFFMAN— CONVENTIONS & EVENTS COORDINATOR
SASHA HEAD—SALES & MARKETING PRODUCTION DESIGNER
DAVID BROTHERS—BRANDING MANAGER
MELISSA GIFFORD—CONTENT MANAGER
DREW FITZGERALD—PUBLICITY ASSISTANT
VINCENT KUKUA—PRODUCTION ARTIST
ERIKA SCHNATZ—PRODUCTION ARTIST
RYAN BREWER—PRODUCTION ARTIST
SHANNA MATUSZAK—PRODUCTION ARTIST
CAREY HALL—PRODUCTION ARTIST
ESTHER KIM—DIRECT MARKET SALES REPRESENTATIVE
EMILIO BAUTISTA—DIGITAL SALES ASSOCIATE
LEANNA CAUNTER—ACCOUNTING ASSISTANT
CHLOE RAMOS-PETERSON—LIBRARY MARKET SALES REPRESENTATIVE

IMAGECOMICS.COM

BITCH PLANET BOOK TWO: PRESIDENT BITCH

First printing. May 2017.
Published by Image Comics, Inc.
Office of publication:
2701 NW Vaughn St., Suite 780, Portland, OR 97210.
Copyright © 2017 Milkfed Criminal Masterminds, Inc.
All rights reserved. Contains material originally published in single
magazine form as BITCH PLANET #6-10. "Bitch Planet," its logos
and the likenesses of all characters herein are trademarks of
Milkfed Criminal Masterminds, Inc.
Unless otherwise noted, "Image" and the Image Comics logos are
registered trademarks of Image Comics, Inc.
No part of this publication may be reproduced or transmitted, in
any form or by any means (except for short excerpts for journalistic
or review purposes), without the express written permission of
Milkfed Criminals Masterminds, Inc. or Image Comics, Inc.
All names, characters, events, and locales in this publication are
entirely fictional. Any resemblance to actual persons (living or
dead), events, or places, without satiric intent, is coincidental.
Printed in the USA.
For information regarding the CPSIA on this printed material call:
203-595-3636 and provide reference #RICH-720401.
For international rights, contact: foreignlicensing@imagecomics.com
ISBN: 978-1-63215-717-1
ISBN DCBS EXCLUSIVE: 978-1-5343-0408-6